Central America

The Future of Economic Integration

edited by
George Irvin and Stuart Holland

Westview Press
Boulder, San Francisco, & London

Series in Political Economy and Economic Development in Latin America

Copyright © 1989 by Westview Press, Inc.

Published in 1989 in the United States of America by Westview Press, Inc., 5500 Central Avenue, Boulder, Colorado 80301, and in the United Kingdom by Westview Press, Inc., 13 Brunswick Centre, London WC1N 1AF, England

Library of Congress Cataloging-in-Publication Data
Central America: the future of economic integration/edited by
 George Irvin and Stuart Holland.
  p. cm.—(Series in political economy and economic
development in Latin America)
 Bibliography: p.
 Includes index.
 ISBN 0-8133-7687-4
 1. Central America—Economic integration. 2. Mercado Común
Centroamericano. 3. Central America—Economic policy. I. Irvin,
George. II. Holland, Stuart. III. Series.
HC141.C378 1989
337.1'728—dc19
                                                        88-36675
                                                          CIP

Printed and bound in the United States of America

The paper used in this publication meets the requirements of the American National Standard for Permanence of Paper for Printed Library Materials Z39.48-1984.

10   9   8   7   6   5   4   3   2   1

Contents

Acknowledgments

The idea for this book originated at a conference on Central American integration held in Managua and cosponsored by the Association for European Research on Central America and the Caribbean (ASERCCA) and the *Coordinadora Regional de Investigaciones Económicas y Sociales* (CRIES). Following the conference, the Commission of the European Community in Brussels requested that the Institute of Social Studies in The Hague carry out a study on aid and trade issues currently being discussed with Central American government officials in the context of the San José Agreement. The decision in Brussels to fund this study enabled members of the research team at the Institute of Social Studies to meet with the heads of Central American integration organizations, ministers and officials in all five republics, members of the U.S. Sanford Commission, and heads of the U.N. Technical Mission on Central American Reconstruction. These contacts were of the utmost importance to our effort to contribute, through this volume, to policy formulation as well as scholarly discussion.

The editors are deeply indebted to the many people who contributed their time, resources, and ideas to the making of this book. In particular, we would like to thank Xabier Gorostiaga, director of CRIES, Dr. Angel Viñas, Mr. Leopoldo Giunti, Mr. Gert Beinhart, and other members of the staff at the Directorate General I of the Commission of the European Community in Brussels. We are also grateful to our editor at Westview Press, Barbara Ellington, and her production team; to J. Kewell for preparing the index; Irene Vos-López for her multilingual word-processing skills; Karen Crawford for preparing the tables; and Linda McPhee for copyediting the final draft.

All contributions to this book were written in a personal capacity, and the recommendations advanced cannot be ascribed to any official body. Errors and omissions are subject to the usual caveat.

George Irvin
Institute of Social Studies
The Hague, The Netherlands

Stuart Holland, M.P.
House of Commons
London, United Kingdom

1

Central American Integration: A Suitable Case for Treatment

George Irvin and Stuart Holland

Introduction

The collection of essays in this volume addresses selected aspects of reconstructing Central American's industrial and trading system. Although all eight essays are by economists, the book is intended primarily for the regional specialist and technical jargon has been kept to a minimum. The general reader who follows Central America should find most of the material readily accessible.

Special attention is given in this book to the role of the European Community (EC) in regional reconstruction and integration. There are relatively few books on European relations with the region and there is only one recent major work on the Central American economies by a European author.[1] Here we focus on the crisis of the Central American Common Market (CACM) and on aid and trade arrangements designed to renew it. We do not address the agrarian issue, particularly the question of land reform, crucial though this is.[2]

The turbulent politics of the past decade, particularly the problems faced by the Sandinista Government in Nicaragua and the ongoing struggles in El Salvador and Guatemala, have generated much concern both in the EC countries and in Scandinavia, and US policies have often been sharply criticised.[3] Moreover, the EC member states, by virtue of their own commitment to economic and political integration, see the revival of a CACM comprising the five republics as an aim worthy of support. The San José process—or annual meeting of EC and Central American foreign ministers which takes its name from the first

George Irvin is Associate Professor of Economics at the Institute of Social Studies, The Hague, The Netherlands. Stuart Holland is a Labour Member of the UK Parliament and Shadow spokesman on Financial Affairs.

of these gatherings held in Costa Rica in 1985—has aimed at strengthening both Europe's political ties with the region and promoting greater intra-regional dialogue. Economically, the EC is Central America's second main trading partner after the US and, if the postwar trend continues, could overtake the US by the end of the century.

In this introductory chapter we do four things. We begin by stating the case for the revival of the CACM, albeit in amended form. Second, we analyze the economic legacy of the 1980s and, in particular, the impact of adjustment policy. Third, we sketch the main arguments advanced in each chapter. Finally, we set out detailed suggestions for EC policy on aid, debt renegotiation and trading arrangements with Central America. These are areas which we consider integral to defining a reconstruction package for the region as called for by the UN General Assembly at the end of 1977.[4] They are also some of the key topics which figure on the economic agenda of 'San José process'; i.e., the annual meeting between EC and Central American foreign Ministers, the most recent of which took place in Hamburg at the end of February 1988.

The Importance of the Central American Common Market

The reader may wonder why we have chosen to focus on industrial growth and integration at a time when the promotion of import-substituting industrialization (ISI) by means of customs-union is out of fashion. The first reason for placing industry at the top of the agenda is because the economic 'cement' of Central American relations, intra-regional trade, has contracted so severely that the Central American Common Market (CACM) is nearly defunct. A decade ago, industry accounted for just over one-fifth of the combined Gross Domestic Product of the five republics while intra-regional trade comprised about one-quarter of total trade. Intra-regional trade consisted almost entirely of manufactured products. Today, regional productive capacity in manufactures quite literally is rusting away. The issues of intra-regional and extra-regional trade, finance and debt are closely related, and a reconstruction package must treat them together.

The second reason for addressing the theme of integration has to do with political modernization. Much of post-war politics in the region centers on the long struggle between the region's traditional rulers, the landed oligarchy, and an emerging alliance of forces concerned with modernizing the state and extending effective rights of citizenship to the majority. The particular configuration of alliances has varied considerably between countries. Only in Costa Rica did the 'modernizers' win an early victory. The role of the United States has at best been ambiguous. At worst, it has been to shore up the forces of reaction for crude, geopolitical motives best expressed fifty years ago by Franklin Roosevelt in his epigrammatic characterization of Somoza.

In the postwar period, if the industrial bourgeoisie cannot be said to have lent its full weight to political modernization, it did at least promote regional integration through the formation of the Central American Common Market (CACM). In turn, industrial development and the urban growth to which it contributed strengthened the coalition of forces demanding an extension of economic and political rights. In this sense integration helped promote modernization. The body which first championed this cause was the Economic Commission for Latin America (ECLA) in the early 1950s. However the CACM which emerged was strongly influenced by the US view of how modernisation was best to be achieved, a view which stressed market forces rather than planned integration.[5] In a sense, history has come full circle and the issues debated in the late 1950s are once again on the agenda.

Thirdly, East-West considerations cannot be ignored. The current crisis has laid bare the schism between the region's traditional elite and the mass of the population, a depth of division accompanied by spiralling insurgency and counter-insurgency. The militarization of the region, for which the Reagan administration bears no small measure of responsibility, has increased economic dislocation and threatens to leave the region bisected. To isolate Nicaragua militarily and politically would leave that country dependent on support from the Soviet Union and institutionalize East-West tensions in Central America. Such a result cannot be in the interests of any of the actors concerned, regional or extra-regional.

The Economic Legacy of the 1980s

Assuming that peace takes root in the region in the remaining years of this decade, what are the prospects of strengthening the economic basis of the peace through renewed growth? At first sight, they appear poor. The key to Central American growth is foreign trade. Commodity export prices show little sign of returning to their mid-1970s level. For several years private net capital flows to the region have been negative and it has only been possible to finance the gap through large aid injections. Equally important, in the absence of any coordinated attempt at adjustment on a regional basis, the attempt by each country acting alone to achieve balance by means of ill-conceived protective and exchange rate management policies has resulted in a downward spiral in regional trade and income.

Since the late 1970s, the region's basic balance of payments (the trade account balance adjusted for long-term capital flows) has deteriorated under the combined impact of the growing net outflow of private capital and an adverse movement in the international terms of trade. Unlike 1974 when the first oil shock coincided with a period of rising commodity prices, the second oil shock in 1979 was followed by a sharp fall in export earnings aggravated by a loss in their purchasing power. The resulting shortage of foreign exchange and the growing external borrowing (and servicing) requirement caused the five republics to stop taking in each others imports.

Cumulative trade contraction in turn contributed to falling per capita GDP which, today, is equivalent to the loss of two decades of growth. This contraction was not inevitable in the sense that it might have been in the 1930s when the region last went through a comparable crisis. Then, unlike today, the region's industrial capacity was negligible and, since adjustment could not be cushioned by switching from imported goods to home production, the only remedy was to let national income fall.[6] What are today's options?

Because the five republics have attempted to adjust to the crisis in quite different ways, it is worth looking briefly at the logic of adjustment. Basically, there are three possible reactions to a fall in import capacity. The first is to borrow abroad to maintain a level of imports consistent with desired consumption and investment (desired absorption). This is a palliative since, unless export earnings recover quickly, debt service obligations can mount making external balance more difficult to achieve.

The second is to adopt protective measures which allow home-produced goods to substitute for imports. Not only does such a course run the danger of provoking retaliation but, where import substitutes have a high import content, the net saving in imports is small.

The third is to reduce absorption and free resources for export. This usually involves some mixture of deficit reduction and devaluation. However, because under typical Central American conditions the export response to devaluation takes time while essential imports cannot easily be cut, the extent of devaluation required may be substantial and imports from the region may be affected more than imports from the rest of the world. Moreover, the countries of the region have been notorious for their reluctance to undertake fiscal reform. Hence the burden of expenditure cuts has tended to fall on civilian welfare spending and the capital budget.

The 1979–1980 crisis combined a rising oil bill, declining export receipts and growing private capital flight. Since none of these proved temporary phenomena, the region could not borrow its way out of the crisis and adjustment policies were required. Broadly speaking, Central America resorted in turn to external borrowing, protection, wage cuts and devaluation.

Devaluation meant belt-tightening, and this was particularly difficult at a time when most countries were trying to contain or suppress social discontent. One country, Nicaragua, was attempting a major programme of redistribution. Since international commercial credit was tight, borrowing was bound to be accompanied by political strings.

Increasing protection might have made sense had it meant raising common protection for a time in order to induce a deepening of extra-regional import substitution. However, Central American industry was already highly protected and therefore relatively costly. Moreover the high import-content of regionally produced goods meant that there was little scope for effecting a net foreign exchange saving through increased common protection.

The result was that the republics sought to adjust at each others' expense by cutting back on regional imports or else simply neglecting to settle their outstanding obligations with the Central American Clearing House. As unsettled intra-regional trade debts mounted, multilateral trade arrangements seized up. Bilateral agreements, in effect amounting to barter trade, took their place. The use of scarce dollars was confined largely to making extra-regional purchases and servicing that portion of debt obligations necessary to remaining creditworthy. Single-country import substitution replaced regional import substitution.

Common policies designed to spread the social burden of expenditure cuts more widely and to co-ordinate real exchange rate reductions would have been less costly. But such policies would have required a high degree of political agreement among the regions' governments, something which was manifestly absent.

Costa Rica, for example, devalued as early as 1980 but attempted to maintain domestic demand through increased public spending and external borrowing. It was only after 1982 that it bowed to IMF pressure and reduced absorption. By 1986 external balance had been restored at a lower level of domestic investment and consumption and at a much lower level of regional trade. In contrast, Guatemala was able to postpone devaluation until 1986 because continued net private capital inflows helped to offset the visible trade deficit.

The only economy in the region which attempted to maintain high, public investment-led growth in the face of adverse terms of trade while eschewing exchange rate adjustment was Nicaragua. The Nicaraguan external deficit was prevented from rising by strict foreign exchange rationing and financed by extensive borrowing. After 1983, the growing need to divert resources to the war effort and the disruption of production led to negative growth with accelerating inflation and, although nominal devaluations took place in 1986 and 1987, the real exchange rate continued to appreciate until February 1988 when a drastic currency reform package was announced. At the time of writing it is too early to say what result the new package will have.

Also, Nicaragua has recently achieved intra-regional trade balance, but its share in total intra-regional trade has fallen to only 2 percent. Its extra-regional trade deficit is larger than the value of total exports. Even supposing military pressure on the Sandinista Government ceases—an assumption supported but not guaranteed by the US Congressional decision to cut off aid to the 'contras'—it will be extremely difficult for Nicaragua both to meet the backlog of pent-up demand and to rebuild the export capacity required to re-establish external balance. A substantial net resource inflow will be required for some years.

In general, then, the regional crisis and the macroeconomic adjustment policies adopted in response to it have weakened integration in three ways. First, a combination of capital flight, depressed commodity prices and increased debt service obligations has reduced the region's import capacity. Given the high import content of Central American manufactures, the supply of regional manufactures has been restricted. Second, because individual countries attempted to adjust by resorting to trade restrictions, regional demand for manufactures has fallen. Such restrictions, once in place, are difficult to dismantle. Third, low demand has drastically curtailed manufacturing investment. This means that existing Central American plant capacity is not being maintained. Since the average age of plant was already considerable at the end of the 1970s,[7] running costs have increased and competitiveness has decreased. Reviving the CACM means, quite literally, rebuilding it.

A Summary of the Contributions

Suppose the region were to return to the growth rates which characterised the 1960s and 1970s. Does it follow that GDP growth in itself would defuse social tensions? On the contrary, it can be argued that the model of integration on which earlier growth was based exacerbated economic inequality and therefore contributed to creating the crisis. If this is so, is there any point in trying to revive the CACM?/ The general view of contributors to this collection appears to be that important changes must occur if the CACM is to act as an instrument for promoting growth with greater equity./

The book begins with a survey of the region's macro-economy by John Weeks. His piece analyzes the causes of the dramatic fall in living standards which the region has undergone since the late 1970s, a decline which contrasts sharply with the high growth rates achieved in the decades following the formation of the CACM. In particular, in order to cover the region's external deficit, commercial and official borrowing has been required on such a scale that the region's debt burden has become unmanageable. Nor has aid always been channelled into additional productive capacity. While the share of savings in regional GDP has been steady or rising, the falling share of investment suggests that the inflow of aid dollars—mainly from the US and the multilateral organisations—has served to finance an outflow of debt service and private capital flight, mainly to the US.

Even more ominously, Weeks argues, the generalized foreign exchange shortage has paralyzed intra-regional trade. Instead of taking in each others goods, countries have sought to substitute domestic production for regional imports and to find new markets for regional exports. Weeks is pessimistic about the coming decade, believing that the CACM will probably disappear.

An historical overview of regional industrial development is provided by Alfredo Guerra-Borges. His paper traces the way in which the early ECLA conception of the CACM—that of planned regional integration built around 'integration industries' producing intermediate and capital goods—gave way to the US-sponsored view of the CACM as a free trade area. Although the CACM achieved record growth for over two decades, much of the region's new manufacturing industry depended on inputs from outside the region. One reason for this dependence, he argues, was that industrial output in general consisted of middle-class consumer goods rather than necessities.

Moreover, the distribution of industry among countries, and hence of the income and employment benefits of industrialization, assumed the character of a Dutch auction. While the region's governments all espoused free-market doctrine, the principle of comparative advantage based on relative resource endowments was bypassed. Neither was industrial location subject to any form of regional planning. Instead, as Guerra-Borges shows, countries vied with each other to offer protected markets, tax holidays and free-trade zones (FTZs). Although the CACM agreements included provisions for a

Common External Tariff (CET) and a Convention on Fiscal Incentives, in practice, the granting of tariff and fiscal exemptions on an *ad hoc* basis by each country became the rule. An incidental cost was the growth of fiscal deficits. The salient point is that many of today's critics of ECLA-inspired import substituting industrialization (ISI) assume that the ECLA strategy failed. Guerra-Borges argues that in Central America it was never tried.

In the current debate on growth strategies, import substituting industrialization (ISI) and export promotion (EP) strategies are usually treated as mutually exclusive. In a chapter with a strong theoretical orientation, Victor Bulmer-Thomas argues that these need not be mutually exclusive since EP can be interpreted in two ways: either as a strategy which requires the dismantling of all protection in order to switch capacity to exports—which he terms 'export substitution' (ES)—or as one which requires protection to be rationalized and an incentive structure to be established which is export-neutral—which he suggests should be the specific meaning of EP.

Bulmer-Thomas then shows that ISI and ES *are* incompatible since it is unlikely that nominal exchange rate reductions will lead to a real exchange rate depreciation sufficient to offset the loss in effective protection to domestic manufacture resulting from dismantling tariffs. *Per contra*, ISI and EP can be combined—and indeed must be combined—if ISI is to proceed. The failure of the CACM is ascribable to inappropriate policies rather than to ISI *per se.*

Formally speaking, while intra-regional trade promotion in the past has depended on maintaining an anti-export biased tariff structure and set of nominal exchange rates, there exists some feasible combination of tariff, exchange rate and tax policies applicable to industrial outputs and imported inputs which will eliminate anti-export bias. Bulmer-Thomas argues that in order to eliminate such bias it is preferable to increase value added in extra-regional export branches rather than to decrease it for home (regional) production since the latter will militate against industrial deepening.

More generally, Bulmer-Thomas argues that the revival of the CACM will depend on the recovery of foreign exchange earnings from traditional exports, the removal of restrictions on intra-regional trade, and the implementation of a complementary package of measures aimed at settling intra-regional debts and financing trade flows under agreed exchange rate arrangements. Most important, the central objective of integration as first envisaged by ECLA must not be lost from view. Growth can only be sustained by deepening industrialization and ensuring that its benefits are equitably distributed.

Juan Alberto Fuentes sees room for guarded optimism. If the 1960s gave rise to exaggerated expectations, the 1970s was a time of 'silent progress,' acceptable if not spectacular. Despite the tumultuous events of the first half of the present decade, there are signs today that silent progress is being made once more. A new Common External Tariff (CET) has been adopted; membership of the Central American Bank for Economic Integration (BCIE) has been broadened and a new intra-regional payments scheme launched. Since the signing of the Cooperation Agreement in November, 1985, the European Community has played a more active role in the region.

In particular, two points stand out in the first part of Fuentes' paper. First, the past decade has seen important changes in the pattern of intra-regional trade which are of political significance for the future of the CACM. El Salvador and Nicaragua, once strongly committed to integration, trade far less within the region. In consequence, the share in intra-regional trade of Costa Rica and Honduras, the countries least committed to integration, has risen. Second, it is misleading to view the region as shifting from a strategy of import substitution to one of export promotion. In fact, the proliferation of intra-regional trade barriers has brought about a switch from regional import substitution to domestic import substitution (or 'single country' ISI). Behind the region's new image of 'openness,' one detects a strong note of *sálvese quien pueda*.

What then are the grounds for the author's optimism? One is the *Derechos de Importación Centroamericanos* (DICA) scheme which, in effect, provides a new instrument for financing CACM trade now that the *peso centroamericano* accounts of the Central American Clearing House (CCC) have ceased to function. Like the *peso centroamericano*, the DICA is a dollar substitute. However, it has the advantage of being an intra-regional convertible currency bought and sold in secondary markets. Its successful introduction would, in effect, establish a dual exchange rate system for intra- and extra-regional trade along the lines conceptualized by Bulmer-Thomas.

More generally, Fuentes argues, any strategy of extra-regional export promotion must lead the region to adopt a common negotiating position both for traditional and non-traditional exports. To a degree, common positions have already evolved in the context of negotiations with the European Community (EC) in such areas as food security, infrastructure projects and technology transfer.

The chapter by Rómulo Caballeros examines the problem of Central American debt. Although some Latin America countries have higher debt service ratios, Central American ratios of debt to GDP are, on average, more than twice as high as the Latin America average and far higher than those of Argentina, Brazil and Mexico. Because Central America trades a higher proportion of its GDP, it is more vulnerable to unfavorable movements in terms of trade. After 1979, a combination of deteriorating terms of trade, a worsening debt structure and rising interest rates forced most countries into renegotiating their commercial debt. In some case, countries were forced to seek agreement with the IMF on terms which, in the view of the author, have weakened the region's long-term debt repayment capacity.

Taking official debt and interest rates at the end of 1986, Caballeros has projected repayment schedules up to 1994. Assuming, furthermore, that export prices and volumes reached by 1994 are equivalent to the highest levels achieved in any year since 1970, he calculates that the region would need to devote about 45 percent of its export earnings to debt service until 1990 and about 30 percent thereafter. Such a target, he argues, is unlikely to be met. Critics may point out that the burden is spread highly unevenly and that few realistic bankers would expect the region's main debtors to meet the schedules projected. Still, it is a valid point that short term restructuring exercises are costly and unproductive. Caballeros argues that what it required is a bold new initiative to deal with the problem.

The chapter by FitzGerald and Croes suggests key elements in the design of such an initiative. But before reviewing their proposals, it is important to understand that they see the debt issue as part of the more general problem of the collapse of the Central American financial system. New financial arrangements are seen as the *sine qua non* for reactivating Central American industry. The authors argue that while the CACM monetary system worked well for two decades, its success was more apparent than real. Monetary stability depended on the self-liquidating nature of the primary commodity credit cycle and no attempt was made to build a common CACM financial system.

In particular, no mechanism existed which would have allowed short-term debt with the Central American Clearing House (CCC) to be refinanced in *pesos*. The Central American Bank for Economic Integration (BCIE) did not deal with intra-trade finance; its exclusive function was to extend long-term dollar loans for productive activities and infrastructure. The Central American Secretariat for Economic Integration (SIECA) dealt mainly with implementing and rationalizing the Common External Tariff without reference to intra-trade. The Central American Monetary Council (CMCA) lacked the power to coordinate the activities of individual central banks. In short, the arrangements governing the functioning of the CACM evolved in a period of economic growth and stability; under crisis conditions, they collapsed.

FitzGerald and Croes propose that creditors, starting with European bilateral donors, should place semi-performing assets in trust and deposit them—possibly in the form of equity shares—in a jointly-administered Central American Reconstruction Fund. At present, a conservative estimate is that Central American obligations to the EC total about US$ 1.7 billion of which about US$ 1 billion consists of bilateral debt. Such a Fund would provide the seed capital for reconstructing Central American trade finance and, if backed by Europe, its leverage could be increased by issuing instruments to 'repatriate' flight capital and purchasing discounted commercial debt.

The final chapter by Cáceres and Irvin makes three main points. First, despite arguments over ISI and the CACM model, the growth of industry in the 1960s and 1970s depended on the prosperity of export agriculture—and this will continue to hold true in the future. Second, the degree of decapitalization of the region is such that a return to 1978 real per capita income levels requires a massive injection of foreign resources. The final point is that it would be unwise for this injection to take the exclusive form of project aid, just as it is unlikely that a significant proportion of total requirements will take the form of private direct investment. In general official assistance will be preferable to commercial credit, and improved trading arrangements will be preferable to more aid.

It would be difficult to disagree with the proposition that export agriculture traditionally has been the Central American engine of growth. The authors' contention, though, is under conditions of labour and land abundance and foreign exchange shortage, export agriculture did not compete with industry but complemented it (unlike the Ricardian case where the existence of a landlord class forces down the rate of profit and slows industrialization). However, as international rent differentials were squeezed after the mid-1970s, the rate of profit could only be maintained by cutting real wages which helped precipitate the crisis.

In practice this means that while greater equity is desirable, it is only affordable if two conditions are met. First, the international community must help foot the bill. Second, the money must be used to diversify export agriculture since only this will lay the basis for improved growth and distribution in the long term.

In requiring the international community to pay, what is being asked for is not charity but compensation for terms of trade and capital flight losses which have accrued as benefits to Central America's trading partners, chiefly the US and the EC. The matter is now of considerable urgency since, between 1979 and 1986, not only has real regional GDP fallen but gross investment has declined continuously leaving the region's productive capacity seriously weakened. The *Banco Centroamericano de Integración Económica* (BCIE) estimates that over the next five years about US$ 4 billion per annum will be needed in fresh finance, a figure broadly in line with the Kissinger Commission estimate. The present multilateral inflow is about US$ 400 million, one-tenth of the requirement.

As regards the role of the European Community, proposals are set out for assistance in three main areas: clearing unsettled intra-regional trade debts (which could easily be tied to the extra-regional debt proposals outlined above); the provision of the extra-regional component of fixed and working capital needed to revive regional industry; and finally, the extension of a STABEX-type facility to the region (STABEX is the export revenue stabilization scheme which the EC operates in favor of Lomé convention countries).

Because of overlapping elements in proposals set out by virtually all the authors in this collection, and because almost all have implications for EC aid in particular, the main elements are summarized in the next section.

Elements of a European Community Package

The key political issue of aid policy towards the region has been 'selectivity'—specifically whether to exclude Nicaragua. Under the Reagan administration, aid has been unashamedly selective and this influence has spilled over into the attitude of some multilateral donors. In this respect, Europe's record is somewhat better although, even when Scandinavian assistance is included, the total flow is considerably smaller than that from either the US or the multilateral agencies. Moreover, much European aid is of a piecemeal nature and it is only recently, largely as a result of the 1985 San José Agreement, that serious thought has been given to a coherent package of measures.

Given the fragility of current peace negotiations, it would be fanciful to hope that the region can attract a large net inflow of direct foreign investment in the near future. This suggests that a recovery package for the region will comprise at least the following items: project aid, balance of payments support, debt relief and more favorable treatment with respect to trade.

Details of the bilateral and multilateral components of the EC aid program are set out in Chapter 8. In the past, the bilateral aid programs of EC member states have totalled more than the EC's multilateral program. Moreover, much of the multilateral total was divided up between the six countries of the Central American isthmus and only a relatively small proportion was retained for region-wide projects.

This balance is now changing. In future, it appears that more aid will be multilateral. Moreover, because of the limited project absorptive capacity of the region, the Central Americans are insisting on a greater proportion of aid being channelled through the region's own integration organizations, chiefly the BCIE.

The main projects currently under discussion are requests for loans totalling ECU 166 million (at the time of writing one ECU is worth US$ 1.15). The total comprises ECU 76 million for modernizing industrial plant and equipment, ECU 40 million for financing extra-regional inputs for industry and ECU 50 million for developing non-traditional exports. These projects are far larger than any previously discussed within the EC multilateral program and, if accepted, would be channelled through the BCIE. Two of the three projects, or a total of ECU 116 million, are to enable intra-regional trade to be revived. Although the phrase 'balance of payments assistance' is avoided, in practice the rapid disbursement of sums of this size would amount to much the same thing.

In addition, Central America has requested EC assistance in helping to refinance intra-regional debt obligations, easing the burden of extra-regional debt and, finally, improving trade arrangements for the region's traditional and non-traditional exports.

Intra-Regional Trade

Progress on reviving intra-regional trade depends on two factors: settling outstanding trade debts and restructuring the regional financial system.

In late 1986, the five republics signed an agreement on the *Derechos del Importación Centroamericanos* (DICA), a scheme designed to restructure the regional financial system. In essence, the scheme is intended to save scarce dollars by allowing each Central Bank to emit dollar denominated import certificates (DICAs) on demand, purchasable in local currency and, upon completion of the transaction, redeemable in the currency of the exporting country. The novel element is that each country's DICA would trade in the open market at a premium or discount according to demand for that country's exports. In effect, were the DICA to become the main instrument for financing intra-regional trade, a new intra-regional exchange rate structure would emerge delinked from the dollar.

However there are snags. For one thing, to date, only the Guatemalan and Salvadorean Central Banks have issued DICAs. The emission of a Costa Rican DICA apparently has been hampered by legal problems. In fact, it appears that Costa Rican officials are concerned that the DICA would divert attention from the problem of outstanding balances owed to Costa Rica and eliminate Costa Rica's surplus in its regional trade account.

For the DICA scheme to work, there would also need to be some agreement between governments at the outset about a 'desirable' intra-regional exchange rate structure and the associated pattern of trade flows. In the absence of such agreement, Central Banks might emit DICAs in quantities just sufficient to maintain the existing exchange rate structure which would negate the whole purpose of the exercise. Finally, any expansion of intra-regional trade would need to be backed by hard currency in order to finance the high extra-regional import component of the region's manufactures. Hence Central America's request for ECU 40 million from the EC.

In short, with or without the DICA, if trade is to be increased and multilateralism restored in the medium term, more mutual planning of trade will be required in the short term. By implication, Central American countries will need to agree on where to invest in production capacity, and particularly whether to invest in Nicaragua which, today, has little to sell to the regional market. This is why it is difficult to see the DICA working except in the context of a wider package of measures.

Extra-Regional Debt

The cornerstone of the package for recycling debt is the creation of the Central American Reconstruction Fund initially worth about ECU 1 million. Under the aegis of, say, the *Banco Centroamericano de Integración Económica* (BCIE) and the *Consejo Monetario Centroamericano* (CMCA), a consortium of creditor nations—starting with those of the European Community—might agree either to a straight swap of official debt of the five Central American governments for equity in the Fund, or to capitalize the Fund from present debt service payments as part of a roll-over operation. As FitzGerald and Croes argue, not only do creditor governments have a political interest in the stabilization of the region but, on any realistic assessment of repayment prospects, such a scheme would be financially advantageous. Moreover there is no reason why multilateral creditors should not join (e.g. the IDB and IBRD) or, indeed, Latin American creditors (e.g. Mexico, Venezuela, Brazil, Argentina) with whom some form of triangulation scheme might be agreed.

In this context, it should be noted that some of the above countries are already members of, or are about to join, the BCIE. Furthermore, since no debt moratorium is involved, it is likely that the international banking community would welcome the scheme, particularly if Fund resources were used to purchase a proportion of outstanding commercial debt now trading at a discount on the international market.

The advantages of such a scheme for Central America are obvious. For one thing, it would provide immediate relief from part of the debt service burden. For another, Costa Rica, the region's main creditor, might be persuaded to write off some portion of its outstanding balances in the Clearing House in return for the recycling of part of its external debt. Finally, the Fund could be used *both* to modernize key CACM industries, provide working capital and provide intra-regional trade finance *and* as a source of pre-finance for traditional and non-traditional extra-regional exports. In short it would fill the functional gap between the Clearing House and the BCIE, a gap which has proved the weakest link in the regional financial system.

The political issue is whether, assuming foreign backing is found, the five republics can agree on a reconstruction plan. In order for the Fund to succeed, it would be necessary not only to reach agreement on dividing the pie, but on what sort of pie to divide. What emerges from Guerra-Borges' account of the early years of the CACM and Fuentes' analysis of the changing pattern of intra-regional trade is that, if the CACM is to be rebuilt, new priorities and objectives will need to be agreed upon. In particular, the integration organizations will need to be backed by some form of regional political body. A 'Central American Development Plan' could be commissioned by the *Consejo Económico* and placed on the agenda of the future Central American Parliament.

Extra-Regional Trade

For many years, a central cannon of progressive orthodoxy in Central (and Latin) America has been that inward-looking and outward-looking development strategies were mutually exclusive in a logical, not merely a rhetorical, sense. As Weeks has noted in an earlier book, to ascribe the decline of the CACM to a fatal combination of internal underdevelopment and external dependency is both wrong *and* inconsistent.[8] What sustained CACM industrialization throughout the first two decades of its existence was the growth and diversification of the region's primary export sector.

Unfortunately, there are no instant cures. Placing non-traditional exports of manufactures on the world market is a worthy goal, but unless a country already enjoys a reasonably diversified and sophisticated industrial base, such a goal is unlikely to be achieved quickly. Further diversification of traditional commodity exports is a more readily attainable goal. So too is the penetration of new markets and the establishment of common marketing and shipping facilities. In the case of those commodities in which the region's market share is substantial, the negotiation of improved terms within one of the world quota systems should be a key policy objective.

As Weeks notes, since 1980 the region as a whole has run a continuous current account deficit averaging about US$ 1 billion annually. Although estimates vary about what proportion of this deficit is ascribable to the deterioration in terms of trade for the region's main commodities, ECLAC estimates that between 1977 and 1984 the region's net barter terms of trade fell by 50 percent.[9] This means that between 1980 and 1984, the region lost about US$ 1.6 billion. Since the EC accounts for about one-quarter of Central American trade, a rough estimate is that, over this same period, Europe gained US$ 400 million, or US$ 100 million per year. We suggest that, prior to entering negotiations about trade concessions, the parties might reflect on the fact that Europe's gain from the region in terms of trade effects over these years is almost certainly larger than the grant element in its total aid to the region over the same period.

Four commodities—coffee, bananas, cotton and sugar—account for over 90 percent of Central American trade with the EC. However, the fact that the Central American countries are not members of the Africa, Caribbean and Pacific (ACP) group (i.e. signatories of the Lomé Convention) does put the region at a serious disadvantage. The only means available to the region for gaining preferential access to the EC market is the Generalized System of Preferences (GSP) which applies mainly to industrial products.

Coffee is by far the region's most important export to the EC and the high quality of the region's product has allowed it to gain a growing share of the European market. At the EC-Central American Foreign Ministers' Meeting held in Guatemala in February 1986, the European side agreed to include green coffee in the GSP. This appeared to be an important concession since it raised the proportion of Central American (and Panamanian) produce subject to preferential EC tariffs from 8 percent to 60 percent. In practice, however, the *ad valorem* tax on green coffee only fell from 5 percent to 4.5 percent. By contrast, in the case of bananas, several EC countries apply a 20 percent tariff which is not applicable to produce from ACP countries. Arguably, their inclusion in the GSP would have had a greater impact.

In the case of sugar, ACP countries enjoy quotas and guaranteed prices. The problem of sugar has become particularly serious for Central America since the collapse of the International Sugar Agreement (ISA) and, in consequence, the very low price which sugar has fetched on the 'free market.' Less than one-quarter of total sugar entering world trade is sold on the free market; the rest is governed by quota agreements which worked well in the 1960s and 1970s but recently have come under increasing strain. Under the EC Common Agricultural Policy (CAP), Europe has become a net exporter of beet sugar and European sales in the free market have helped to depress prices. Moreover, the ISA cannot be revived without European co-operation which really means that unless the CAP is reformed and the ISA revived, sugar prices are unlikely to recover. The problem is further compounded by the recent major cut in the US sugar quota.

Ideally, Central American membership of Lomé would allow more favourable access to markets, would help secure more stable export earnings (through STABEX) and would give the region access to credit from the European Investment Bank (EIB). Such membership is unlikely, however, since it is opposed by the ACP countries, in any case, Europe is reluctant to bear the extra costs involved. In the short to medium term, it would appear more fruitful for Central America to concentrate on gaining a limited number of concessions from the EC. For commodities, a most important concession would be extension of STABEX-type facilities to the region.

Recently, the European Commission has established a small fund of ECU 100 million (COMPEX) to stabilize the purchase price of commodities from the very poorest LDCs. The only country of the Caribbean region to have benefited, however, is Haiti. One semi-official European research institute puts the cost of extending STABEX to Central American coffee, cotton and bananas at US$ 60 million per annum.[10] The estimate given in Chapter 8 is ECU 40 million per annum but applies to coffee alone. In any event, such a figure could be accommodated easily within the increase in the multilateral aid budget requested at San José IV (Hamburg). Thus, there appears to be some room for maneuver in the area of commodity price support.

The 1986 extension of the GSP to the region is important for the future of non-traditional exports (i.e. full and semi-manufactures). However, only a proportion of Central American exports to Europe consists of manufactures, and textile exports (particularly important for a country like El Salvador) are restricted by the Multifibre Agreement.

Much the same criticism has been made of the US-sponsored Caribbean Basin Initiative; few regional manufactures are exported to the US and of those that are, 87 percent already enjoy duty-free access. Moreover, both in the case of Europe and in the US, such progress as has been made in removing tariff barriers to LDC products tends to have been offset by new forms of non-tariff discrimination. This is one of the factors limiting potential gains to LDCs from the Uruguay round of GATT negotiations. As in the case of the GSP, the GATT is principally concerned with liberalizing trade in manufactures.[11] Only one Central American country, Nicaragua, is a full member of GATT.

Concluding Remarks

In the past decade, Central America has experienced social, political and economic upheaval on a scale arguably greater than that experienced in the 1930s. The cost to the region has been enormous, not merely in financial terms but in terms of human life. One result is that today the region is more politically divided and economically dependent on external aid for recovery than it was two decades ago. Ostensibly, such conditions are not favorable to re-establishing the momentum towards integration.

At the same time, changes occurring in several main areas provide ground for cautious optimism. First of all, there has been political change within the region even in those republics not noted for enlightened regimes. US opposition to the left-wing government in Managua, echoed to varying degrees in the other Central American capitals, should not obscure the extent to which internal processes have weakened the traditional alliance between the oligarchy and the military and helped to re-enfranchise modernizing coalitions in the region.[12]

In the field of regional and external relations, the high point of 1987 was the signing of the Arias peace plan by the five republics. The mood in 1988 stands in marked contrast to that five years ago when the Contadora draft was opposed by a majority of the countries of the region. Despite strong opposition from within the Reagan administration, Central Americans have taken the initiative in resolving their political differences, an initiative supported by new political actors from Latin America and Europe.

Central America's 'new voice' is one product of limited though tangible political and social reforms. The pent-up demand for such reform was, of course, illustrated most vividly nearly a decade ago by the overthrow of Somoza in Nicaragua and the protracted struggles which developed in El Salvador and Guatemala. While progress has been unevenly distributed and democratic gains remain fragile, it is unlikely that there will be a complete return to the 'oligarchic despotism' characteristic of the region's domestic politics nor to the unquestioning subservience to US interests characteristic of its foreign relations.[13]

The second area of change is in the region's economic structure. The Central American economy has been set back by two decades or more and almost all actors would agree that reducing the region's extreme vulnerability to external shocks—or what some would refer to as excessive dependence on the agro-export model of growth—is a desirable end. However there is less agreement about the means.

One response to external vulnerability or 'dependence' is to diversify export destinations and products, in particular promoting non-traditional (i.e. semi-processed) exports. Successful export diversification and promotion will involve, *inter alia,* choosing a set of commercial policy instruments which make the production of tradables at least as attractive as non-tradables. But although the removal of anti-export bias may be a necessary condition for achieving long-term growth, it is not a sufficient condition and indeed may prove harmful to growth if it results in de-industrialization. For this reason, primary attention is paid in this book to a regional growth strategy in which industrial integration plays a central role.

The legacy of the 1980s crisis is a harsh one. Just as a common adjustment policy would have reduced the cost of the crisis, a common reconstruction program will be preferable to each country attempting to 'go it alone.' Reconstruction, is not merely a matter of funding projects. Reconstruction involves finding the foreign exchange which will enable trade barriers to be dismantled at the same time as helping further diversification of regional exports to take place. Renegotiating external debt is a key element too. Not only would a debt-swap arrangement be a low-cost strategy for creditors but, as we have argued, it could prove the key to unlocking the problem of outstanding intra-regional debt. New trade arrangements are also vital. As several contributors to this book argue, the regional economy is most vulnerable to fluctuating export earnings. The extension of a STABEX-type facility to the region, particularly if operated as a buffer fund, would not involve additional net costs to the EC. To the extent that price stabilization stimulated growth, both trading partners would benefit; i.e. the appropriate analogy is not a zero-sum but a positive-sum game.

Finally, reviving regional integration does not mean reviving the original model of the CACM. The old model was underpinned by weak institutional arrangements and produced illusory growth. At the level of the member states, individual countries were unwilling to relinquish traditional prerogatives even where these were clearly inconsistent with the collective good. At the level of class, the interests of landed capital were never subordinated to those of the coalition of forces supporting an industrialization project. At the same time, the old model has nurtured new forces and produced political confrontations which, today, have cleared the ground for a more vigorous modernization project to be launched.

The various essays which follow, and which are summarized above, share the core principles of ECLA's initial vision of regional integration. If future integration measures are combined with sensible commercial policies, a stronger regional financial system and, in particular, new arrangements for dealing with intra-regional trade imbalances, reviving the CACM will not just mean increased trade. It will mean securing a more equitable distribution of the benefits of trade both among the five republics and among their citizens.

Politically, the European Community has played a limited but constructive role in helping to promote a negotiated settlement in the region. If a durable peace is to be achieved in Central America, Europe has an historic opportunity to help underwrite it economically. In this respect, it is important to think not only of the regional economy but also to keep sight of a joint recovery policy for the global economy.[14]

Notes

1. Examples of books by European authors on the region's politics are Grabendorff, Krumwiede and Todt (1984) and DiPalma and Whitehead (eds) (1986); the book on the Central American economy referred to is Bulmer-Thomas (1987b). An extensive bibliography on European-Latin American relations is IRELA (1985).

✳✳ 2. The argument that 'excessive' reliance of export agriculture is the heart of the Central American crisis, and that agriculture therefore must be reformed, has been put by various authors. In particular, see Williams (1986) and Bulmer-Thomas (1987b).

3. For a particularly vitriolic attack on Europe's challenge to traditional US prerogatives in the region see Kristol (1985).

4. On 7 October 1987, the UN General Assembly passed Resolution 42/1 agreeing to back the call for "aid for peace" issues by the five Central American presidents at their meeting in Esquipulas on 7 August, 1987. On 18 November 1987, a Commission of the UN General Assembly requested of the Secretary General that an emergency aid program be drawn up for the region and presented to the General Assembly no later than 30 April, 1988.

5. The classical account of competing ECLA and US views which determined the nature of the CACM in its formative years is Cohen (1982b). For an excellent short analysis of the inegalitarian pattern of growth resulting from the CACM, see Delgado (1981).

6. An excellent discussion of the 1930s crisis is to be found in Bulmer-Thomas (1987b) which also contains a most useful analysis of the different adjustment policies adopted since 1979.

7. See SIECA/BCIE/ICAITI (1987).

8. See Weeks (1985b).

9. ECLAC estimates that over the 1977–1984 period, the region's terms of trade fell by 50 percent and the purchasing power of exports by 30 percent. See ECLAC (1985).

10. See IRELA (1987).

11. See Valdés (1987).

12. For an excellent account of the contradictory nature of capitalist modernization in the region see Weeks (1986a).

13. The phrase is attributed to Baloyra; see, for example, Baloyra (1983).

14. See Holland (ed) (1983); also see the 'Manley Commission Report, Manley and Brandt (1985).

2

A Macroeconomic Overview of the Central American Economies

John Weeks

Introduction

Taken as a whole, the Central American region has suffered from economic decline and stagnation since 1978. While all of the Latin American countries have endured growth performances varying from poor to disastrous over the last ten years, the situation in Central America has been considerably worse. Further, while it could be plausibly argued that there are optimistic indications for a number of countries of the hemisphere, rare are the experts who foresee a sustained recovery of the Central American region in the near future. The purpose of this survey is to consider the recent macroeconomic performance of the Central American region and in doing so to understand why immediate prospects are so dismal.

At one level the particularly poor growth performance of the Central American region can be explained by the obvious fact that no other part of the hemisphere is so torn by armed conflict and social strife. However, the region's difficulties are deeper than this, and to an extent, war and civil disturbance are symptoms rather than causes. Particularly the four northern Spanish-speaking Central American countries (Guatemala, Honduras, El Salvador, and Nicaragua), have been in this century among the most underdeveloped in the hemisphere, in terms of economic, political or social indicators. To a great extent, the dismal growth performances are part of the transition of the region out of a legacy of dictators and dependency.[1]

John Weeks is Professor of Economics at Middlebury College in Vermont.

Identifying Trends

Now, at the end of the 1980s, it is appropriate to assess the economic developments of the decade in Central America.[2] While it is obviously not possible to predict the course of future events in the region, one can identify a number of clear trends and tendencies which provide the context for economic developments toward the end of the century. In this section I consider the most important macroeconomic trends, first listing them, then elaborating each in turn with reference to available data.

— The first trend one can clearly identify is *the accelerating collapse of the regional integration project*. It is thirty years now since the first concrete steps were taken to form a Central American free trade zone, and twenty-five years since the general customs and tariffs agreement went into effect. While only one of many trade groupings of developing countries, the Central American Common Market was unique in that it represented the economic integration of countries which at one time had formed a single country, and to an extent could be viewed as the continuation of the goal of Central American unity. Among both nationalist dreamers and many practical politicians of the region such a unity has been seen for a hundred years as the hope for economic and political sovereignty.[3] Whatever promise Central American economic integration might or might not have had in the long run, it has joined the ranks of lost causes for the foreseeable future. Intra-regional trade has collapsed (to the extent that countries have declared periodic unilateral trade embargoes), and at a recent meeting of the governing body of the CACM steps were taken to dismantle regional protectionism on major commodities.[4]

— Closely related to the first trend has been a second: *the tendency for the governments of the five CACM countries to follow economic-crisis-management strategies which are mutually exclusive and will generate competition rather than cooperation among the five countries.* Costa Rica has sought its *salida* from the regional economic crisis by expansion of the internal market; Guatemala has vigorously pursued the path of 'non-traditional' exports and trade liberalization; strife-torn El Salvador and Nicaragua have adopted closed-economy policies in response to war; and only in Honduras is the general thrust of economic policy unclear and possibly consistent with a return to regional integration. Notwithstanding these different strategies, the range of options open to governments in the use of specific policy instruments is more limited now than at any time since the end of the Second World War. The major multi- and bilateral lending agencies have reached a close consensus as to 'appropriate' tariff, exchange rate, monetary and fiscal policy for Central American governments. The consensus has resulted in these organizations attempting to dictate to the governments of the region a common policy package representing an extraordinarily ideological and right-wing interpretation of mainstream economics.

— Third, in all countries of the region except Costa Rica *investment in productive assets both by the public and private sectors has tended to decline.* With regard to the public sector, the decline reflects pressures to reduce expenditure (usually in the context of multilateral-supported structural adjustment programmes). Perhaps private sector lack of enthusiasm, despite extensive incentives provided by governments, reflects a judgement about the economic and political future of the region made by business groups both domestic and foreign. The fourth major trend is *towards increased macroeconomic instability for the countries of the Central American region.* All five countries are now more open to the international economy than a decade ago (and it must be remembered that these economies have always been more open than those of other Latin American countries). This opening has occurred at a time when the international economy has itself been particularly unstable./Instability has manifested itself with regard to primary commodity prices and interest rates, and also in terms of fluctuating growth rates of the OECD countries and increased developed country protectionism. Given greater openness and increased international economic volatility, it is hardly surprising that the tiny economies of the region have suffered from instability.

— Fifth, *the governments of the region have found it increasingly difficult to meet their external debt payments.* Compared to the other countries of Latin America, the countries of the region have tiny debts. However, an unfavorable conjuncture of circumstances makes the debt problem extremely grave for Central American governments and citizens (and the latter ultimately make the sacrifices to service the debt). Traditional exports suffer from low prices with little likelihood of substantial rise relatively to the world price level in the foreseeable future.[5] In addition some (i.e. sugar and beef) have fallen victim to protectionism. Non-traditional exports, even where they have shown promise (i.e. Guatemala and Costa Rica) would require new investment and perhaps a decade of development in order to become major foreign exchange earners. If the debts are to be serviced, little help can be anticipated from the capital account either. New capital inflow in the form of direct investment is unlikely to be forthcoming in large amounts (except perhaps to Costa Rica). Fresh commercial credit is extremely scarce and available on increasingly hard terms when forthcoming. Indeed, much of the measured financial inflows to Central American countries in recent years have been mere ledger entries resulting from debt rescheduling. For these reasons, ECLA has warned that by the end of the decade the Central American region may become a net exporter of capital, as Latin America as a whole has been since 1982.[6]

— Sixth, *the standard of living of Central Americans has declined drastically* (catastrophically one might say). Further, this decline in income per head has not been the result of a sudden and short-run catastrophe (though these have occurred in the region in the form of war and natural disasters), but the consequence in most cases of a consistent and persistent decline. Evidence indicates that living standards have fallen in both rural and urban areas. In urban areas real wages have declined and unemployment has increased (except in Costa Rica; see Tables 2.5 and 2.6).

In the following section the trends identified above will be discussed in further detail. In this section the trends have been presented in an order implied by the analytical progression of the discussion. Since some are more strictly quantitative and others qualitative, they are elaborated in a different order in what follows.

Review of the Evidence

Declining Living Standards

For almost three decades, 1950–1978, the countries of Central America enjoyed robust growth records (see Table 2.1). Only for Guatemala and Honduras during the 1950s and Nicaragua during 1970–1978 was the rate of growth of GDP not considerably above the rate of growth of population. Over the entire 29 years, Costa Rica had the highest rate of GDP growth, and its advantage in per capita income growth was even greater because it had the lowest rate of population growth in the region. While the other countries also had quite respectable growth records by hemispheric comparison (particularly El Salvador and Guatemala in the 1960s and 1970s), there is a virtual consensus among experts that lower income groups benefited little if at all.

Empirical evidence indicates that in El Salvador, Guatemala, Honduras, and Nicaragua real wages were stagnant or declining during the two decades of rapid growth. In addition, the evidence is overwhelming that a drastic concentration of land occurred, increasing substantially the number of landless and land-poor peasants.[7] Speaking of Guatemala, Hintermeister concluded that no significant improvement could be made in the condition of peasant smallholders without land redistribution.[8] It is in this context that one must consider the dismal growth performances of the 1980s. While national output had grown rapidly in the 1960s and 1970s, it is quite likely that the majority of the citizens of Central America were no better off in 1980 than they had been in 1960, though on average real family incomes had risen.[9]/Since 1980, the vast majority of Central Americans have certainly suffered falls in real income./

\Table 2.1 demonstrates one of the trends identified: the decline in living standards in Central America./During 1950–1978 a negative annual growth rate of GDP represented an extraordinary event. From 1979 to 1986 for the five countries in the table (thirty-five observations) negative growth occurred thirteen times. Further, in only eleven of the thirty-five cases did per capita income rise in a year. In the 1980s it has been a relatively unusual event for income per inhabitant to rise in any country, having occurred only three times since 1983 (twice for Costa Rica). The final line of the table provides a rough estimate of the change in per capita incomes during the 1980s, which has been negative in all cases.

Economic Instability

This decline in living standards has gone along with sharp fluctuations in growth rates. For Costa Rica and El Salvador the spread between the lowest and highest growth rate for the 1980s is in excess of fifteen percentage points, and almost ten for Nicaragua. Even the modest-by-comparison six and seven point swings for Guatemala and Honduras would have been judged as extraordinary in the 1960s and 1970s.\To a great extent this extreme volatility of growth rates reflects the instability of the world economy. The relationship is most obvious in the case of Costa Rica. Without exception from 1980 through 1986 the Costa Rican economy expanded when its external terms of trade improved and contracted when they deteriorated. Further, the slight improvement in growth rates in 1986 for several of the countries was significantly influenced by sharp but brief increases in coffee prices.

Sectoral performances demonstrate a similar volatility. Due to data limitations it is not possible to separate peasant production from large-scale agro-business, which one would want to do in order to judge the effect of agricultural growth on rural welfare./However, it is worth noting that in no country in the region has the growth of agriculture kept pace with the growth of population (see Table 2.2)/ Also, the post-war development of agriculture involved shifting some of the region's best land out of food production into export crops. In consequence, the need to import basic staples, first evident in the 1970s,[10] has increased for the region as a whole. With regard to the export sector, the sometimes violent swings in the rate of agricultural growth (e.g. Costa Rica 1983–1984) reflect in part the instability of primary product prices.[11]

ᵗThe manufacturing sectors of the region have been if anything even more unstable than the agricultural sectors ᵗ(Table 2.3A). Again the spread between highest and lowest growth rates is quite extraordinary: over twenty percentage points for Costa Rica and Nicaragua, and about ten for El Salvador, Guatemala, and Honduras. Translated into levels of output, these manufacturing growth rates tell a depressing story (Table 2.3B)—the de-industrialization of the countries of the Central American Common Market. For three of the five, El Salvador, Guatemala, and Honduras, the peak level of industrial output was reached in 1980 or 1981, and for Costa Rica 1986 was the first year in which real output exceeded the level of 1980.

Declining Investment

The instability of economic growth can be as depressing to private investment as slow growth. Since Central America has suffered from both of these, another of the identified trends—the decline in productive investment—is hardly surprising. An inspection of the first four lines of Table 2.4 shows declines in all of the countries but Costa Rica for 1982–1985. The most dramatic fall has been in Guatemala (despite substantial government incentives), where the change is negative in all four years.[12] Equally dismal has been the performance of private investment taken alone (the last four lines of the table). Only in the case of El Salvador has private investment been consistently positive, but these statistics must be viewed with a critical eye. Despite positive rates of change for private investment as a whole, private investment in plant and equipment was negative overall for the period and in three of the four years. This suggests that what investment occurred involved inventory accumulation and commerce-related activities rather than expansion of capacity. Further, it must be remembered that the decline in investment rates were from the already-depressed levels of the early 1980s, and were coincident with extensive closures of bankrupt factories and capital flight.[13]

Increasing Debt Service Burden

Economic instability, declining investment, and capital flight have placed great pressure on the balance of payments of the Central

American countries and made debt service increasingly difficult (the fifth trend listed above). Table 2.9 shows the trade balances of the seven countries, which have been consistently negative. Over seven years and five countries, a positive trade balance has been recorded in only six of thirty-five cases (five of the six being enjoyed by Costa Rica and Guatemala). In all cases except Nicaragua trade balances improved in 1986, in part due to the short-lived improvement in coffee prices.[14] These trade deficits, along with further current account deficits on 'invisibles' (insurance, transport, and profit outflows) provoked the accumulation of further debt (see Table 2.10). From 1980 to 1985, the foreign debt of two countries in the region doubled (Guatemala and Nicaragua). Two countries also reduced their foreign debts in some years: Costa Rica and Guatemala (in 1986 in both cases). All declines were minuscule.

Debt service burdens remain extremely high with no sign of a downward trend (Table 2.11). All the countries of the CACM were paying 35 to 55 percent of their export earnings to foreign creditors in 1985–1986 except for Nicaragua (which has declared a moratorium on payment to certain types of creditors). For El Salvador, Guatemala, and Honduras the debt service ratio for 1985–1986 was considerably more than double its 1981 level. In part the rise in debt service ratios represents the dubious benefits of rescheduling, as renegotiated liabilities have 'ballooned' in the second half of the 1980s. Guatemala is a case in point: despite enjoying in 1986 the second largest trade surplus of any country in the region during the 1980s, its debt service ratio for 1986 would actually rise if all obligations were met. The likelihood of all debt obligations being met is relatively slight. Meeting a substantial proportion would probably make the region an exporter of capital.[15] From time to time financial journalists have speculated about the unspeakable consequences for the Western monetary system were major debtor countries to default. In terms of the human condition, even more unspeakable would be the consequence of the Central American countries paying their full debt obligations.

All the economies of the region are growth-constrained by debt service. This constraint takes two important forms. First, in order to service the debt, exports must increase, and this requires shifting resources from the production of domestically-consumed products to commodities for sale abroad. Such a shift of resources usually involves among other things a restriction of domestic demand.[16] Second, since the reallocated resources produce commodities which are exported but cannot finance imports, debt-service payment involves a net reduction in the availability of commodities on the domestic market. This process necessarily generates inflationary pressures. The exports which pay the debt service generate an income equivalent in value to those commodities in domestic currency. The domestic currency injection creates excess effective demand which, if governments are to compensate, must be eliminated by reducing real expenditure.[17]

Debt service payments also have produced a distortion of the government budgets in the region which is frequently misinterpreted as lack of fiscal discipline. Characteristically, the debt service is carried in government budgets as a current expenditure by the Ministry of Finance, which it is in terms of foreign currency (i.e. the actual payment in dollars to the creditor). However, the domestic currency equivalent of debt service which appears in the government accounts is no expenditure at all, but merely a ledger entry. Debt service in domestic currency does not enter the domestic expenditure stream and is not itself expansionary. What is expansionary is the domestic currency equivalent of debt servicing exports (explained above), which is in private hands. The proportion of the fiscal deficit accounted for by debt service represents too much potential expenditure by the private sector, not the government. The condition on IMF loans that governments must reduce their fiscal deficits because they are expansionary is singularly inappropriate in many cases.[18]

Collapse of Regional Integration

Along with economic instability, falling living standards, and increased foreign debt has gone the collapse of the regional integration project. In the mid–1970s, intra-regional trade accounted for about a quarter of the total commodity trade of the five countries of the CACM, and in 1980 edged over US$ 1 billion. Since that time trade among the five countries has dropped dramatically, to about a third of the peak level (see Table 2.8). On a formal diplomatic level, there have apparently been attempts to facilitate intra-regional commerce, for example through the creation of a Central American cousin of the IMF Special Drawing Right.[19] In practice the five governments have proceeded on the basis of the *de facto* disintegration of the CACM. Over the last several years trade between members of the CACM has occasionally been suspended by embargoes (e.g. between Guatemala and Costa Rica) usually prompted by the failure to service bilateral debts.

Prospects for a rejuvenation of intra-regional trade were dimmed by the decisions taken at the December 1986 meeting of the CACM, where it was agreed to reduce normally-scheduled tariffs on textiles and apparel from 100 to 65 percent and from 70 to 45 percent, respectively. In an apparent attempt to further facilitate extra-regional imports of these commodities, an accord was reached to reduce their tariffs to only nominal levels (five to fifteen percent) should circumstances be such that domestic production could not meet local demand.[20] These decisions represented considerably more than tariff adjustment. Protection of the textile and clothing sectors had been central to the strategy of creating a regional market from which entrepreneurs could reap the advantages of economies of scale. Reducing these tariffs responded to pressures from interest groups with quite another strategy in mind, that of 'take-back' industries in which semi-finished articles would be imported into Central America and re-exported after some degree of processing. This type of limited manufacturing processing is not new to the Central American isthmus, being particularly important in Panama and associated with 'duty-free zones' (*zona franca* in Nicaragua during the Somoza dictatorship). There is considerable and not particularly encouraging international experience with this type of manufacturing exports. Whether or not it would be a vehicle for the re-industrialization of Central America is debatable. That it conflicts with the creation of a protected regional market if pursued on a considerable scale is obvious.

Competitive Crisis-Management Strategies

As the Central American economic crisis has deepened and the economies have settled into low-level stagnation, governments in the region have placed less and less practical importance on regional cooperation. The tendency of the early 1980s for each government to seek a separate peace with the international economy has become more pronounced.[21] The countries of the region have embarked upon divergent paths both as a result of and in spite of pressures by the major multilateral organizations for them to pursue *de facto* a similar package of policies. Except for Nicaragua, the members of the CACM have come under pressure to liberalize trade policy, which in the Central American context means reducing preferential treatment of intra-regional commodities. Further, the view of the IMF that fiscal deficits are always undesirable and should be reduced has led to policies that depress regional demand.[22] While demand reduction might release resources for extra-regional exports, its domestic effect is to restrict the market for the products of regional industry.

The implementation of superficially similar adjustment policies has not prevented governments of the region from following different strategies. Most successful in terms of reviving growth has been the strategy of the Costa Rican government. This strategy has involved maintaining protectionism (in face of multilateral and bilateral pressure to the contrary) and expanding the internal market. Reference to Table 2.1 shows that Costa Rica had the least-worst overall growth record after 1982, averaging 3.5 percent per annum during 1983–1986 (the only country whose rate of GDP growth exceeded the rate of population growth for the period). Costa Rica also had the fastest average rates of growth for agriculture and manufacturing for these years (see Tables 2.2 and 2.3). As noted above, only Costa Rica has had a consistent (albeit slow) expansion of the manufacturing sector, reaching an all-time high in 1986.

The ravages of war have forced upon the governments of El Salvador and Nicaragua relatively autarchic policies. Whatever the benefits or costs of economic liberalization in other contexts, in El Salvador and Nicaragua the primary result would be capital flight and exchange rate depreciation. The economic policies of both governments demonstrate a recognition of this reality. In El Salvador the state monopsony on the marketing of coffee (established in 1980) remains in effect although there is strong pressure from growers to abolish INCAFE, the parastatal marketing agency. In general the country's private sector has not cooperated with the Duarte government's attempts at economic stabilization programs (including tax reform); indeed, the opposition has been quite virulent, including a one-day business close-down in January 1987 to protest government policies.[23] The most striking difference in economic policy between Nicaragua and El Salvador is the heavy stress given to softening the impact of adjustment on the poor in the former country and the complete absence of such a priority in the latter. To take but one example, in recent years the Nicaraguan government has vigorously pursued a land-to-the-tiller land redistribution program, while the much-heralded Salvadorean land reform law is a dead letter.

The often bitter conflict between business and government in El Salvador is in sharp contrast to the qualified support given by the private sector to the new economic policies of the Cerezo administration. It is in Guatemala that one finds the most clearly defined program to establish a new growth strategy. In March 1986 the newly-elected government announced an economic plan which on paper involved a unique mixture of economic liberalism and populism. With respect to the private sector, the plan sought a re-orientation of industry and agriculture away from the regional market and traditional exports towards 'take-back' industries and the production of luxury agricultural products for the US market (taking advantage of trade preferences under the Caribbean Basin Initiative).[24] However, such products are unlikely to be substantial foreign exchange earners in this decade, accounting for less than three percent of export revenue in 1985. While the economic liberalization half of the economic plan has been implemented with vigor, one has yet to see any evidence of the populist portion. In May 1986, Cerezo announced a public works program designed to create 40,000 jobs, but over a year later it remains at the level of a proposal. To an extent the government can claim that the project fell victim to multilateral organisations' pressure for expenditure reduction.[25] But tax reform proposals have been opposed by the business elite and, in the Autumn of 1987, this led to a businessmen's strike. In addition, given the precarious position of the country's civilian government vis-à-vis the military, Cerezo may be forced to abandon his popularity-raising program which would have serious implications for the government's ability to rule.

In the case of Honduras the general thrust of economic policy is considerably less clear. As noted above, policies have been implemented to shift relative profitability toward extra-regional exports, but within this policy to continue to rely on traditional agricultural exports. In mid-1986 the government announced a new set of incentives for coffee, cotton, and beef producers, including a reduction of taxes. Concessions were also granted to two foreign-owned banana enterprises, though the companies continue to press for total exoneration from export duties.

Honduran governments over the past several years have come under strong pressure to liberalize and deregulate an economy always known for the limited role played by the state in economic affairs. In early 1986 a USAID loan of US$ 50 million was held undisbursed, awaiting the implementation of certain economic reforms by the Suazo government (e.g. devaluation and liberalization of foreign exchange controls).[26] The present government does not seem to be opposed in principle to these policy changes, so one can anticipate further liberalization measures.[27]

Concluding Remarks

This survey of economic policies should indicate the diversity of strategies being pursued in the region in response to the economic trends identified at the outset of this chapter. With the possible exception of Costa Rica there is little indication that any of the economies of the region are on the verge of a sustained recovery from the 'long night' of the Central American economic crisis. Few observers except the most ideological on the right or left foresee such a sustained recovery as imminent.[28] One tends to rebel against such pessimism, particularly in light of the long and sustained growth performances of the Central American economies after the Second World War. However, the conditions which produced that growth cannot be re-created (and few would desire it given the political models involved). A new basis for growth has yet to be established, for old plant and equipment have deteriorated without a compensating accumulation of new investments. Further, the projection for growth rates of developing countries toward the end of the century is hardly optimistic.[29] Weak, vulnerable to external shocks, and racked by social strife, the Central American region could hardly be anticipated to grow faster than the average for the developing world.

TABLE 2.1   Central America: Growth of Gross Domestic Product, 1950--1986
             (percent)

Year	Costa Rica	El Sal- vador	Guate- mala	Hon- duras	Nica- ragua
1950--1960	6.4	4.8	3.7	2.8	5.4
1960--1970	5.9	5.5	5.2	5.0	6.5
1970--1978	6.3	5.4	6.0	4.7	3.9
1979	5.3	-1.2	4.7	6.0	-24.5
1980	0.9	-8.1	3.7	0.6	4.6
1981	-2.3	-8.3	0.7	1.0	5.4
1982	-7.3	-5.6	-3.5	2.6	-0.8
1983	2.7	0.8	-2.7	1.1	4.6
1984	7.9	2.3	0.6	3.5	-1.6
1985	0.9	2.0	-1.0	2.7	-4.1
1986	3.0	1.0	0.0	3.0	-0.4
1987*	[2.0]	n.a.	[1.0]	n.a.	n.a.
Cum. Y/P (1980--1986)	-5.0	-35.0	-23.0	-9.0	-29.0

Notes: Figures for 1986 are preliminary. 'Cum.Y/P' refers to the
accumulated change in per capita income over the years indicated. These
figures for per capita income should be taken as rough orders of
magnitude, since they are based upon estimates of population growth in
non-census years.
    *Projections are by government agencies in both cases. The initial
2 percent projection for Guatemala was subsequently revised in light of
the fall in coffee prices. Taken in order of countries, the growth rates
are calculated on the basis of constant prices of 1966, 1962, 1958, 1978,
and 1980.

Source: IDB (1987). Similar figures using different base year prices in
some cases are found in CEPAL (1987a) and in CEPAL (1986c).

TABLE 2.2   Central America: Growth of Agricultural Value Added,
             1980--1986 (percent)

Year	Costa Rica	El Sal- vador	Guate- mala	Hon- duras	Nica- ragua
1980	-0.5	-5.2	1.6	0.8	-19.0
1981	5.1	-6.4	1.0	0.1	9.5
1982	-4.7	-4.7	-3.0	-1.7	2.8
1983	4.0	-3.2	-1.7	2.1	5.8
1984	10.1	3.3	1.6	1.1	-5.3
1985	-2.9	-1.1	-0.8	1.9	-4.8
1986	0.0	-2.1	0.0	1.6	-5.4

Note: Figures for 1986 are preliminary.

Source: IDB (1987).

TABLE 2.3   Central America: Growth of Manufacturing Production,
             1980--1986

A. Rates of Change of Real Output (percent)

Year	Costa Rica	El Sal- vador	Guate- mala	Hon- duras	Nica- ragua
1980	0.8	-10.7	5.6	-2.9	14.7
1981	-0.5	-10.4	-3.1	-2.2	3.0
1982	-11.4	-8.4	-5.2	-3.6	0.1
1983	1.8	2.0	-1.9	5.1	5.6
1984	10.4	1.3	0.5	3.6	0.4
1985	3.2	3.7	-0.2	2.4	-4.7
1986	2.7	2.4	0.5	1.6	1.6

B. Value Added (millions of 1982 US dollars)

Year	Costa Rica	El Sal- vador	Guate- mala	Hon- duras	Nica- ragua
1980	855	688	1627	443	646
1981	851	616	1576	447	664
1982	754	564	1494	415	653
1983	763	559	1466	400	683
1984	827	583	1476	409	694
1985	852	609	1476	400	654
1986	875	623	1464	406	664

Notes: Figures for 1986 are preliminary. The percentage changes in Part
A may not correspond exactly to the value added figures in Part B because
the former are based on indices of physical production for different base-
year prices.

Source: IDB (1987).

TABLE 2.4   Central America: Rate of Change of Gross Fixed Investment at Constant Prices, 1982--1985 (percent)

Year	Costa Rica	El Salvador	Guatemala	Honduras	Nicaragua
(Public and Private)					
1982	-27.8	-10.1	-10.9	-19.0	-19.4
1983	4.2	-7.5	-27.0	2.1	8.7
1984	25.9	2.3	-11.8	7.1	-4.6
1985	5.2	5.0	-3.3	-6.6	-14.7
(Private)					
1982	n.a.	0.3	-4.2	-35.9	n.a.
1983	n.a.	7.2	-2.4	-3.6	n.a.
1984	n.a.	11.2	2.4	-4.1	n.a.
1985	n.a.	16.2	-1.2	1.0	n.a.

Note: The positive percentages for private investment in El Salvador hide a measured decline in investment in plant and machinery in three of the four years (a cumulative decline of about 25 percent).

Source: CEPAL (1986a), pp. 196, 319, 343, 391 and 456.

TABLE 2.5   Rates of Urban Unemployment in Central America, 1980--1986 (percent)

Year	Costa Rica	El Salvador	Guatemala	Honduras	Nicaragua
1980	6.0	16.1	2.2	8.8	22.4
1981	9.1	25.0	2.7	9.0	19.0
1982	9.9	30.0	4.7	9.2	19.9
1983	8.6	30.0	7.6	9.5	18.9
1984	6.6	30.0	9.7	10.7	21.1
1985	6.7	30.0	11.9	11.7	22.3
1986	6.7	30.0	12.0	12.4	21.7

Notes: Figures for 1986 are preliminary. In the case of Honduras, the government also reported 'equivalent unemployment' (which includes a measure of underemployment). This second series of figures follows that above in its direction of movement if not its level. For 1983--1986, the figures are respectively: 22.0, 23.9, 24.5, and 25.0.

Source: CEPAL (1986c) and CEPAL (1986a).

38

TABLE 2.6   Rates of Change of Real Wages in Central America, 1980--1985
             (percent)

Year	Costa Rica	El Salvador	Guatemala	Honduras	Nicaragua
1980	0.8	9.0	0.2	-8.3	-15.0
1981	-11.7	-0.6	19.8	5.0	1.4
1982	-19.8	-11.8	6.0	-0.5	-12.7
1983	10.9	-12.9	-7.6	-7.7	-12.7
1984	7.8	2.1	-0.7	-4.5	0.1
1985	8.9	-19.4	-11.5	-3.3	-18.9

Notes: In the case of Honduras, manufacturing is included only for 1980--
1982.   Working population covered varies from country to country.   The
Nicaraguan data are most restricted, covering only those employees under
the social security system.

Source: CEPAL (1986c) and CEPAL (1986a).

TABLE 2.7   Rates of Inflation in Central America, 1980--1986 (percent)

Year	Costa Rica	El Salvador	Guatemala	Honduras	Nicaragua
1980	18	19	9	12	25
1981	65	12	9	9	23
1982	82	14	-2	9	22
1983	11	16	15	7	33
1984	17	10	5	4	50
1985	11	31	32	4	334
1986	14	32	42	4	778

Note: Figures for 1986 are preliminary.

Source: CEPAL (1986c) and CEPAL (1986a).

TABLE 2.8   Intra-Regional Exports for the Countries of the CACM,
1980--1986 (millions of current US dollars)

Year	Costa Rica	El Salvador	Guatemala	Honduras	Nicaragua	Total
1980	270	296	404	84	75	1129
1981	238	206	356	66	71	937
1982	164	174	320	52	52	763
1983	187	168	308	61	33	758
1984	175	177	290	57	43	742
1985	145	96	208	18	24	490
1986	98	93	148	19	12	370

Source: CEPAL (1987a).

TABLE 2.9   Trade Balance for the Countries of Central America,
1980--1986 (millions of US dollars)

Year	Costa Rica	El Salvador	Guatemala	Honduras	Nicaragua
1980	-374	178	47	-104	-353
1981	-89	-100	-249	-115	-416
1982	64	-122	-114	-4	-317
1983	-45	-96	36	-67	-350
1984	-66	-179	-60	-78	-396
1985	-69	-231	-17	-124	-470
1986	53	-170	150	-20	-570

Note: Figures for 1986 are preliminary.

Source: CEPAL (1986c) and CEPAL (1986a).

TABLE 2.10   Central America: Foreign Debt by Country, 1981--1986
(millions of US dollars)

Year	Costa Rica	El Sal- vador	Guate- mala	Hon- duras	Nica- ragua
1981	3360	1471	1305	1708	2566
1982	3497	1710	1560	1986	3139
1983	3848	1891	2130	2162	3788
1984	3955	1949	2463	2392	3901
1985	4084	2003	2644	2615	4616
	[526]	[174]	[76]	[347]	[5]
1986	4000	2120	2530	2880	5260

Notes: Figures for 1986 are preliminary. Those in brackets for 1985 give the amount of new debt contracted by the private sector.

Source: CEPAL (1986c) and CEPAL (1986a).

TABLE 2.11   Estimated Debt Service as Percent of Export Earnings
for the Countries of Central America, 1981--1986

Year	Costa Rica	El Sal- vador	Guate- mala	Hon- duras	Nica- ragua
1981	26.5	18.4	19.7	16.1	41.3
1982	21.2	26.2	20.2	48.4	45.4
1983	63.7	66.0	25.1	38.0	22.2
1984	31.7	52.0	34.7	39.0	18.7
1985	41.2	56.8	46.0	39.2	19.8
1986	36.0	52.0	48.0	36.0	31.0

Notes: Estimates for 1986 are based upon scheduled obligations and average interest rates for the year. Effects of re-negotiations and default are not included, except in the case of Nicaragua where it is assumed that government continued its policy of repaying only those lenders who continued to extend new credits.

Source: CEPAL (1986a).

Notes

1. This transition is alluded to in CEPAL (1986b) and in an earlier version of the same, CEPAL (1984). The particularly reactionary nature of the Central American dictatorships is treated explicitly in Baloyra (1983) and in Weeks (1986a).

2. Perhaps more important are the social and political developments (foremost among which are war and civil strife), but these lie beyond the scope of this paper.

3. CEPAL writes, "The fragmentation of Central America since the short-lived federation broke up has . . . contributed to the fact that each of the countries has resigned itself historically to having a scanty margin of action with regard to its own fate, due to the preponderance of factors beyond its control." CEPAL (1986b), p. 11.

4. I refer to the December 1986 meeting at which tariffs were reduced substantially for textiles and clothing, and other steps taken to facilitate extra-regional imports of these items.

5. See Singh (1983) and World Bank (1983). Despite the reference to Africa in its title, the first paper provides a good discussion of world market prospects for products relevant for Central America.

6. See CEPAL (1986c), p. 33; and CEPAL (1986b), pp. 27–28.

7. The evidence is summarized in Weeks (1985b), Chapter 5; and Weeks (1987), 'Rural Poverty, Growth, and Equity,' paper prepared for the FAO document, *Agriculture: Toward 2000* (Washington, February 1987), available from author. Detailed analysis of conditions in the agricultural sectors of the six Spanish-speaking countries of the region can be found in Peek (ed) (1987).

8. See Hintermeister (1987).

9. "The fruits of the long period of economic expansion which took place after the war were distributed in a flagrantly inequitable manner . . . preventing any significant relief of the extreme poverty which persists in the region." CEPAL (1986b), pp. 11–12.

10. See Weeks (1985b), pp. 105–107.

11. "Although some agricultural products for export received the stimulus of increased prices, the effects of the downward trend of international prices in previous years, which had affected investment and production decisions, continued to be felt." CEPAL (1987a), p. 2.

12. Preliminary estimates show that private investment in Guatemala declined by a further 5.3 percent in 1986. See *This Week: Central America and Panama* (Guatemala City), 2 February 1987.

13. One estimate is that US$ 9 billion left Central America as capital flight during 1978–1986. See *Central American Report* (Guatemala City), 20 June 1986. The tip of the iceberg is the measured increase of US$ 1.4 billion increase in deposits in US banks by Central American nationals from June 1979 to June 1984. See CEPAL (1986b), p. 28.

14. Due to the drought in Brazil coffee prices rose in 1985 to a peak level of US$ 245 per quintal (one quintal equals one hundred pounds). The rush of coffee-

producing countries to take advantage of the higher price (largely ignoring quotas set by the International Coffee Agreement) resulted in a glut on the world market and a decline to US$ 182 per quintal in July 1986. However, because of lags between contraction of sales and delivery, the price gain showed up in 1986 export earnings for several countries.

15. "International banks appear to be extremely reluctant to commit fresh funds in a subregion in which high risks are considered to prevail; on the other hand, commitments originating from external debt service are so high that the possibility of the region becoming a net exporter of capital cannot be discounted." CEPAL (1986b), p. 33.

16. For example, in Honduras for the last two years small farmers primarily involved in production of basic grains have complained that their government has favored large scale producers of cotton, coffee, and beef in its agricultural policy. Perhaps the best example of this is the guaranteed price of cotton. See *Central American Report* (Guatemala City), 16 May 1986.

17. From the point of view of the residents of a country taken as a whole, debt involves the unrequited surrendering of production to foreign debtors (i.e. the export earnings are not available for imports). However, the exporters of these commodities are paid for them. The domestic currency they receive goes into the domestic expenditure stream without finding any equivalent goods and services.

18. For example, in 1986 Guatemala's fiscal deficit was 735 million quetzales, of which 270 million represented a ledger entry for debt service. In terms of cash flow, the government current account was in slight surplus. Even more striking is the case of Costa Rica, where the IMF was demanding a reduction in government expenditure (e.g. civil service lay offs) to reduce the fiscal deficit. The overall deficit on the current and capital accounts was four billion colones, slightly less than debt service payments measured in colones. Therefore, on the basis of cash flow, the total budget was balanced.

19. In August-September 1986 the finance ministers of the CACM countries met to create the 'Central American Import Certificate' (*Derechos de Importación Centroamericanos, DICA*). These can be issued by the various Central Banks and are accepted as payment among the member countries. See *Central American Report* (Guatemala City), 8 September 1986.

20. See *Central American Report* (Guatemala City), 9 January 1987; and CEPAL (1987a).

21. Brief surveys of economic policy by country for the early 1980s are found in Weeks (1985b), Chapter 8; Weeks (1985a) and Weeks (1986b).

22. Failure of governments to pursue such policies with vigour sufficient to satisfy the IMF has led to suspension of stand-by agreements (Guatemala and Honduras in 1984). See CEPAL (1986b), p. 28. Commenting on the multilateral organizations' programs, CEPAL writes, "Foremost among the internal factors which have restricted economic activity is the implementation of adjustment policies which . . . have had marked recessionary consequences." CEPAL (1987a), p. 1.

23. See *Central American Report* (Guatemala City), 13 January 1987.

24. Representatives of the Guatemalan private sector have complained that

the trade preferences of the CBI are in fact relatively trivial, covering only three percent of the value of Guatemalan exports to the US in 1985. See *Central American Report* (Guatemala City), 19 December 1987.

25. The Inter-American Development Bank has been supportive of the Cerezo government's populist program. It is not accidental that the IDB alone among the major multilateral lenders has come under great pressure from the US government to change its policies and system of governance.

26. See *Central American Report* (Guatemala City), 24 January 1986. In another version, a London newspaper alleged that the loan was held up over disputes about the presence of the 'contra' army in Honduras; *The Guardian* (London), 22 December 1985.

27. In January 1986 the new president of Honduras, José Simón Azcona Hoyo, endorsed IMF austerity measures. See *Central American Report* (Guatemala City), 10 January 1986.

28. CEPAL summarizes the situation as follows: "It is difficult to make any forecasts as to the likely evolution of the Central American economies. On the one hand, the exhaustion of their international monetary reserves, the burden of the external debt, the shrinkage in imports and the depressed levels of all macroeconomic variables . . . considerably narrow the margin of action available to economic policy; on the other hand, the restrictions of external and subregional origin affecting Central American development are subject to a whole range of factors which further heighten the uncertainty looming over all the countries." CEPAL (1986b), pp. 33–34.

29. See, for example, FAO (1987).

3

Industrial Development in Central America, 1960–1980: Issues of Debate

Alfredo Guerra-Borges

Introduction

The present work is divided into three main sections. Broadly speaking, the first section is concerned with why Central America was a late industrializer and what forces shaped the CACM. The two decades following 1960 were characterized by rapid industrial growth, but the resulting pattern of import substitution industrialization was deeply flawed. Although these flaws are sometimes ascribed to the prescriptions of ECLA, it would be truer to say that ECLA's prescriptions which emphasized balanced industrial growth were largely ignored.

The second section begins with a brief description of the institutional machinery of the CACM and goes on to consider some of the anomalies in the tariff and fiscal arrangements which emerged and their implications for industrial structure. In particular it is shown that the CACM tariff structure favored the production of luxury consumption goods at the expense of intermediate and capital goods. Moreover, the failure to implement common fiscal policies and the recourse to free-trade zones to attract foreign capital was costly both in terms of lost government revenue and in terms of the price competitiveness of industry.

Recent debates on industrialization are the subject of the third and final section. Here it is argued that the dichotomy between inward-

---

Alfredo Guerra-Borges was for many years chief economic advisor to SIECA and is, at present, Professor Emeritus at the *Instituto de Investigaciones Económicas* of the *Universidad Nacional Autónoma de México*.

and outward-looking development strategies is both theoretically unhelpful and practically misleading. While it is true that greater attention must be paid to export promotion, new industrial exports are most likely to develop in such lines as timber, food products, clothing, and footwear, all of which grew under the CACM. Moreover, it is unlikely that foreign capital can be relied upon to provide the bulk of the required finance. A precondition for any growth, obviously, is peace which will enable scarce foreign exchange to be re-channelled towards meeting economic priorities.

SECTION I

The Point of Departure

Although a small number of industrial enterprises existed in Central America at the beginning of this century, it is only after the Second World War that a genuine process of industrialization took hold. In Guatemala and El Salvador, brewing industries were established at the end of the nineteenth century, and textile production appeared in the 1920s. Otherwise, regional industry was confined to sugar mills, the most important being the San Antonio Mill in Nicaragua which, as late as 1952, refined seventy-seven percent of that country's production. Before 1945 there was also a thin scatter of firms producing such things as cigarettes, cement and plastics. But the bulk of industrial output originated in the artisan sector; i.e. in workshops employing less than five full-time workers equipped with simple means of production.[1]

A variety of factors helps explain why industrial development took place so late in Central America. For one thing, the size of the population and the low level of per capita income made for a narrow domestic market. In 1950, the five Central American countries together had only 8 million inhabitants and the regional gross domestic product was a mere 1.4 billion US dollars, or US$ 175 per head. According to United Nations data, the average annual income of the bottom ninety percent of households in El Salvador was US$ 92. In Guatemala the figure was US$ 80.[2]

More than two-thirds of households lived in rural areas, typically, in scattered villages. Urban centers were small. With the exception of Guatemala City and San Salvador, in 1960 no city in Central America had more than 100,000 inhabitants.

A further constraint on industrial development was the absence of an adequate transport infrastructure. Before modernization began in the 1960s, the region's network of roads and railways was limited and served principally to carry merchandise to the ports. Electricity generating capacity was a further problem. In 1960, annual per capita electricity consumption ranged from 74 KW-hours in Guatemala to 355 KW-hours in Costa Rica in contrast to a figure of 398 KW-hours for Latin America as a whole.

Rates of illiteracy were high and skilled workers and supervisors were in extremely scarce supply. This, together with the narrowness of the domestic market, was an important reason why at the beginning of the 1960s existing industrial plant capacity was severely underutilized. According to estimates of the Joint Programming Mission (*Misión Conjunta de Programación*) published in 1962, the degree of underutilized capacity was 18 percent in Nicaragua, 37 percent in Honduras and, on average, 27 percent in Guatemala, El Salvador and Costa Rica. Financing industrial investment depended very largely on private venture capital. In good years, a landowner in the export sector might provide a personal loan to an industrial entrepreneur. In general, though, little finance capital flowed directly from agriculture to industry.

A more important source of finance to industry was commerce; indeed, a number of industries were set up specifically to serve the needs of the commercial sector. As a rule, the banking and financial sector only provided working capital to industry. A report of the World Bank notes that, in the 1960s, most lending to the industrial sector was for periods of less than eighteen months even though the credit requirements for fixed investment had risen greatly.[3]

Industrialization and Integration

It was not until the post-war years that new social and political conditions emerged favoring industrial development. As power gradually slipped from the hands of the traditional oligarchy, modern ideas took hold and new social currents grew in strength, particularly in the progressive climate prevailing at the end of the Second World War. On the 16th of June, 1951, the Economic Commission for Latin America (ECLA) approved Resolution 9 (IV) calling for the promotion of industrialization through integration. As much as any other event, this event marks the conception of the Central American Common Market (CACM).

The impulse towards integration did not come from Central America's propertied classes, still less from the governments whose interests they represented. The notion that industrialization would enable Central America to decrease its reliance on monoculture, to shed its 'banana republic' image, came from ECLA. Integrationist ideas were introduced and spread by a new generation of young, well-educated *técnicos*.

One sign of the times was a law passed by the Costa Rican Parliament in 1940 quixotically entitled the 'Law Favoring the Establishment of Totally New Industries' (*la ley que favorece el establecimiento de industrias totalmente nuevas*). In Guatemala, the first Industrial Development Act (*Ley de Fomento Industrial*) was passed in 1946 and similar legislation soon followed in neighbouring countries. Further evidence of a new climate of opinion is to be found in the spate of banking and monetary reforms adopted in the five republics during the period 1945–1950. Integration became synonymous with industrialization. The integration movement grew to encompass various groups—ECLA-influenced intellectuals, local businessmen, traders, foreign companies—groups whose interests were by no means compatible. Such differences, though dimly perceived initially, soon became clear and ultimately changed the course of industrial development in a manner unforeseen by ECLA.

Early Notions of Integration

For ECLA, regional integration was a necessary but insufficient condition for industrial development. In order to thrive, industry must be distributed among countries so as to make the best use of resource endowments *and* ensure that the benefits of growth are equitably distributed. Since economies of scale were significant in some lines of manufacture, ECLA insisted that investment in such lines should proceed according to an agreed regional plan. The establishment of such 'integration industries' was central to the ECLA vision. The development of industrial branches where economies of scale were less important could be left to private enterprise.

While ECLA's economic logic was sound, it failed to consider the ideology of the business community, both local and foreign, which regarded the notion of 'planned development' with suspicion. When the US Government set out alternative proposals for regional integration which emphasized free trade and capital mobility, there was little doubt which proposal would win the day. The General Treaty of Central American Economic Integration (GT), drawn up in 1960, superseded the Multilateral Treaty of Free Trade and Economic Integration (MT) of 1958 which had incorporated the Integration Industries Convention (IIC). In contrast to ECLA, which wanted planned development of integration industries linked to gradual trade liberalization, the US administration wanted:

intra-regional free trade as the norm with any exceptions to be explicitly listed (the opposite of MT) and by implication the elimination of the monopoly status of designated integration industries.[4]

A 1959 agreement on trade liberalization had envisaged this process taking place over a ten-year period. In the GT of 1960, the target period for trade liberalization was reduced to five years. Although the Integration Industries Convention was retained in the GT, it was never implemented. Moreover, the Alliance for Progress established under President Kennedy provided US financial backing for the integration organizations set up under the GT, thus giving Washington a decisive say in shaping the CACM.

Industrialization under the CACM

A particular feature of Central American industrialization is its close association with the integration process. This is not to say that industrial growth can be attributed exclusively to the setting up of the CACM. Rather, the form which economic integration took was of key importance to the pattern of industrial development.

Under the CACM, manufacturing growth soared. Measured at constant 1970 prices, industrial output grew by 8.5 percent per annum over the period 1960–1970 subsequently falling to 6.4 percent for the period 1970–1978. (Average figures for 1979 and 1980 are excluded because they reflect the virtual collapse of the manufacturing industry in Nicaragua during the uprising against Somoza.) For the period 1960–1970, the rate of growth of industrial value added was 1.5 times that of value added as a whole. For 1970–1978, a figure of only 1.2 reflected the general slowdown in economic activity.

A further index of the rapid rate of industrialization is provided by measuring industrial output per capita, bearing in mind that the rate of population growth was high. In 1960, per capita industrial output was US$ 100. Measured at 1970 prices, the figure had risen to US$ 156 in 1970 and US$ 207 in 1978.[5]

One result of rapid industrial growth was the destruction of artisan employment. By the mid-1970s, artisan output accounted for only 18 percent of Central American industrial output, down from 30 percent in 1960. Moreover, the structure of industry changed significantly.

The share of non-durable consumer goods in total manufacturing output declined while that of intermediate goods rose. The former had accounted for 73 percent of regional industrial production in 1960. By 1978, the share of non-durable consumer goods had fallen to 57 percent. The share of intermediate goods rose from 22 percent to 36 percent over the same period. Moreover, changes in the non-durable consumer goods sector included the introduction of new technologies, larger plants and a more diversified product range.

Using the Central American Industrial Census of 1968, SIECA showed that in key sectors, most output originated from plants set up after 1960. For example, 71 percent of the paper and paper products manufactured in the region in 1968 originated from plants and machinery acquired since 1960, as did 56 percent of rubber and rubber-based products, 50 percent of industrial chemicals, 55 percent of non-ferrous metal products, and 69 percent of ferrous metal products.[6]

By contrast, the production of intermediate goods hardly grew at all. In 1968, engineering and durable consumer goods output accounted for less than 6 percent of total manufactures. Many new industries used relatively simple technologies and concentrated on products at the end of the production chain. Only in exceptional cases can one speak of an industry showing any significant degree of vertical integration.

Nevertheless, the 1960s was a period of rapid progress and the resulting changes are aptly characterized in a World Bank Report prepared in 1972:

> Viewing the industrial landscape in 1970, the mission was impressed by the transformation that has taken place in the composition of industrial production in Central America. The traditional lines of manufacture—food, beverages, tobacco, clothing, footwear—retained their importance in the overall structure, but superimposed on the scene was a wide array of new activities and new products. However, it is easy to be misled by all the novelty and statistics. A balanced view has to recognize that Central American industrialization to date is skin-deep, so to speak. There is scarcely any production capacity in capital goods nor in the heavier categories of intermediates. A large number of plants have come into existence, many of less than optimal size, which have bitten off a tiny chunk of value added at the finishing end of the processing operation.[7]

Import Substitution

Much as elsewhere in Latin America, the chosen path to industrialization in Central America has been via import substitution. As is evident from Table 3.3, over the period 1960–1978 the share of extra-regional manufactures in total manufacturing imports declined, particularly that of manufactured intermediate products which fell from 59 percent to 39 percent.

The share of extra-regional non-durable consumer goods in total imports was low at the outset: 8 percent in 1960 declining to 6.5 percent by 1978. Similarly, modest reductions were registered in the shares of durable consumer goods as well as those of machinery and equipment.

However, an alternative way of gauging the extent of import substitution is to look at how the share of intra-regional imports in total imports increased over the period 1960–1978. Looking at Table 3.4, the 1960 figure is 5 percent while the 1978 figure is 21 percent. Consumer and intermediate goods account for the greatest part of this increase.

As to the main characteristics of the import-substitution process, a number of observations are apposite. First, there was no genuine attempt to develop coherent industrial policies at the regional level. This is reflected by the high extra-regional import content of much production for final demand, particularly in the 'touching-up' industries (*industrias de toque final*). The latter's contribution to raising average industrial value added was minimal. The balance of payments contribution of such industries was questionable. Where touching-up (sometimes called 'take-back') industries were MNC-owned and the percentage of remitted profits was high, the overall balance of payments effect was often negative.

Of course, legislation was passed in each country regulating industrial development and, in 1969, the Central American Convention on Fiscal Incentives for Industrial Development (*Convenio Centroamericano de Incentivos Fiscales al Desarrollo Industrial*) was adopted. But in practice, the political influence of local and foreign investors prevailed over the limited regulatory powers of the administrators. Such legislation more often than not was simply disregarded.

It should be noted that the statistical aggregates tell only part of the story. The breakdown of imports does not reveal the degree to which, in the case of certain products, regional demand increased so rapidly that regional production was unable to keep pace. In other cases, regional production was constrained by problems of adapting and incorporating new technologies.

These features were particularly characteristic of new products. Much of the increase in aggregate demand over the period is explained by the rising income of a growing but still tenuous middle class. Moreover, the composition of demand changed radically as North American consumption patterns spread. The manufacture of new products generally required the use of sophisticated machinery and other inputs in a manner which was difficult to accommodate with existing resource endowments given the region's relatively low level of development.

Hence, although the initial share of non-durable consumer goods imported from outside the region was low (and fell somewhat over the period), the most significant characteristic of the industrialization process is that it was geared to meeting the rapidly changing consumption requirements of a narrow segment of the population.

A final point concerns import substitution in the case of intermediate inputs for industry. Although considerable import substitution took place, both the absolute and the relative shares of industrial inputs purchased outside the region rose. One might observe that this feature has been characteristic of import substituting industrialization (ISI) in much of Latin America. New final-goods production capacity fueled the demand for foreign inputs and technology. First-stage ISI generally was not foreign-exchange saving but, on the contrary, increased net foreign exchange requirements. Ultimately, the industrialization process was impeded or exhausted by a balance of payments constraint. However, in our view, it is incorrect to ascribe the shortcomings of ISI to ECLA. It is precisely because ECLA's call for balanced industrial growth went unheeded that ISI did not live up to its original promise.

Industrial Location and Specialization

A general feature of Central American industrial growth is that the pattern of regional specialization which emerged within the CACM bore little relation to the relative resource endowments of the countries concerned. Because of the highly liberal policy adopted with respect to importing extra-regional industrial inputs, local resource endowments played only a minor role in the location of industry. This is not to say that industrial location was not influenced by considerations of scale, labor availability, infrastructure and the like. However, the overriding consideration was nearly always political— which government was prepared to offer most?—particularly in the case of foreign companies.

Much research has been carried out on industrial specialization within the CACM from the point of view of intra-regional trade. In general, the implicit assumption of such research has been that the country acting as the region's main supplier of a given line of products would possess the most installed capacity in that line; i.e. that inter-industry specialization was the norm. Measurement conventions differ somewhat from one study to the next but the common point of reference has generally been the relative share of each country in regional trade flows between industries.[8]

Such studies reveal, for example, that Guatemala has been Central America's principal supplier of pharmaceuticals, textile threads, tires and glassware. For two decades EL Salvador was the second most important regional trading nation, producing such things as paper and cardboard containers, clothing, textiles and a range of electric appliances. Table 3.5 shows the position of each country with respect to trade in selected industry groups.

However, a study by Bela Balassa of three countries—Costa Rica, Honduras and Nicaragua—has revealed a high degree intra-industry specialization which suggests that the greater part of Central American industrial trade takes place between firms belonging to the same industry in different countries (intra-industry) rather than, as commonly supposed, between firms belonging to different industries (inter-industry).[9] This fact helps explain why the establishment of the CACM gave rise to such similar patterns of investment activity in the five countries. Undoubtedly, the duplication of industry has helped inject a healthy dose of competition into regional production. On the other hand, competition has often taken the form of simple product differentiation, typically between MNCs and mainly for the purpose of gaining a foothold in the regional market.

The Destination of Industrial Output

In speaking of the 'local market' it is necessary to specify whether one is referring to a single country or to the region as a whole. In certain branches of industry, the nature of the product limits the market to the country of production; e.g., cement. In other branches, the bulk of production is for export within the region; e.g., glassware and most industrial chemicals. Most 'local market' industries are regional in nature and, in the absence of access to the market of the five countries, would almost certainly collapse.

A most interesting aspect of Central American industrialization is the degree to which firms have acquired the capacity to place products outside the region. With reference to manufactures—leaving aside semi-manufactures such as processed food products—over the period 1960–1969, the average annual rate of growth of extra-regional manufacturing exports was 12.4 percent. By contrast, manufacturing exports within the region grew at over twice that rate, or 28.6 percent in real terms. In the subsequent period, 1970–1976, the reverse was true. Intra-regional exports grew by only 6.6 percent annually while extra-regional exports growth jumped to an annual average of 22 percent. Then, over the years 1976–1979, average growth rates fell to 4.8 percent and 2.7 percent respectively.[10]

Looking at the growth of manufacturing exports (measured at constant 1970 prices) and their share in trade, total manufacturing exports for the region jumped from US$ 286 million in 1970, of which 10 percent was extra-regional, to US$ 1.051 billion in 1979 of which 22 percent was extra-regional. Hence, by the late 1970s one-fifth of manufacturing export production was being placed outside the region—and it should be borne in mind that over 95 percent of processed agricultural exports (e.g. sugar, meat, lumber) went to the rest of the world.[11]

Today, the question of placing manufactured exports in the world market has become central in the debate over the region's future. Both the Reagan Administration and the World Bank have conditioned the terms of this debate. There are also those business groups who, by reason of their strong antipathy towards the Sandinista revolution, consider it the divine mission of Central America to place exports in the US market.

SECTION II
Policy Instruments

Having reviewed key features of the industrialization process in Central America, it will be useful to examine the main policy instruments used in its promotion. These include the setting up of free trade zones (FTZs), the adoption of a Common External Tariff (CET) and the use of fiscal and financial incentives.

Institutionally speaking, important roles in the fields of finance and technology, respectively, have been played by the Central American Bank for Economic Integration (BCIE) and the Central American Institute of Research and Industrial Technology (ICAITI). The BCIE, which was set up mainly to finance infrastructure projects, did much in the 1960s to establish the modern road network necessary to expedite the physical movement of goods. To facilitate the financial settlement of trade obligations between countries, the Central American Clearing House (*Cámara Centroamericana de Compensación*, CCC) was established. At the summit of the organizational chart of 'integration organizations' is the Economic Council (*Consejo Económico*), which comprises senior economics ministers, followed by the Executive Council (*Consejo Ejecutivo*) which is composed of deputy-ministers (*viceministros*). These two councils act as the executive branch and are assisted by the Permanent Secretariat of the General Treaty of Central American Economic Integration (SIECA).

When the General Treaty came into effect on 4 June 1961, 81 percent of dutiable trade between the members was freed of all restrictions; by the early 1970s, the figure had risen to 96 percent. Taking so large a step in so short a time was greatly assisted by the fact that the countries concerned had much the same economic characteristics and possessed relatively little industry. The dismantling of industrial protection encountered little resistance simply because there were few vested interests to overcome. Such initial resistance as was encountered soon crumbled. By contrast, in the 1970s the integration organizations were forced to cede ground more than once when confronted by the combined forces of new interest groups.

The free trade zone (FTZ) was one of the key instruments used to promote industrialization. A coalition of interest groups promoted the FTZ idea. First of all, there was the local bourgeoisie which perceived the FTZ as offering a golden opportunity for utilizing existing spare capacity and exploiting new, low-risk investment opportunities. By the same token, this group rejected any scheme which smacked of regulation. This view was shared by foreign capital, the other main group behind the FTZ, whose influence grew steadily throughout the 1960s filling, so to speak, economic space as yet unclaimed for the banner of 'free enterprise.'

The Common External Tariff (CET), consolidated and extended during the first decade of the CACM, provided useful protection for investors and eliminated some of the discrepancies between the protective structures of individual countries. It also reflected the interests of a newly emerging bourgeoisie. Not only did the CET provide protection relative to third countries, but the level of common protection was higher than that of the national tariff levels it superseded. The highest level of nominal protection (an average of 106 percent) was established for non-durable consumer goods while, in the case of industrial inputs, an intermediate band of 36 percent was established. For capital goods, average nominal protection was only 11 percent, reflecting the need to acquire such goods cheaply. There was little interest in promoting local capital goods production.

Given the difference in nominal rates applicable to industrial outputs and inputs, average effective protection was high and the effective rate of protection (ERP) varied significantly between industries. The same was true between countries since the five countries did not all adopt the CET at the same time. A further curious feature of nominal tariff protection is that most articles were dutiable both by weight and on an *ad valorem* basis. In 1972, the *ad valorem* component accounted for only about 60 percent of tariff revenue and as inflation accelerated after 1974, the level of nominal protection fell.

However, the factor which played havoc with the attempt to construct a uniform tariff structure for the region was the use of tariff exemptions as an incentive to industrial investment. By the 1970s, exemptions had become the rule as countries competed with each other to attract investors. The case of Guatemala is instructive. It is estimated that, in 1980, only 31 percent of total imports paid any duty.[12]

The fiscal implications of such exemptions are evident; Guatemala has the lowest ratio of fiscal revenue to GDP of any of the CACM countries.

The Central American Convention on Fiscal Incentives for Industrial Development (*Convenio Centroamericano de Incentivos Fiscales al Desarrollo Industrial*) came into effect barely a year and a half after the signing of the General Treaty. Fiscal incentives were graduated in such a way as to encourage investment in capital goods and raw material producing industries as well as industries using a high proportion of inputs originating in Central America. But the fact that seven years elapsed between the adoption and application of the Convention suggests a serious conflict of interests existed between entrepreneurial groups in the different countries. Each sought the support of its own government to gain maximum advantage from existing fiscal incentives. When the Convention eventually was applied, existing concessions were maintained and a special provision was included to ensure that where tariff dispensation was higher under existing legislation than under the new Convention, the former would apply.

Undoubtedly, incentives such as tax holidays and tariff dispensations did stimulate investment in the early years. But as these were extended over time, temporary relief turned into permanent subsidy. Ultimately, fiscal laxness on the part of Central American authorities served to paper over an uncompetitive cost structure. For those industries where costs were competitive, fiscal stimuli were redundant. The policy was ultimately self-defeating since, applied indiscriminately, it failed in its original purpose which was to encourage the setting up of new industry. As to its usefulness in attracting foreign investment, a number of studies have shown that fiscal incentives were a relatively minor consideration in choosing to set up operations in the CACM. MNCs invested in order to secure a place in a new and growing market.

Ultimately, the structure of incentives adopted involved serious costs over and above the loss of government revenues and subsidized inefficiency entailed. The abolition of import duties on raw materials was stimulus to the use of raw material intensive technologies, often of a primitive nature. Moreover, the combined effect of tax and tariff exemptions strengthened the position of MNCs *vis-à-vis* local enterprise and did little to encourage local acquisition of MNC technology and know-how. In sum, it is debatable whether the CACM possessed any coherent industrial policy. Such policy as there was, far from stimulating the process of industrialization, may in certain respects have constrained it. As has been argued elsewhere:

Paradoxically, what most impeded the quality of industrialization in the region was the high rate of profit. With investment concentrated in those sectors where the payback period was shortest and where the narrowness of the regional market fostered market concentration, there was little incentive for investment funds to flow into areas which would have promoted industrialization in depth.[13]

Industrialization in Depth

Shortly after the initiation of the integration process, ECLA and SIECA, in a joint report, had this to say:

> If industrialization continues to be confined to those branches of industry producing consumer goods along traditional lines, opportunities for development will be limited. . . . Such branches of activity will tend to grow relatively slowly in keeping with the rate of growth of population and the growth of incomes generated from the agriculture export sector. . . . It is evident that if the required rate of industrialization is to be achieved, investment should be channelled towards other branches of activity including those producing inputs for the consumer goods industry. These matters are closely linked since the new capital-goods and intermediate industries required are those capable of generating a pattern of growth under which the consumer goods industry would utilize a higher proportion of Central American input as well as benefiting from the advantages of specialization and the absorption of new technology.[14]

The central idea was to complement the development of the consumer goods sector by setting up basic industries; i.e., capital goods and raw material production.

> This is basic in the sense of creating the material conditions for the development of the manufacturing sector which, supported by the exploitation of natural resources specific to the region, would free other sectors from the potential constraint imposed by the capacity to import necessary manufactured inputs. . . . The main characteristic of basic industries is that they help to foster the internal articulation of the economy's productive sectors.[15]

Both ECLA and SIECA considered that a first step in this direction would be the setting up of industries likely to play a strategic role in the next phase of regional industrialization, principally in such branches as light engineering and chemicals, although "one might also include export-oriented industries as well as those component-assembly industries which, in some cases, represent the first phase in the establishment of basic industries on a regional scale."[16]

This view of industrial development strategy found little resonance in the private sector and was certainly too far-sighted for myopic governments. The existing strategy had created new vested interests. First, the incipient nature of industrial development meant that a wide spectrum of 'easy' opportunities for highly profitable investment existed. Then too, local entrepreneurs generally lacked the experience and expertize required to set up basic industries for intermediate and capital goods. More important, overseas investors, who certainly did not lack experience, had other things in mind. In general, foreign capital saw in the CACM an opportunity to exploit a new, protected market. Moreover, given that MNCs generally occupied an oligopolistic position in this market, a high level of profit in the consumer goods industries was virtually guaranteed. The implementation of a far-sighted industrial policy would have required the presence of a strong, developmentalist state prepared to underwrite basic industry. Such a state did not exist in Central America.

SECTION III

The 1980s

In the 1980s, for the first time, the region as a whole has experienced a crisis of such proportions that the future of industrialization *per se* is in doubt. A serious downturn in regional economic activity first became evident around 1978. In some countries the political crisis was already manifest. The effect of deteriorating world market conditions was evident throughout the region. Current account deficits began to mount and balance of payments difficulties were aggravated the growing flight of capital. The crisis deepened under the impact of the 1979 oil shock. Over the period 1980–1982, combined international reserves of the five countries fell by US$ 1.33 billion dollars, a figure equivalent to 152 percent of total reserves in 1979. In effect, net reserves for the region were negative. The most serious aspect of the economic crisis, though, was the contraction in intra-regional trade caused by the foreign exchange shortage. Industry was the sector which suffered most given that 90 percent of intra-regional trade consisted of industrial products.

The political aspect of the crisis, equally evident by the late 1970s, can be divided into two phases. In the first phase, the countries most affected were, on the one hand, Nicaragua and, on the other, El Salvador and Guatemala. In the latter two countries, the social divisions underlying the conflict had long been evident. In Nicaragua, the uprising against Somoza comprised a broadly-based class alliance.

Ostensibly, the nature of the crisis was more political than social. The second phase began after 1981. At this point, not only did the political crisis spread throughout the region, but its trajectory was molded increasingly by forces outside the region, chiefly by the Reagan Administration. And as tensions mounted, the political dimension of the crisis became all-embracing. Economic plans were scrapped; lending agreements were abrogated; capital flight intensified; military spending increased. The foreign exchange necessary to fuel continued industrial activity was diverted to the apparently more urgent task of strengthening national security. In 1986 alone, the US Congress dealt with funding requests for Central America equivalent to one-sixth of total postwar US aid disbursements to the region.

On the economic front, there are two broad schools of thought on how to deal with the crisis. The first school which is increasingly influential and enjoys the support of the IMF, the World Bank and USAID, believes that the region can only survive by promoting new exports and placing them in new markets. Little is said about the CACM. Import-substituting industrialization is treated as an historical curiosity. The other school, which appears to have the support of some bilateral donors, chiefly from Scandinavia and within the EC, emphasizes the need to revive the CACM and promote further industrial integration. On this view, export promotion has a complementary role to play in industrial development, it does not supersede it.

Obviously, there can be little disagreement over the need for Central America to increase its total exports to the rest of the world and the share of industrial exports within this total. Extra-regional export activities are a necessary complement to domestic and regional sales and can help soak up underutilised capacity. Moreover, such exports force regional manufacturers to be more competitive, lowering unit costs and increasing product quality. Export promotion is all the more important if the region is to pay its own way. Current levels of aid will not be available indefinitely. Neither can the trade gap be closed by further cuts in imports given the region's dependence on foreign raw materials, intermediate and capital goods.

Nevertheless, one may accept such arguments without concluding that an outward looking strategy means abandoning industrial integration and the CACM. First, all studies of the region's export potential suggest that primary commodities will account for the bulk of total export earnings for many years to come. The list of typical processed or manufactured products will continue to comprise such items as food products, clothing, timber, leather, glassware, etc. New manufactures may be added to the list in time, but at the moment it is difficult to speak of any major breakthrough. The only concrete suggestion emanating from the proponents of non-traditional export-led growth is to set up *maquiladoras;* i.e., plants representing an intermediate stage in the manufacturing chain making intensive use of cheap, unskilled labor.

This is precisely the sort of industrial activity envisaged in Title II of Act 98–67, more commonly known as the Caribbean Basin Initiative. The Act calls for the elimination of US tariffs on all goods (with some exceptions such as petroleum and derivative products) originating in the countries to which it applies. However, prior to its passage in 1984, over 80 percent of the products in question were already non-dutiable. Confronted with this problem, supporters of the CBI argue that the real purpose of the Act is to stimulate new export lines. What is not added is that, in order to do so, Central America must attract private capital. The problem is that the wage differential between Central America and competing regions is insufficient to compensate for the risk of political upheaval and the lack of a common border. Central America is unlikely to attract large amounts of direct investment in the near future.

In summary, the prospects for placing new exports on the US market in particular, and the world market in general, are not encouraging. World trading arrangements in manufactures continue to discriminate against new entrants. As to the prospects for agricultural exports, to quote a recent report of the Inter-American Development Bank, "the principal exporters—Argentina, Brazil, Colombia and Central America—will experience a period of intense competition in markets for temperate products and livestock, while real prices will decline for most tropical products."[17]

The alternative, what we shall refer to here as 'integrating industrialization,' sees export promotion and import substitution as opposite sides of the same coin. Given current regional and world market conditions, an import-substitution strategy would still appear recommendable, though it needs to be complemented by export promotion. In most cases, Central American industry has no option but to produce for the regional market, or else disappear, since it enjoys neither the economies of scale nor the technology required to produce export-quality products. Also, about one-third of Central American industry is foreign-owned. So far, foreign capital has shown little interest in turning the region into an export platform.

If industrial integration of the region is allowed to wither, further stages of industrialization necessary to achieve sustained development will not be possible. Nevertheless, the underlying concept of integration needs to be modified in a manner which reduces the disparities generated by the CACM model of the 1960s and 1970s. Clearly, the principle of free trade will continue to be basic. But there will certainly be a need for other principles ensuring that a renewed CACM will be stronger, more cohesive and less prone to internal divisions than in the past.

One final reflection is on a point of central concern to all actors: it is impossible to deal with these matters realistically while abstracting away from the question of US policy towards the region. There can be no economic development in Central America unless the question of peace is resolved. At the time of writing, all attempts at reaching a negotiated settlement have been blocked or undermined by the US. As long as a new relationship does not emerge between the region and its neighbour to the North, it would be imprudent to speak of new perspectives for industrial development. At this stage, considerable patience and perseverance is required merely to hold on to what exists. Nevertheless, it is clear that when economic development returns once again to the agenda, the challenge to Central Americans will be to redesign and renew the political and institutional framework of regional cooperation in a manner which avoids a repetition of the present crisis, a crisis which but for lack of regional cohesion, might have been avoided.

62

TABLE 3.1 Central America: Real Rates of Growth of Industrial
Product, 1960--1978

	Central America	Guate-mala	El Sal-vador	Hon-duras	Nica-ragua	Costa Rica
1960–1970	8.5	7.7	7.8	7.0	10.9	9.2
1970–1978	6.4	6.4	5.5	5.8	5.0	8.9

Note: Industrial Product at 1970 prices.

Source: Author's calculations based on CEPAL (1983).

TABLE 3.2 Central America: Percentage Share in Total Industrial
Output by Major Category of Good: 1960, 1978

	Non-Durable Consumer Goods	Intermediate Goods	Consumer Durables & Capital Goods
1960			
Central America	72.6	21.6	5.8
Guatemala	73.4	21.4	5.2
El Salvador	72.9	19.6	7.4
Honduras	68.2	21.7	10.1
Nicaragua	74.6	24.0	1.4
Costa Rica	72.2	22.5	5.3
1978			
Central America	57.2	35.7	7.1
Guatemala	57.6	37.0	5.4
El Salvador	48.3	42.7	9.0
Honduras	62.7	30.0	7.3
Nicaragua	63.1	34.0	2.9
Costa Rica	57.5	31.8	10.7

Note: Industrial output valued at 1970 prices.

Source: Author's calculations based on CEPAL (1983).

TABLE 3.3   Share of Extra-Regional Imports in Total Demand by
            Major Category of Industrial Good: 1960, 1970, 1978

	Total Demand	Non-Durable Consumer Goods	Intermediate Goods	Consumer Durables & Capital Goods
1960	33.2	8.3	59.0	79.1
1970	28.3	5.3	38.1	73.0
1978	31.5	6.8	39.3	75.1

Note: Regional demand equals gross value of regional industrial output minus extra-regional exports plus extra-regional imports (cif), all at 1970 prices.

Source: Author's calculations based on CEPAL (1983).

TABLE 3.4   Value of Extra- and Intra-Regional Imports by Category of
            Goods: 1960, 1970, 1978

Category Year	Extra-Regional			Intra-Regional		
	1960	1970	1978	1960	1970	1978
Non-durable	67	74	157	9	79	96
Intermediate	268	458	846	13	174	301
Durable & Capital Goods	148	337	696	2	22	45
Total	483	869	1699	24	275	442

Year	1960	1970	1980
Value Total Imports of which Extra-regional Percentage Share is:	24	1144	2141
		(percent)	
Non-Durable	12	52	38
Intermediate	5	28	26
Durable & Capital Goods	1	6	6
Share in Total:	5	24	21

Note: Imports valued at 1970 prices. All values in millions of US$.

Source: Author's calculations based on CEPAL (1983).

TABLE 3.5 Central America: Principal Product Groups Exported and Country Rank in Intra-Regional Exports, 1982/a

SIIC/b	Country/Product Group	Value of Trade (US$ 1000)	Regional Rank	Percentage of Regional Trade
	- GUATEMALA/*			
3522	Pharmaceutical products	26633	[1]	[48-67]
3211	Threads and Yarns	23999	[1-2]	[34-75]
3512	Insecticides and Disinfectants	19056	[1]	[78]
3551	Tires	12290	[1]	[59]
3620	Glass/Glass Products	10301	[1]	[78]
3523	Soaps/Cosmetics	9388	[2]	[41]
	TOTAL	101667		
	*/ % Guatemalan products selected (54); % of SIECA sample (22); % of CACM trade in manufactures (14)			
	- EL SALVADOR/*			
3412	Paper and Cardboard Containers	13729	[1]	[46-75]
3220	Clothing other than Footwear	9539	[1]	[47-73]
3213	Stitched Undergarments	7112	[1]	[63-74]
3211	Textile Yarns	7053	[1]	[71]
3839	Electrical Appliances and Parts	7018	[1]	[66]
	TOTAL	44451		
	*/ % Salvadorean products selected (54); % of SIECA sample (9); % of CACM trade in manufactures (6)			
	- HONDURAS/*			
3223	Soap and Washing Preparations	9819	[1]	[42]
3121	Edible Maize Starches	1918	[1]	[79]
3113	Fruit Juices	1748	[1]	[48]
	TOTAL	13485		
	*/ % Honduran products selected (67); % of SIECA sample (3); % of CACM trade in manufactures (2)			
	- NICARAGUA/*			
3513	Artificial Resins and Plastic Materials	8514	[1]	[47]
3112	Dairy Products	4182	[1]	[100]
3511	Industrial Chemicals	2369	[1]	[99]
	TOTAL	15065		
	*/ % Nicaraguan products selected (56); % of SIECA sample (3); % of CACM trade in manufactures (2)			

3839	Electric Appliances and Parts	5411	[1-2]	[33-90]
3121	Food Products, various	5139	[1-2]	[30-93]
3511	Aromatic Concentrates/other Chemical Products	5105	[1]	[97]
3819	Metal Products excluding Machines	5007	[1]	[55-67]
3211	Textile Yarns	4013	[2]	[29]
3311	Wood and Wood Products	3732	[1]	[43]
3117	Bakery Products	2223	[1]	[43]
	TOTAL	44201		

*/ % Costa Rican products selected (54); % of SIECA sample (9); % of CACM trade in manufactures (6)

NOTES: Percentage shares in regional trade represent shares in specified products, not in all products belonging to SIIC group shown; the SIIC number is given merely to facilitate comparisons with other studies.

a/ The SIECA sample survey covers the principal export products of each country. The total value of trade covered by the sample was US$ 470.4 million. Total CACM trade in industrial products for 1982 was valued at US$ 728.9 million.

b/ SIIC signifies Standard International Industrial Classification. The code indicates the industry of origin, at four digit level, of the product groups selected. Product-group definitions used above have been shortened.

c/ Where two figures are shown, these indicate the respective shares of the most important and least important product appearing in the SIECA sample of the group in total exports for the group. A single figure means that only a single product-line, i.e., that shown in the Table, has been included in the SIECA sample.

Source: Author's calculations based on SIECA (1982), 'La Complementación Industrial en Centroamérica,' Guatemala: Secretaría de Integración Económica Centroamericana.

Notes

1. See Torres Rivas (1984); also see Guerra Borges (1968).
2. See CEPAL (1956), p. 6.
3. See World Bank (1967), para. 84.
4. See Bulmer-Thomas (1987b), pp. 173–174.
5. See CEPAL (1983a), p. 6.
6. See SIECA (1974), p. 23.
7. See World Bank (1972), para. 28.
8. See Guerra Borges (1975); also see World Bank (1972), vol 1, Table 7; and SIECA (1985a).
9. See B. Balassa (1979).
10. See CEPAL (1983b), p. 15.
11. See CEPAL (1983b), p. 11 and Table 10.
12. See Guerra Borges (1986), pp. 21–27. This paper also appears in a set of collected essays on tariff exemptions; see *Exenciones Arancelarias e Integración,* (Buenos Aires: Instituto para la Integración de América Latina, 1986), pp. 260–71. With respect to tariff exemptions, Guatemala was considered broadly representative of Central America as a whole given the relative development of its industrial sector and the country's high import coefficient.
13. See Guerra Borges (forthcoming); this paper was prepared when the author was Visiting Professor at the Center for Latin American Studies, Florida International University, and was first presented in January 1987.
14. See CEPAL/SIECA (1964), p. 121.
15. See CEPAL/SIECA (1964), p. 122.
16. *ibid.*
17. See BID (1986), p. 87.

4

Can Regional Import Substitution and Export-Led Growth Be Combined?

Victor Bulmer-Thomas

Introduction

The focus on import-substituting industrialization (ISI) within the Central American Common Market (CACM) in the 1960s was always seen by policy-makers as a prelude to manufactured exports towards the rest of the world (ROW). During the 1970s, tentative efforts were made in several republics to combine the two industrialization strategies, although the results were generally disappointing. Today, governments in each republic are under considerable pressure from external and internal forces to abandon the inward-looking strategy and focus exclusively on manufactured exports to ROW as a way of promoting industrialization.

This paper addresses this issue and is divided into three parts. The first examines whether strategies of ISI within a regional framework and of increasing extra-regional manufactured exports[1] are mutually exclusive or whether they can coexist within the same policy framework. The second part considers the current difficulties of the CACM and asks whether its decline can be reversed without distorting the allocation of resources away from increasing extra-regional exports. The third part examines the question of whether economic cooperation at the regional level can be conducted outside the framework of CACM and, if so, in what areas.

It is appropriate to begin, however, with some definitions. The term ISI is straightforward and covers the process of import substitution in industrial goods either at the national or regional level. In the latter case, it is assumed that imports are replaced by regional production

Victor Bulmer-Thomas is Reader in Economics at Queen Mary College, the University of London.

behind a tariff or protective barrier which applies equally to all countries of the region. In the former case, imports are replaced at the national level by local production behind a protective barrier which applies only at the national level. In the case of regional ISI, therefore, it is assumed that the movements of industrial goods between countries is not subject to restrictions additional to those that apply at the national level.

There is much greater ambiguity, however, regarding the term "export diversification." Where a strategy is contemplated of dismantling a national protective structure in order to increase extra-regional exports, I shall talk of export substitution (ES). Where the strategy contemplates maintenance, by and large, of the national protective structure coupled with encouragement of extra-regional exports, I shall refer to export promotion (EP). Regional ES, therefore, refers to a situation where a group of countries acting together dismantle their national protective structures and regional EP to a situation where the regional protective structure remains intact and the countries of the region coordinate their policies in favor of EP.

SECTION I

Are Regional Strategies of ISI and ES/EP Mutually Exclusive?

If it is possible to combine ES/EP with ISI, the combined strategy must overcome at least some of the worst failings commonly associated with ISI. It is appropriate, therefore, to begin by recognizing the problems of ISI in general and, in particular, the difficulties raised by regional ISI in CACM.

A major problem is that ISI, far from reducing balance of payments (BOP) problems and foreign exchange bottlenecks, frequently increases them. The reasons are threefold: first, ISI is itself very import-intensive and new industrial activities typically generate a high demand directly and indirectly for imports from ROW as intermediate goods, spare parts, capital equipment, etc.; second, the policies designed to favor ISI frequently discriminate against exports, so that the *supply* of foreign exchange is lower than it might otherwise be; third, ISI (which almost always begins with consumer goods) shifts the structure of extra-regional imports in favor of intermediate and capital goods, any reduction in which is much more damaging than in the case of consumer goods.[2] As Table 4.1 shows, this was a serious problem for CACM as early as 1970 with 55 percent to 74 percent of all earnings from extra-regional exports swallowed up by industry's need for foreign exchange to buy intermediate and capital goods.

\A second problem, related to the first, is that the success of the ISI strategy becomes heavily dependent on the performance of traditional exports./In other words, ISI—far from competing with the traditional export-led growth model based on primary products—is actually complementary to it. This criticism is supported by the experience of CACM, in which the most successful years coincide with a boom in primary product (traditional) exports and the least successful with the reverse.[3]

The third problem is the bias associated with ISI against production of intermediate and capital goods in favor of production of consumer goods. The structure of protection adopted under ISI involves changes in the nominal rate of protection (i.e. changes in nominal tariffs). The combination of changes in tariffs on firms' inputs and outputs has the effect of altering their value added or net output; economists describe the change in value added relative to the free trade situation as The Effective Rate of Protection (ERP).[4] The higher the ERP, the higher the incentives for industrialists to produce the goods in question.

The ERP varies from sector to sector. Where nominal tariffs are low, however, on intermediate and capital goods and high on consumer goods, the ERP will typically be much higher for consumer goods than for other branches of industry. This was certainly the case for CACM (see Table 4.2). There is, therefore, the danger that the ISI process becomes exhausted following import-substitution in consumer goods (the so-called "easy" stage of ISI) and is unable to advance into more complicated industrial ventures because of the bias built into the structure of protection. Thus, one of the main aims of regional integration is undermined, because the regional grouping was designed to achieve a market large enough to support production of intermediate and capital goods.

The fourth problem concerns the bias against manufactured exports under ISI. The ERP for any given sector (V_j') measures the percentage change in value added per unit of output in the post-tariff situation compared with the pre-tariff free trade situation (V_j), i.e.

$$ERP_j = [(V_j' - V_j)/V_j] \times 100; \qquad j = 1...n \qquad (1)$$

If in the post-tariff situation industrialists try to export their output outside the region, they lose the protection offered by the nominal tariff on their output, but continue to be subject to tariffs on their inputs. Thus, their value added per unit of output on exports (V_j^e) will be less even than value added in the free trade situation (under the latter at least inputs are not subject to tariffs). If we now define the bias against exports (B_j) as the percentage by which value added per unit of output in the post-tariff situation exceeds value added per unit of output in extra-regional markets, i.e.:

$$B_j = [(V_j^i - V_j^e)/V_j^e] \times 100; \qquad j = 1...n \qquad (2)$$

then it will always be the case that the bias against exports in any given sector will be at least as great as the ERP in the same sector, i.e.:

$$B_j > ERP_j; \qquad j = 1...n \qquad (3)$$

The extent of the bias against manufactured exports clearly depends on the size of the ERP Table 4.2 suggests, however, that in the CACM (particularly for consumer goods) the ERP has been quite high. Thus, there has been a bias against exporting *outside* the region precisely those commodities that have done well *inside* the region

The fifth problem associated with regional ISI (very important in the case of CACM) is the difficulty of providing an institutional framework which guarantees that all countries in the region receive an equitable share in the distribution of net benefits. The most careful and thorough study of the CACM (see Cline, 1978) concluded that it had indeed generated net benefits at the regional level, but that the distribution of these net benefits was very unequal. This is frequently given as a major reason for Honduras' departure from the CACM in December 1970. The problem is a very old and very familiar one: exclusive reliance on market forces will ensure that the most developed countries within the region receive the lion's share of regional net benefits, while interference with market forces to ensure a more equitable share of the benefits may lower the growth rate of the most developed members.

It would be easy to continue listing difficulties associated with ISI in general and CACM in particular, but the above problems are the major ones. In addition, a successful regional ISI policy presupposes some harmonization of exchange rate policy between the countries of the region, which may be inconsistent with the exchange rate flexibility demanded by an ES or EP strategy.

It is very tempting, when faced with such a formidable list of problems, to conclude that any form of export diversification is preferable to ISI. In the matter of trade policies to be adopted by less developed countries (LDCs), however, there are no easy options and it is salutary to remind ourselves that export diversification strategies also involve major problems. Consideration of ES strategies will illustrate this point.

Under an ES strategy (such as was followed in the southern cone of Latin America in the late 1970s), tariffs are systematically lowered or dismantled, producing a depreciation of the nominal (and hopefully real) exchange rates. Whatever the stimulus for non-traditional manufactured exports, it is more than likely that a substantial part of the industrial base will be wiped out by imports (that is sometimes called negative ISI). Some of these firms forced to close will be high-cost, inefficient producers, which could never be expected to compete internationally under free trade; others, however, might have made the transition to international competition under different circumstances, had negative ISI not lead to their permanent closure.

The shift in the allocation of resources within an ES strategy encourages industrial specialization. There is the danger, however, that the country will become as dependent on a few manufactured products as it previously was on a few primary commodities. Exploitation of the opportunities for forward and backward linkages in the industrial sector (potentially very great) will be impossible if the industrial base rests on a handful of manufactured products.[5]

Nowhere is this problem more vividly illustrated than in the free trade zones (FTZs) established by a large number of LDCs (including Central American countries) in the last decade. In return for duty-free imports, cheap labor and tax holidays, companies (often foreign-owned) export their output to earn valuable foreign exchange. As a strategy for earning hard currency, it has some arguments in its favor; as a strategy for industrialization it is very weak, because it allows little or no opportunities for the exploitation of backward and forward linkages.

The depreciation of the nominal exchange rate associated with the ES strategy sets up inflationary pressures, which require further large nominal depreciations to achieve a small real depreciation of the exchange rate. The latter is bought at a high price, however, in the form of an acceleration of inflation and (usually) a fall in real wages together with a deterioration in the distribution of income in favor of greater inequality. The latter changes aggravate the bias against production for the home market under the ES strategy and may provoke further deindustrialization.

Finally, no discussion of the ES strategy would be complete without reference to market access. It is precisely in those commodities where LDCs might be expected to have a comparative advantage (e.g. textiles) that protectionist barriers in the developed countries (DCs) are at their greatest. These obstacles consist more of non-tariff barriers

(NTBs) than of tariffs and LDCs have lobbied for years for their removal, The results have been mixed; while the LDCs have secured the Generalized System of Preferences (GSP), the Lomé Convention and the Caribbean Basin Initiative (CBI) as partial compensation for the spread of NTBs, protectionist sentiment among the DCs has increased rather than decreased in recent years. The result is that a successful ES strategy (e.g. Taiwan) needs to be supported by a formidable trade lobby in the capitals of DCs in order to guarantee access for an increased flow of manufactured exports.

Given that there are no easy options for LDCs in the matter of trade policy, it is now appropriate to consider whether the ISI strategy can be made consistent with export diversification in such a way that it offers the advantages of both without the disadvantages of either. We must, therefore, consider the possibility of (1) linking ISI with ES and (2) linking ISI with EP.

The possibility of linking ISI with an ES strategy is remote. Almost by definition, an ES strategy implies negative or reverse ISI and, in practice, most of the instruments favoring one strategy discriminate against the other. Only in the case of real exchange rate depreciation (RERD) does the same instrument favor both sets of strategies, but RERD is unlikely to be sufficient to compensate industrialists producing for the home market for the reduction in ERP consequent upon the lowering of nominal tariffs.

This was the combination of strategies favored by several Central American republics in the 1970s and the results were very disappointing. In the *Plan Nacional de Desarrollo* published in Costa Rica in 1974 (while Oscar Arias Sánchez was Minister of Planning), projections for manufactured exports implied that the growth of extra-regional exports would be the same as intra-regional exports. (See *Oficina de Planificación, Plan Nacional de Desarrollo, Sectores Productivos, B. Sector Industrial,* Cuadro 6, San José, 1974), but the actual performance of extra-regional manufactured exports fell short of projections.

Despite the disappointment of the 1970s, the combination of ISI and EP strategies is in fact feasible and the failures of the 1970s are due more to an inappropriate combination of policy instruments than to any logical inconsistency between the two strategies.

Let us return to equation (2). As long as $V_j^i > V_j^e$, there will be anti-export bias and a preference for sales to the home market. Analytically, therefore, a combination of ISI and EP strategies requires a choice of policy instruments pushing V_j^i and V_j^e towards equality—at least in those sectors where extra-regional exports are considered feasible.

What policy instruments do V'_j and V^e_j depend on? Taking the former first, it can be defined as:

$$V'_j = P_j e_j (1 + t_j) - \sum_i a_{ij} e_i (1 + t_i) \qquad (4)$$

where:

P_j is the world (dollar) price of the jth commodity.

e_j is the nominal exchange rate applied to imports of the jth commodity.

a_{ij} is the requirement of the ith commodity per unit of output in the jth commodity at world (dollar) prices.

e_i is the nominal exchange rate applied to imports of the ith commodity.

t_j is the nominal tariff on the jth commodity.

t_i is the nominal tariff on the ith commodity.

In equation (4), value added per unit of output in the post-tariff situation is seen to depend on six variables, four of which (e_j, e_i, t_j, t_i) are instruments controlled by the authorities. The latter can lower V'_j by lowering e_j and t_j and by raising e_i and t_i.

The definition of value added per unit of output if exported (V^e_j) is:

$$V^e_j = P_j e_j - \sum_i a_{ij} e_i (1 + t_i) \qquad (5)$$

which is similar to equation (4) except that the output is now sold in world markets and, therefore, loses the protection offered by the nominal tariff on competing imports (t_j). From equation (5), we can see that the authorities can raise V^e_j by raising e_j and by lowering e_i and t_i.

There therefore appears to be a possible conflict in the use of some instruments. The authorities, it is assumed, wish to lower V'_j and raise V^e_j in order to make firms in the jth sector equally willing to sell to the (protected) regional market and to the (unprotected) world market. A lowering of e_j, however, and a raising of e_i and t_i lowers V'_j, but also lowers V^e_j. Similarly, a raising of e_j and a lowering of e_i and t_i raises V^e_j but also raises V'_j.

This dilemma can only be resolved by distinguishing between exchange rates and tariffs by end use. Thus, the authorities need to operate one set of exchange rates for goods sold in the regional market (e^r_j, e^r_i) and one for goods sold overseas (e^o_j, e^o_i). Similarly, the nominal tariffs of inputs need to vary for the same reason. Thus, t^r_i would be the nominal tariff on the ith commodity used in products sold in the regional market, while t_i^r would be the nominal tariff on the ith commodity used in goods sold abroad.

It is, therefore, possible to rewrite equations (4) and (5) to take account of these qualifications. Before doing so, however, it is necessary to introduce one further complication. Industrial firms will respond to the value added per unit of output net of direct taxes; by taxing V_j^i and V_j^e at different rates, the authorities have two further instruments for moving V_j^i and V_j^e towards equality.

Equation (4) now becomes:

$$V_j^{'*} = r_j^r V_j' = r_j^r [P_j e_j^r (1 + t_j^r) - \sum_i a_{ij} e_i^r (1 + t_i^r)] \tag{6}$$

where r_j^r is the direct tax rate on value added for the jth commodity when sold in the regional market and V_j' is the post-tax value added for the jth commodity when sold in the regional market and equation (5) now becomes:

$$V_j^{e*} = r_j^o V_j^e \approx r_j^o [P_j e_j^o - \sum_i e_{ij} e_i^e (1 + t_i^o)] \tag{7}$$

when r_j^o is the direct tax rate on value added for the jth commodity when sold in the world market and V_j^{e*} is the post-tax value added for the jth commodity when sold in the world market.

The authorities' task is now to choose some combination of instruments such that $V_j^{'*} = V_j^{e*}$. Since there is in principle a large number of possible combinations, it is worth setting out the options to the form of a box diagram (Table 4.3). Although in principle many combinations of instruments can achieve the desired objectives, the authorities' choice will be guided by other considerations. Thus, for example, any combination which relied exclusively on decreases in $(V_j^{'*})$ would run counter to the ISI strategy (under the latter, incentives must be available for "deepening" ISI through production of intermediate and capital goods). Similarly, the authorities may well find it unduly complicated to work with "2n" exchange rates (two for each commodity) and may prefer to operate with only two exchange rates (e^r, e^o) which vary by end-use, but not by commodity.

We can now use Table 4.3 to evaluate what has been done in Central American in order to combine ISI with EP strategies. Most republics at various times have worked with differential tax rates $(r_j^r > r_j^o)$; typically, this has been achieved through *Certificados de Abono Tributario* (CAT) estimated as a fixed percentage of the FOB value of exports. Most republics have also discriminated between tariffs on inputs through drawback schemes favoring firms which export all their production (in the extreme case $t_i^o = 0$). Similarly, some republics have allowed exporters to sell part of their foreign exchange earnings at more favorable rates of exchange than applied to firms selling the same output in the regional market. Finally, efforts have been made to lower nominal tariffs on competing imports.

The impact of all these changes, however, has been very modest and has not been sufficient to bring $(V_i^{'*})$ into equality with (V_j^{e*}). The CATs, for example, have been insufficient to compensate for the tax holidays and widespread exemptions enjoyed by many firms selling in the regional market. The advantages conferred by lowering (t_i^o) have been small, because (t_i^r) has also been very low; the exchange rate privilege has applied, in general, to exporters of non-traditional *agricultural* products rather than manufactured goods.

The most serious problem, however, has been the adoption of the new *Arancel de Aduanas* on 1 January 1986. Although the new *Arancel*, currently applied by Costa Rica, El Salvador and Guatemala, has the great merit of using *ad valorem* rather than specific tariffs and has also been accompanied by a sharp reduction in the tax holidays and exemptions offered to existing firms selling to the regional market, it has on balance probably increased (t_j^r) rather than lowered it. The situation has been aggravated by the decision of some countries to calculate the tax due on the local currency cost at the parallel exchange rate; this has the effect of raising $(V_j^{'*})$ and increasing the gap over (V_j^{e*}).

The most effective way for the authorities to achieve the desired equality is through a rise in e^o (or e_j^o), a fall in t_j^r, an increase in r_j^r and a fall in r_j^o. A change in e^r is not desirable, because the regional ISI strategy works best when members maintain fixed exchange rates within the region; changes in input tariffs are unlikely to be very effective, because the starting rates are so low. Finally, the combination of rising r_j^r with falling r_j^o will help to prevent a fiscal shortfall as a result of extending tax privileges to extra-regional exports.

The ease with which these instruments can be changed varies enormously. Changes in nominal tariffs (e.g., t_j^r) require regional cooperation, since the basis of a Customs Union/Common Market is a common external tariff (CET). Changes in tax rates (e.g., r_j^r) may require regional cooperation if the member countries are subject to fiscal harmonization; finally, differential exchange rates (e.g., $e_j^o > e_j^r$) are unpopular with international financial institutions, such as the International Monetary Fund and the World Bank, and external financial support is sometimes made conditional on their removal.

It is worth re-emphasizing, however, that there are no easy trade policy options for LDCs in general and Central America is particular, and that despite the difficulties outlined in the previous paragraph, it *is* possible to make the necessary changes and combine an ISI with an EP strategy. This is likely to be preferable to an ISI or ES/EP strategy on its own for reasons already given.

An ES strategy minimizes state intervention, which is a major source of attraction for many policy-makers. An ISI/EP strategy cannot work in this way, however, because market forces cannot be relied on exclusively; by definition, market forces in the post-tariff situation favor production for the regional market; interference with market prices (using the instruments described above) can reduce or eliminate the bias against extra-regional exports. The bias, however, varies from sector to sector; if the authorities eliminate the bias against exports in the sector with the greatest comparative *disadvantage,* they will offer too much incentive to those sectors with greater prospects for extra-regional exports.

The authorities must, therefore, use *selective* discrimination. They must identify those sectors with the highest potential dynamic comparative advantage in international trade and adjust their policy instruments so as to eliminate anti-export bias in those sectors.

The record of governments in "picking winners" is not a good one. The authorities have typically been ambiguous about the criteria employed to determine "potential dynamic comparative advantage." A brave attempt to resolve this problem can be found in the Brookings Institution Study of the CACM (see Cline 1978, Chapter 6). In that study, a series of indicators are used to identify out of 75 industrial sectors the 25 with the greatest potential dynamic comparative advantage (see Table 4.4).

The Brookings Institution Study, for lack of suitable data, did not use what I believe to be the most appropriate methodology for identifying sectors in need of export promotion. This, the Domestic Resource Cost (DRC) criterion, works as follows: for each industrial sector, an estimate is made (using input-output tables) of the direct and indirect foreign exchange requirements needed to earn one dollar's worth of exports; the difference between the two then gives net earnings of foreign exchange. For each sector, an estimate is then made of the direct and indirect domestic factor requirements (e.g., capital and labor) needed to produce one dollar's worth of exports. These factor requirements are then valued at their shadow or accounting prices and added together. By dividing the total for each sector by the net earnings of foreign exchange, one obtains the value of domestic resources in each sector needed per net unit of foreign exchange earned (i.e., the DRC criterion). Sectors with a high DRC are inefficient and should not be promoted, because they require "excessive" domestic resources to earn foreign exchange; sectors with low DRCs should be promoted, because they are very efficient at converting domestic resources into scarce foreign exchange. The equilibrium exchange rate is sometimes used to provide the dividing line between sectors with high and low DRCs.[6] Needless to say, the choice of which sectors to promote should also be influenced by considerations of market access. It is no use promoting textiles, for example, even if the sector enjoys a low DRC, unless there are realistic chances of overcoming protectionist barriers in overseas markets.

SECTION II
The Decline of CACM: Can It Be Reversed?

The value of intra-regional trade within the CACM has been declining in relative terms since 1970 and in absolute terms since 1980. This decline is a very serious matter and its causes will shortly be investigated. Nonetheless, it must be put into perspective. Intra-regional exports still account for nearly 20 percent of total Central American exports, varying from a low of 10 percent in Nicaragua to a high of 25 percent in Guatemala; the fall in the value of intra-regional exports (38 percent between 1980 and 1984), although extremely severe, is still much less than the decline in intra-regional trade within the Andean Pact.

The decline of CACM in the 1970s was only relative; the value of total trade increased more rapidly than intra-regional trade, but this was due above all to favorable prices for traditional primary products. In 1980, however, the CACM experiences a huge increase ($215 million) in intra-regional imports; this was almost entirely due to a 171 percent increase in Nicaraguan imports from CACM as the war-torn Nicaraguan economy began the work of reconstruction.[7]

The 1980 Nicaraguan level of CACM imports could not be sustained and the value of trade fell in 1981, although still exceeding 1979 levels. The real crisis of the CACM began in 1982, however, with a series of adverse shocks all combining to produce an eighteen percent fall in the value of intra-regional trade.

The most important of these shocks was the decline in the value of extra-regional exports, which began in 1981 as the world economy went into recession; this had a predictable effect on the external terms of trade for Central America (which had in any case been falling since 1977 when the coffee price peaked) and on the volume of demand. Since intra- and extra-regional trade are complementary in Central America (see above), the value of CACM trade was dragged down by the fall in extra-regional exports.

The second shock was the adjustment and stabilization program, which all Central American countries were running in 1982. The initial response to the first shock had been to increase domestic demand through an increase in public expenditure; this had produced unsustainable levels of budget deficits, inflation and public external indebtedness, forcing all republics to adopt adjustment programs.[8] In 1982, real GDP fell in all five republics—the first such occurrence since 1932.[9] The fall in real GDP was accompanied by an even sharper decline in real consumption per head with a predictable impact on the value of CACM trade.

The third shock has been a series of unilateral and *ad hoc* measures designed to aid each country's balance of payments problems by restricting CACM imports; these include exchange rate changes, exchange control, delays in the issue of licenses and, above all, non-payment of debt arrears. The last problem has been particularly severe; the "surplus" countries (Nicaragua, El Salvador and Honduras) have on occasions unilaterally restricted CACM *exports* in order to force a reduction in the debtor status of trading partners. The impact of all these measures has been to restrict regional trade, while increasing the importance of counter-trade.

The final shock has been civil war and political unrest; while the first two shocks reduced the *demand* for regional exports, civil war and political unrest has restricted the *supply* of regional exports. Thus, part of the decline in CACM exports from Nicaragua and El Salvador has been due to war-related supply constraints, although in the former case mention should also be made of the unrealistic exchange rate offered exporters to CACM, which has appreciated sharply in *real* terms since 1979.

It will be noted that I have not attributed much importance to the regional political crisis as such in accounting for a decline in intra-regional trade. Hostility between countries is not a sufficient reason for a decline in intra-regional trade and the value of trade has declined between "friendly" countries as well as between "hostile" ones; since 1980, for example, the decline in Costa Rican imports from all other Central American republics has been very similar.[10] Thus, the decline in CACM is due fundamentally to economic factors and this is very important for consideration of how recovery might be promoted.

It is clear that a radical restructuring of the CACM, along the lines proposed by the *Comité de Alto Nivel* (CAN) in the early 1970s, is not currently feasible. Radical changes presuppose a degree of political consensus among the member countries, which is manifestly absent at present. At the same time, the current emphasis should be on making the CACM merely a dynamic factor (along with extra-regional manufactured exports) rather than *the* dynamic factor (which was the CAN's proposal); thus, a more modest set of reform proposals is both more realistic, and more desirable.

It should also be clear that a necessary condition for the revival of CACM is a recovery in extra-regional exports and regional growth rates. The essential complementarity between intra- and extra-regional trade will remain for some time, because only the latter can provide the scarce foreign exchange on which the former depends.

The prospects for extra-regional trade, given the fall in oil and the rise in coffee prices, are better now than they have been for some time; although this is a necessary condition for the revival of CACM, it is unlikely to be sufficient. The latter requires that CACM countries start to dismantle the barriers they have erected against intra-regional trade since 1980.

The biggest barrier is the accumulation of debt arrears between pairs of CACM countries, because it restricts both CACM imports *and* CACM exports. In the hierarchy of unpaid debts, those owed by one LDC Central Bank to another are given the lowest priority; this has to be changed and international financial institutions and international agencies should give the same priority to intra-CACM debts as is currently given to debts owed to international commercial banks, while at the same time Central American countries need to implement more flexible arrangements for settling inter-country debts than currently exist through the regional clearing house (CCC). It is a matter for regret, therefore, that the IMF—which in 1983 had agreements with four of the five republics—did not include as a condition of its lending the settlement of intra-CACM debts.

The second barrier is the uncertainty surrounding exchange rates and the frequent changes in rates applied to CACM trade. Central America's reputation as a region of stable exchange rates and low inflation has now disappeared. The promotion of extra-regional exports (including manufactured goods) requires flexible exchange rates, but this conflicts to some extent with the stability required to promote regional trade. The only solution (as suggested in Section I) is to operate a two-tier exchange rate with target zones set for the exchange rates applied to intra-regional trade. The zones should be set in such a way as to minimize the risk of one republic emerging as a persistent deficit or surplus country within the CACM.

The third barrier relates to the failure to implement a Common External Tariff (CET). Not only is the new *Arancel de Aduanas* being applied by only three countries; there is also no agreement on which exchange rate to use to convert dollar prices into local currency prices before applying the tariff. Thus, Guatemala has been applying the parallel exchange rate so that an extra-regional import competing with Guatemalan production is first subject to an implicit tariff (the parallel exchange rate) and then to an explicit tariff (drawn from the *Arancel de Aduanas*).

The removal of these barriers, coupled with the revival of extra-regional exports and regional growth, should go some way towards reversing the decline in CACM. Coupled with the EP strategy, it would deal with some of the criticisms of the CACM mentioned in the first part of this chapter (e.g. the dependence of the CACM/ISI strategy on the performance of traditional exports). It would not, however, eliminate either the problem of ensuring an equitable distribution of net benefits among members, or the problem implied by the bias in structure of protection against intermediate and capital goods. Both problems remain very difficult to resolve.

Ever since the demise of the regional integration industries' scheme[11] and the failure to adopt a fiscal incentives scheme which favored the weaker members of CACM, the only major institutional mechanism for countering the impact of market forces on the distribution of net benefits has been the Central American Bank of Economic Integration (BCIE). Since its creation, BCIE's lending has favored the economically weaker states in Central America (Honduras, Nicaragua) over the stronger, but this has not been sufficient to counteract the impact of market forces in favor of the dominant countries.

One easy, but misguided, way to resolve this dilemma would be to restrict CACM membership to the stronger countries (i.e., Guatemala, El Salvador and Costa Rica), because in that case market forces would probably achieve an equitable distribution of net benefits. It is misguided because CACM (like other regional integration schemes) cannot be judged purely in economic terms. The continuation of Nicaraguan membership is very important if Nicaragua is not to become even more isolated within Central America, while the re-entry of Honduras into CACM is an important goal for those who wish to see Central America speak with one voice in international trade and finance negotiations. The anomalous position of Honduras has, in any case, become a source of friction as other countries (notably Guatemala) have reacted to the preferential status accorded to Honduras after 1970.[12]

There is, therefore, a strong case for reviving the Integration Industries' Convention (IIC), under which firms can be granted a regional monopoly subject to various controls on their behaviour. The

IIC was always intended as a counter to market forces, since no country would be allowed a second regional monopoly until all other countries had received one. The IIC fell into disuse for various reasons,[13] but it would suit the next stage of ISI admirably. While there is little justification for a regional monopoly in the case of firms producing consumer goods, the same is not true of firms producing intermediate and capital goods. Significantly, the three regional monopolies set up in the 1960s under the IIC all involved intermediate goods (tires, caustic soda, glass).

The IIC would, therefore, meet two targets with one instrument; it would go some way towards ensuring an equitable distribution of net benefits, while at the same time pushing the CACM towards the next stage of ISI. In addition, the fact that the Convention already exists (and needs only to be revived) means that a long and difficult debate over the introduction of new policy instruments can be avoided.

The final question to be resolved in this part concerns the optimal size and character of the CACM. Although it has always been called a "common market," this is misleading because free movement of labor and capital is not permitted. At best, it has operated as a customs union, although in recent years the absence of a CET has meant that "free trade area" would be a more accurate description.

The CAN in the early 1970s pressed for a genuine common market. This is now unrealistic, because "free movement of labor and capital" could be used to justify wholesale out-migration on the one hand and capital flight on the other. A customs union remains a realistic goal, but means the adoption of a CET by all members; as a first step, therefore, all states must implement the new *Arancel de Aduanas* and harmonize the exchange rate basis on which trade taxes are collected. A genuine customs union also implies the removal of any remaining restrictions on intra-regional trade (e.g. in agricultural products).

The *de facto* membership of CACM at present is three countries: Costa Rica, El Salvador, and Guatemala. Nicaragua is a member in name only, while Honduras has not yet rejoined. I have already argued above that these two countries should be urged to become full and active members again bringing the total back to the original five.

Should other countries be asked to join? The only possible candidates are Panama and Belize. Membership by the latter presupposes a settlement of the Anglo-Guatemalan dispute (which now looks feasible), but would complicate the problems of CACM enormously. It would be difficult to apply the IIC if Belize were a member and Belize's size (population of 160,000) means that national ISI has not been a serious option: thus, the structure of the Belizean economy is very different from the rest of Central America and the economy is much more export-orientated.

Panama's service-based economy is also very different from the rest of Central America. Panama, however, has pursued national ISI (although it has produced major inefficiencies). Regional ISI coupled with an EP strategy could prove attractive to Panama, since there are good reasons for Panama to be hesitant about an ES strategy. Average real income in Panama is high and the extension of CACM southwards would, therefore, prove attractive to the rest of Central America. Interestingly, the recent Cooperation Agreement between the European Community (EC) and Central America (see next section) treated Panama as part of CACM.

Regional Economic Cooperation Outside the CACM

Although I have argued that the "first-best" policy for Central America is an ISI/EP strategy with ISI conducted at the regional level through CACM, there are many obstacles which block progress towards this goal. In this section, therefore, we shall examine a "second-best" policy consistent with either an EP or ES strategy, but more likely to accompany the latter.

What are the obstacles blocking progress towards the "first-best" policy? The main one is geopolitical: a strengthening of CACM would benefit all members, while the main thrust of current US policy has been to isolate the Sandinista government in Nicaragua. (This contradiction was explicitly recognized—but not resolved—in the Kissinger Report). Thus, the US administration is not prepared to support the increase in capital flows at the *regional* level which would be needed to revive CACM.

This is a serious problem, although it is not decisive. While the current US administration is unlikely to give active support to CACM, it is now clear that it will not try to block *other* initiatives to revive regional integration. Thus, for example, the recently signed Cooperation Agreement between the EEC and Central America envisages a "substantial" increase in multilateral aid which will be used to promote *regional* projects and programs (from which, in principle, Nicaragua will also benefit). Although US Secretary of State Schultz had tried in September 1984 to block the possibility of EEC aid benefiting Nicaragua, the diplomatic consequences have led the US to drop its original objections.

Nevertheless, the revival of CACM without US support would be very difficult; the two regional powers (Mexico and Venezuela) can no longer be expected to provide substantial capital flows to Central America, without which the elimination of debt arrears will be difficult to achieve. US support is also important, because direct foreign investment to take advantage of regional ISI is needed and much of this would almost certainly have to come from North America; although these are private capital flows, the leverage of the US administration remains considerable.

Another major obstacle blocking progress towards the "first-best" policy is the lack of trust between various Central American countries. The most important example is the tension between Nicaragua on the one hand and Costa Rica, El Salvador and Honduras on the other; there is also a lack of trust between Honduras and El Salvador, whose border dispute has still not been resolved.

Finally, one must mention ideological and political differences among the countries of the region. The basic issue, of course, is the possibility of cohabitation between a Marxist government in Nicaragua and non-Marxist governments elsewhere, although it would be foolish to rule out the possibility of a return to military rule in some republics and the tensions this would create.

The problems posed by a Marxist Nicaragua can be exaggerated. Past experience has shown that this has not ruled out collaboration between all Central American countries on a range of issues (e.g., the joint approach to the European Community (EC) in September 1983 under the auspices of the Inter-American Development Bank). However, the revival of CACM does presuppose a harmony of interests between the members which might be very difficult to achieve under present circumstances.

Thus, it is realistic to explore the possibility of regional economic cooperation outside CACM. Furthermore, this is a very topical question since the recently opened EC office in San José is expecting to receive requests for funding regional projects which need not be directly linked to CACM.

There are several areas where regional economic cooperation is desirable and—given the political situation in Central America—feasible. The first is energy projects; the huge hydroelectric geothermal projects begun in the 1970s, when external funds were cheap and easily available, are now coming on line. With regional cooperation, the efficiency of these projects could be increased through external trade in energy; the political benefits are also likely to be considerable, because one country will now have a vested interest in political stability in its neighbors (the destruction by the *contras*, for example, of electricity pylons in northern Nicaragua has disrupted Honduran energy exports).

The second is education; the export diversification strategy—whether EP or ES—requires the acquisition of new skills and techniques by the labor force. There are substantial economies of scale in these forms of vocational and technical training, which can only be enjoyed through regional cooperation.

A third area is the elimination of diseases, both those that afflict the human population and the animal/plant kingdom. A program to eliminate coffee rust, for example, is much more likely to succeed if neighboring countries participate. The same is true of malaria control and the elimination of other tropical diseases.

A fourth area is transport and communications. This is familiar territory, since Central American countries have been collaborating on these social infrastructure projects since the 1950s (e.g., the Pan-American Highway) and in some cases even earlier (International Railways of Central America linked El Salvador with Guatemala in the 1920s). Much remains to be done, however, as technological progress in these two fields has generated new demands.

Regional economic cooperation could also bring substantial benefits in international negotiation. A joint CACM position, for example, could help Central America in negotiations under the International Coffee Agreement (ICA), the International Sugar Agreement (ISA) and even the Multifibre Agreement (MFA). The experience of the *Unión de Países Exportadores de Bananos* (UPEB) in the 1970s showed what could be done through cooperation, and—even more—what could be lost through lack of cooperation.

Finally, regional cooperation could help to strengthen the Cooperation Agreement with the EC. The Agreement, scheduled to run until 1990 in the first instance, is subject to annual review at ministerial level; a strong regional negotiating position could do much to extend the scope and impact of this Agreement (currently rather limited). The EC, a regional body itself, finds it easy to negotiate with other regional bodies and the EC remains a vital potential market for any export diversification strategy.

TABLE 4.1   Import Intensity of Industry in Central America, in 1970
(millions of US dollars)

	Costa Rica	El Salvador	Guatemala	Honduras	Nicaragua
(1) Total Imports of Raw Materials for Industry	111.3	80.8	107.8	75.0	68.1
(2) Percentage of (1) from Outside CACM	76.9	74.3	76.1	76.2	76.2
(3) Total Imports of Capital Goods for Industry	51.5	27.1	43.9	32.3	32.6
(4) Percentage of (3) from Outside CACM	98.6	95.0	97.7	96.5	96.6
(5) Extra-regional Imports for Industry as percentage of:					
(a) Extra-regional Imports	55.0	56.0	57.0	53.3	56.1
(b) Extra-regional Exports	73.7	55.4	66.5	58.3	62.9

Source: Derived from SIECA, VII Compendio Estadístico Centroamericano, Guatemala, 1981.

TABLE 4.2   Average Effective Rates of Protection for Costa Rica

	1965-- 1967	1968-- 1969	1970-- 1971	1971-- 1974
All Manufacturing	65.9	78.8	65.9	98.6
Intermediate Goods	32.1	39.9	32.1	49.5
Capital Goods	32.3	49.1	32.3	58.8
Consumer Goods	81.8	95.7	81.8	120.2

Source: Bulmer-Thomas (1979).

TABLE 4.3 Policy Instruments for Combining ISI with EP

	Increases in (V_j^{e*})	Decreases in $(V_j'^{*})$
e_j^r		Down
e_j^o	Up	
e_i^r		Up
e_i^o	Down	
t_j^r		Down
t_i^r		Up
t_i^o	Down	
r_j^r		Up
r_j^o	Down	

Source: author.

TABLE 4.4   Twenty-Five Industrial Sectors Ranked Highest for Overall
             Comparative Advantage, Central America

Sector	Description	Combined Rank, Static and Dynamic Comparative Advantage
3839	Electrical Apparatus not elsewhere specified	75
3140	Tobacco Manufactures	74
3131	Distilled Spirits	73
3832	Radio, Television, Communication Equipment	72
3111	Meat (slaughter, preparation)	71
3512	Fertilizers, Pesticides	70
3843	Motor Vehicles	69
3312	Wooden Containers	68
3114	Canned, or preserved Fish	67
3559	Rubber Products not elsewhere specified	66
3113	Canned, preserved Fruits and Vegetables	65
3813	Structural Metal Products	64
3521	Paints, Varnishes	63
3311	Sawmills, planing mills	62
3823	Metal- and Wood-working machinery	61
3213	Spinning, Weaving, Finishing Textiles	60
3831	Electrical Industrial Machinery	59
3116	Grain Mill Products	58
3411	Pulp, Paper, Paperboard	57
3132	Wine	56
3118	Sugar	55
3412	Paper, Paperboard Containers and Boxes	54
3134	Soft Drinks	53
3710	Iron and Steel (basic)	52
3551	Rubber Tires and Tubes	51

Source: Cline (1978), p. 282.

Notes

1. During the 1960s and 1970s, the value of both intra-regional and extra-regional exports increased rapidly; the latter, however, was based on primary products. The main concern now is whether it is possible to combine an increase in intra-regional trade with an expansion of extra-regional *manufactured* exports.

2. These arguments are developed more fully in Bulmer-Thomas (1982a).

3. In the Central American context, "traditional" primary product exports include coffee, bananas, cotton, sugar and beef.

4. For a case study of the ERP in Central America, see Bulmer-Thomas (1976).

5. Backward and forward linkages are of enormous importance for an understanding of the industrialization process in LDCs. For a fuller treatment, see Bulmer-Thomas (1982b).

6. See Bulmer-Thomas (1982b).

7. See Bulmer-Thomas (1986a).

8. Even Nicaragua adopted an adjustment program in 1982, although it was not subject to IMF conditionally. See Medal (1985).

9. I have estimated real GDP for the five Central American Republics for the inter-war years and linked it to the official statistics published for all countries since 1950. See Bulmer-Thomas (1987b).

10. Costa Rican imports from CACM fell by 48 percent between 1980 and 1984. The decline in imports from each country was: Guatemala (42 percent), El Salvador (54 percent), Honduras (56 percent) and Nicaragua (50 percent). See Consejo Monetario Centroamericano (1985).

11. For a comprehensive treatment of the scheme, see Ramsett (1969).

12. After 1970, Honduras signed bilateral trade treaties with is former privileges as CACM membership, but allowed her to charge duties on imports from those countries.

13. See Ramsett (1969).

5

Central American Economic Integration: Renewed Prospects in the Midst of Crisis

Juan Alberto Fuentes

Introduction[1]

Recent developments suggest that there may be new hope for regional economic cooperation. Clearly, such cooperation is vital if the region is to accomplish the twin tasks of negotiating a durable peace settlement and revitalizing internal and external trade.

Since intra-regional trade (IRT) is the main indicator of the state health of Central American economic integration, this essay begins with a review of some hypotheses explaining the decline of such trade. We argue that adjustment policies based largely on non-tariff barriers to trade have resulted not only in trade contraction but also in a new geographical pattern of trade in which those countries whose share in total IRT has risen are those which, in the past, were least committed to economic integration. Nevertheless, there are signs that economic cooperation between the five republics may improve. The rate of IRT contraction is slowing, new arrangements have been agreed upon which would reduce structural imbalances in IRT and avoid the need to settle obligations in dollars, a new common external tariff (CET) has been agreed which rationalizes effective protection and, finally, a common regional position is emerging with respect to trade negotiations with the rest of the world.

Juan Alberto Fuentes was formerly SIECA representative in Europe and professor at CEMLA (Latin American Centre of Monetary Studies) in Mexico. At present, he works as consultant to the United Nations Development Program (UNDP) in Suan José, Costa Rica. He is also a member of the United Nations Mission on Central American Reconstruction charged with reporting to the General Assembly in April 1988.

We conclude by arguing that, although all countries of the region must become more 'outward looking,' the promotion of exports to third countries can best be accomplished done within the context of a renewed Central American Common Market (CACM).

A Crisis of Expectations

It is commonly argued that the process of regional economic integration entered a state of 'permanent crisis' over fifteen years ago. The reasons cited are various and include the unequal distribution of the benefits of integration, the war between El Salvador and Honduras in 1969, weaknesses in the institutional structure of the CACM and excessive foreign dependence.[2] In addition, the particular form which economic integration took is said to have held back development of domestic markets, enhanced the unequal distribution of income, perpetuated the concentration of land ownership, encouraged inefficient forms of protection and opened the door to exploitative multinational firms. How far these ills are ascribable to the CACM is a moot point. What is true is that, unlike the 'golden age' of the 1960s, today there is widespread scepticism about the future of the CACM.

This mood has been strengthened by what the Economic Commission for Latin America (ECLA) has referred to as the Central American 'crisis of expectations.' The main 'expectation' was that, with the creation of the CACM, Central America was set on a path which could only lead to full economic integration. However, as ECLA has noted, such a notion was never envisaged in the General Treaty of Economic Integration.

> In reality, the General Treaty does not contain a single clause calling for the unification or harmonization of economic policies at all levels. Rather, it tends towards an arrangement based on partial commitments to facilitate the formation of relatively loose arrangements over objectives of limited scope—the establishment of a free trade zone and adoption of a common tariff within five years—all of which was accomplished.[3]

Despite the prevailing mood of pessimism—particularly among social scientists—an alternative account of the effects of the CACM during its first two decades has gradually emerged.

> First, integration was the best option facing the Central American countries in the early fifties to accelerate economic growth; second, if all the countries derived important benefits from the process, the relatively less-developed countries such as Honduras did so in much smaller

proportion than those countries which were economically more advanced; third, integration has had positive effects such as promoting change in the structure of production through the process of industrialization.[4]

True, there is disagreement over how far the pattern of specialization resulting from the CACM was optimal. Some writers— see chapter 3 of the present volume—have characterized country specialization as more intra- than inter-industrial in nature, with competition within the region taking the form of superficial product differentiation. Such a pattern is contrasted, unfavorably, with a hypothetical pattern which might have resulted from the pursuit of inter-industrial specialization based on the exploitation of local natural resources and taking full advantage of economies of scale.

Nevertheless, the pace of industrial growth in the 1960s and 1970s was impressive, particularly the growth of intra-regional trade in manufactures. Although regional income growth slowed in the second half of the 1970s, over the decade the value of intra-regional exports climbed from US$ 286 million to more than US$ 1 billion.[5] Although attempts to effect a major restructuring of the CACM were unsuccessful, in general the experience of integration during the 1970s may be regarded as positive, particularly with respect to achieving a stronger a 'project focus.'[6] Integration in the 1970s achieved what Hirschman has called "silent progress;"[7] i.e. progress which was significant though not spectacular.

In the 1980s, the integration process has shown a remarkable ability to survive despite the fact that the region has experienced one of the most convulsive periods in its history. But the setbacks experienced in the first half of the 1980s imply that the crisis is no longer merely one of expectations. Some figures will serve to illustrate the magnitude of the crisis.

Intra-regional trade (IRT) has contracted to a point where, in 1986, its value in current dollars was lower than ten years earlier (see Table 5.1). The value of intra-regional exports has fallen even more than the value of extra-regional exports; hence, the share of IRT in total trade has fallen from an average of 23 percent in the 1970s to 15 percent in 1985.[8] Moreover, since 1981, there has been a serious decline in the proportion of intra-Central American transactions settled through the Central American Clearing House. The proportion of settlements within total transactions fell from 100 percent in 1980 to approximately 70 percent in 1985 to 45 percent in 1986, the greatest fall being in registered trade with Nicaragua.[9] The fact that IRT has tended to bypass the Clearing House reflects, in turn, the difficulties which certain countries have experienced in meeting their settlement obligations to the Clearing House (e.g. Nicaragua, followed by El Salvador), and the desire (above all by Costa Rica) to avoid the further accumulation of payments outstanding.

These factors have turned what once was a regional settlement system into a regional credit system under which Costa Rica has become the main creditor. Since Central Banks in debtor countries have been unable to finance IRT (by selling further dollars for imports at the official rate) and Central Banks have been reluctant to do so given their own extra-regional obligations, IRT registered with the Central Banks and passing through the Clearing House has contracted more sharply than actual IRT. The growth of parallel and black markets in dollars has allowed Central American products to be imported which otherwise could not be acquired. Moreover, counter-trade—i.e. bilateral barter trade agreements—has spread considerably. But there has been a marked reluctance to trade with Nicaragua given the limited capacity of that country to supply the Central American market. In consequence, Nicaragua's has virtually ceased trading with the region.

The failure to meet obligations to the Clearing House is reflected in the growth of intra-regional trade debt (the bulk of which is between Central Banks). Outstanding debt, in turn, has been a major obstacle on reaching agreement on how to revive IRT. At the end of 1986 this debt amounted to slightly more than US$ 700 million.[10] Of this total, approximately US$ 500 million corresponded to Nicaraguan debt, owed mainly to Costa Rica (US$ 217 million). Total Salvadorean debt with the rest of Central America was US$ 85 million. Costa Rica was the region's principal creditor with credits outstanding of US$ 368 million, followed by Guatemala with $ 237 million.

The Principal Causes of the Decline in Intra–Central American Trade

There are four main interrelated causes of the decline in IRT: falling incomes; overvalued exchange rates combined with trade restrictions; shrinking productive capacity; and the deterioration in extra-regional terms of trade, particularly the fall in price of traditional commodity exports. Of the above, the latter is key since the commodity export sector has been—and continues to be—the engine of growth of the Central American economy.

If the reduction in intra-regional trade were fully explained by the fall in regional income, one might question whether a crisis of intra-regional trade existed as such.[11] The fact that many Central American manufactures are luxury goods and have an income-elasticity greater than unity implies that the fall in the value of trade should be proportionally greater than that in income. This appears to be true in the case of Costa Rica and Honduras where the figures show a significant relationship between the growth rates of per capita GDP and intra-regional imports over the period 1977–1984.[12] But for Guatemala this relationship is weaker.[13] It is nonexistent in the case of El Salvador and Nicaragua, which suggests that other factors explain the contraction of their imports from the rest of Central America.

A second factor that helps to explain the precipitous decline in IRT is the difference in exchange rate policies pursued by the five republics; these differences reflect the more general problem of the lack of common adjustment policy. In general, the early 1980s saw an attempt to maintain official exchange rates (traditionally pegged to the US dollar) in the face of sharp differences in domestic rates of inflation. This resulted in the general overvaluation of Central American currencies, a phenomenon exacerbated by the appreciation of the dollar relative to the currencies of other world trading partners.[14]

A third factor adversely affecting intra-regional trade has been declining industrial production capacity. The decline has been most serious in those countries experiencing widespread socio-political unrest or military intervention, notably El Salvador and Nicaragua. El Salvador accounted for 27 percent of intra-Central American exports in 1977, but only 23 percent in 1986. Nicaragua went from 17 percent to 3 percent over the same period.[15] In absolute terms and at current prices, Salvadorean exports to the region fell from US$ 211.6 million to US$ 97.5 million while Nicaraguan exports fell from US$ 134 million to US$ 10.5 million. In Nicaragua, the range of export goods available also contracted substantially.[16]

With respect to non-tariff barriers, two developments are particularly important. First, before 1984, the most general short-term device used to defend the balance of payments was import restrictions. Starting in 1984, given the growing backlog of unsettled accounts in the Central American Clearing House, creditor countries restricted their exports to debtors. First Costa Rica, then Guatemala, insisted on counter-trade agreements. Costa Rican restrictions on exports to Nicaragua subsequently were extended to its exports to other countries. Second, bilateral trade relations acquired new importance. When Honduras left the CACM at the end of the 1970s, it re-established trade relations with the four remaining members on a bilateral basis. In the 1980s, multilateralism disintegrated and was replaced with bilateral arrangements. The bilateralization of Costa Rican trade with El Salvador and Guatemala at the end of 1985 is an example of this phenomenon.

The four factors cited above—e.g. falling incomes, overvalued exchange rates, shrinking productive capacity and foreign exchange shortages—lie at the root of the decline in intra-regional trade. The recent deceleration in the contraction of income has reduced the relative importance of the first factor. However, since large discrepancies persist between official and parallel exchange rates, trade expansion is difficult. Some progress is now being made on this front, notably in the cases of El Salvador and Guatemala. Losses in productive capacity as a consequence of war, or the more general economic crisis, continue to constrain the supply of exports in Nicaragua and El Salvador. But the principal obstacle to increased trade is the generalized shortage of foreign exchange. Econometric evidence, based partly on the use of gravity models, demonstrates the significance of each of the variables identified above.[17]

While it is important to analyze the regional determinants of the contraction in intra-Central American trade, it is evident that this phenomenon is part of the wider global economic crisis. Faced with this crisis, the Central American economies have experienced grave difficulties in adjusting to a new and harsher international economic order. These difficulties have been compounded by political and military conflict and the growing flight of capital from the region. A combination of trade restrictions and deflationary stabilization policies have followed.

The Changed Intra-Regional Trade Pattern and Its Consequences

The crisis has hurt some countries far more than others, as reflected in the important changes which have occurred in traditional trade patterns. In 1986, the value of Nicaragua's exports to the region was less than in 1970, while Guatemalan and Costa Rican exports were equivalent to levels attained in 1976 and 1975 respectively (see Table 5.1). In 1976, intra-regional exports from Nicaragua accounted for more than 18 percent of total intra-Central American exports; the figure fell to 10 percent in 1979 and to 3 percent in 1986. By 1981, Honduras had replaced Nicaragua as the fourth largest regional exporter. This is explained in large part by war damage to Nicaraguan industry and, after 1979, the loss of key markets such as El Salvador.

In 1986, El Salvador's share of intra-Central American exports was 23 percent as compared to 30 percent in 1979. In value terms, 1986 export levels were equivalent to those obtaining nearly 15 years earlier. In 1981, Costa Rica had already replaced El Salvador as the second most important country in intra-regional trade after Guatemala. Guatemala not only maintained its position as the principal intra-regional exporter, but actually increased its share in IRT despite a transitory setback in the late 1970s.

In 1979, Costa Rica was in deficit with all countries of the region except Honduras. By early 1981, it had displaced El Salvador and joined Guatemala at the top of the league table, running a surplus with all countries. Meanwhile, Nicaragua was in deficit with all countries. El Salvador, which together with Guatemala had traditionally enjoyed a trade surplus, went into overall deficit with the region at the beginning of 1982. Its large deficit with Guatemala was similar to that of Nicaragua with El Salvador and Costa Rica. Guatemala stayed in overall surplus but experienced deficits with Costa Rica from 1982 to 1985.[18]

Those countries most dependent on intra-regional exports during the 1970s were Guatemala, with an average share of 31 percent of intra-regional in total exports, and El Salvador, with 30 percent. Nicaragua followed with 23 percent, Costa Rica with 21 percent, and Honduras trailed a distant fifth with 7 percent.[19]

The displacement of El Salvador by Costa Rica and of Nicaragua by Honduras implies that, with respect to IRT, the relative share of those countries historically least dependent on such trade has increased. This phenomenon may prove particularly important in the sense that those countries which have most weight in Central American integration negotiations are those which least depend on it. In short, changes in trade patterns do not augur well for the CACM.

Another important change in the regional trade pattern is that regional imports have been replaced by domestic substitutes. Domestic import substitution for regional imports (as opposed to regional substitution for extra-regional imports) has been criticized by those who argue that it is the antithesis of integration; that it has prevented potential economies of scale from being exploited fully. Others have replied that domestic import-substitution is the only vehicle available for expanding the industrial sector of Central America, or indeed, of any LDC, under present conditions.[20]

In its more dynamic form, the argument for single-country ISI envisages a process in which, once factories producing for the regional market have been established and domestic markets have begun to grow, initially established factories are complemented by new factories producing for each national market.[21] However, one complication is that single-country ISI might not lead to increased regional trade, but instead, to increased imports from the rest of the world. Ultimately, single-country ISI might be trade-diverting at the regional level.

Available evidence suggests that all Central American countries—with the exception of Nicaragua—have gone through a process of domestic industrial import-substitution throughout the 1978–1984 period of crisis and recession.[22] For Central America as a whole, the share of domestic production directed towards satisfying domestic industrial demand increased from 58.0 percent in 1978 to 64.1 percent in 1984. Over this same period, the share of intra-regional imports in domestic industrial demand fell from 8.3 to 5.7 percent while the share of imports originating in the rest of the world fell from 33.7 percent to 30.2 percent.

In Nicaragua, over the period 1978–1984, little industrial import substitution took place. Nevertheless, the share of extra-regional imports in domestic industrial demand increased from 28.2 percent in 1978 to 43.2 percent in 1984, while the share of domestic production fell from 62.0 percent to 52.0 percent. The share of intra-regional imports fell from 9.9 percent to 4.8 percent.

As the Central American economies move from a period of contraction to one of mere stagnation, the emphasis is now on unilateral trade liberalization vis-à-vis the rest of the world rather than on integration. Thus, in addition to the erosion of intra-regional trade by single-country ISI, Central American imports are being displaced by imports from the rest of the world. Special export-credit lines provided by developed countries (and certain NICs) lend further impetus to this process. In short, unless new life can be breathed into the CACM, the outlook for intra-regional trade is bleak.

The Prospects for Economic Integration

One way to evaluate the prospects for further economic integration is to compare current conditions with those obtaining at the beginning of the 1960s when the Central American Common Market was created. At that time, the prevailing consensus of economic opinion favored ECLA-style arguments for integration. Also, the example of European integration was much admired.

Today, opinion is sharply divided. Most important, the position of the United States has changed. Early enthusiasm for the CACM—albeit, a CACM which differed from that envisaged by ECLA—as exemplified by the San José meeting of the Central American presidents with President Kennedy in 1963, has given way to qualified support for a CACM from which Nicaragua would be excluded. The Caribbean Basin Initiative and the economic boycott of Nicaragua are opposite faces of the same coin.

For Central America, the crisis of the world economy has meant deteriorating terms of trade, rising interest rates and a large net outflow of private capital. The current external indebtedness position and the conditionality of aid contrast starkly with an earlier period characterized by generous inflows of official aid and direct private investment. Although monetary policies in the region have always been 'orthodox,' the region is experiencing an unprecedented period of belt tightening. Current skepticism about further integration seems is understandable.

In 1985, however, two events gave new impetus to the process of economic integration. The first was the adoption of a new Common External Tariff (CET). The second was the signing of a Cooperation Agreement between the European Economic Community (EEC) and Central America and Panama (or what is now called the Central American isthmus). On a third front, that of intra-regional debt, no formal agreement has been reached but 'silent progress' is being made in its restructuring.

In December 1984, the governments of Costa Rica, El Salvador, Guatemala and Nicaragua signed the Agreement on the Central American Tariff and Customs Regime. This established the normative framework for the new Common External Tariff (CET). The details were agreed in October, 1985, and the CET took effect in January, 1986. The CET had been the subject of more than ten years of study and negotiation, with strong technical support from SIECA. Agreement was prompted by the possibility that Costa Rica might apply a new unilateral tariff following its adoption of the structural adjustment program proposed by the World Bank.

The main effect of the new CET is to reduce differences in effective protection between countries. Under the previous tariff structure, the effective rate of protection (ERP) varied markedly both among countries and among industries in the same country. Apart from Guatemala where effective protection under the earlier tariff structure was reasonably uniform, in the rest of Central America the standard deviation of the ERP was of the order of 100 percent. Under the new CET, nowhere does the standard deviation exceed 50 percent.

With the exception of Costa Rica, the CET does not lower average effective protection. Even for Costa Rica, reductions in the rate of effective protection are significant only in two product groups, processed food and industrial chemicals. This helps explain the lack of opposition to the CET from the Central American private sector. In Guatemala, the new tariff arrangement actually increases average effective protection but does not significantly alter its dispersion. Hence, the CET has managed to satisfy both Costa Rica's concern to reduce protection and Guatemala's desire to avoid any such reduction. It should be noted that because the new CET also eliminates fiscal incentives in the form of tariff exemptions on imported industrial inputs, the ERP on final goods is reduced while it rises for intermediate products and capital goods.

In Honduras, the private sector has expressed interest in the CET, having rejected an earlier proposal for a separate national tariff structure. Various factors help explain this: the higher average protection offered by CET compared to the current tariff structure; the gradual and flexible incorporation of new signatories allowed for by the Treaty; and the emerging view that in future Honduras might enjoy greater benefits from intra-Central American trade.

However, there are still important difficulties. First, Article 26 of the Central American Tariff and Customs Regime allows for the application of non-tariff measures at each government's discretion "based on national legislation." In addition, there does not appear to be consensus about how flexibly the CET is to be applied. Neither is there agreement over the principle of gradually lowering the *average* ERP which is favored by Costa Rica.[23] Finally, there are fears that Article 26 may be interpreted in too lax a manner, particularly the provision allowing duty-free access to extra-regional imports where a temporary supply shortage is deemed to exist.

On balance, the CET agreement has considerable merit. Agreement was achieved by means of a gradual process of negotiation which excluded political issues from the agenda. An important by-product of the agreement is that it paves the way for defining a common Central American position in trade negotiations with the rest of the world.

The second positive achievement is the signature of the Cooperation Agreement between the European Community (EC) and Central America (including Panama). This agreement was signed after more than a year of negotiations, beginning with the Ministerial Summit held in San José on 28–29 September 1984, and followed by a further Summit in Luxembourg on 11–12 November 1985.

The expectations raised were considerable, some less realistic than others. It was hoped that the Agreement would mark a major step forward in both the political *and* economic fields, Central America achieving preferential status in the latter. Instead, the Agreement provided for "cooperation in a non-preferential framework" and established that EC development assistance would be granted within "the framework of those programs destined for non-associated developing countries;" i.e. without a truly political component.

Nevertheless, the negotiations and resulting Agreement strengthened Central American economic integration. The negotiating process forced Central American countries to adopt joint positions on issues of economic and social development, and various ministries and national and regional institutions participated. Within the Agreement, four of the twelve paragraphs in the Preamble on principles make explicit reference to support for Central American economic integration. The role of integration in promoting development and stability stands out; reference is made to the reinforcement of coordinated and complementary regional economic development, the need to arrest the decline of intra-regional trade and the need to increase the productive capacity of those countries in chronic deficit on intra-regional trade account.

Unfortunately, on the question of economic cooperation, the Agreement is vague. For example, as regards access to the EC Generalized System of Preferences (GSP), Central American (and Panamanian) interests are to be "accommodated." The only detailed provisions are those pertaining to development assistance. Particular emphasis is given to aid for integrated rural development, common training facilities, food self-sufficiency, and improved health provision. In summary, the Agreement supports integration efforts in social areas, but not in the areas of foreign trade and finance where the scope for promoting Central America integration is greatest.

Alternative Payments Mechanisms for Intra-Regional Trade

In recent years a number of studies have been carried out on proposed alternatives to the Central American Payments Clearing House (*Cámara Centroamericana de Compensación*).[24] The Clearing House effectively ceased to be multilateral in 1982. Intra-regional debt has continued to mount since each country has given priority to servicing its extra-regional debt. To date, little progress has been made other than in recognizing that such discrimination must stop and in accepting the need to separate the issues of servicing existing debt and repaying the principal. It is also recognized that there is no single solution to the payment problem—but rather that there are several and a package must be negotiated soon.

The best-known proposal calls for the creation of Central American

Import Certificates (*Derechos de Importación Centroamericanos,* or DICAs) to complement the existing payments system. The idea was first proposed by the Costa Rican Chamber of Industry and then developed in detail by the Secretariat of the Central American Monetary Council (*Consejo Monetario Centroamericano,* CMCA). In general, the scheme has been viewed with favor by both the public and private sectors though doubts have been expressed about its multilateral and negotiable character.

The logic of the scheme is as follows. A DICA, bearing the stamp of the country of issue but denominated in US dollars, would be issued by the Central Bank of, say, country A. Businesses in A wishing to import from some other country of the region, say B, could purchase DICAs in their local currency. Upon taking delivery of the merchandise, importer A would pay exporter B in DICAs. The latter would present them to Central Bank B either for redemption in local currency or for validation. Validation would enable exporter B either to use the DICAs to import directly from country A, or else to sell them in the open market to anybody in any country wishing to import from country A.

The gap between the supply of DICAs (the amount issued based on import requests) and their demand (the demand for exports from the country of issue) would determine whether a country's DICA sold at a premium or a discount. Where a country was in trade surplus, its DICA would command a premium. This would be equivalent to an upward adjustment in the country's exchange rate thus bringing the country back into balance. The same logic holds for a deficit country whose DICA would sell at a discount, thus tending to make its exports more competitive.

In effect, the DICA is meant to have two functions. First, it serves as a new regional trading currency which substitutes for scarce dollars. Second, the system introduces an automatic exchange rate adjustment mechanism meant to eliminate trade imbalances within the Central American region. In addition, the scheme allows the private sectors in each country to grant each other credit to the extent that the DICAs delivered to an exporter are not immediately used for imports.

However, the DICA cannot eliminate trade deficits caused by a shortage in productive capacity in the export sector. In the case of Nicaragua, for example, given the domestic export-supply constraint and the lack of demand for Nicaraguan DICAs in other countries, the Nicaraguan Central Bank would need to restrict the issue of DICAs in order to avoid a precipitous fall in their market value. Hence, any proposal to expand intra-Central American trade will need to be accompanied by policies aimed at strengthening the productive capacity of the relatively less-developed countries, or of those countries where the productive sector has suffered physical damage.

Another problem which the DICAs fails to resolve is that of financing the exchange requirements of export products with a high import content. The problem would not exist if Central America produced intermediate products which were close substitutes for imports from the rest of the world. This is not the case. Traditionally, most IRT has consisted of consumer goods with a high import content, so that even if the DICA were to stimulate IRT, extra dollars would be needed to finance its extra-regional import component.

Finally, a key problem which the DICA leaves unresolved is the settlement of outstanding regional trade debt. Since much of this debt is owed to Costa Rica, it remains to be seen whether Costa Rica will not insist upon reaching agreement on outstanding debt as a prior condition to issuing the DICA.

These problems are indicative of the difficulties involved in restoring free trade in the region. An immediate return to free intra-regional trade is simply not viable. At the same time, it is impractical to try to codify and regulate all forms of trade.[25] The creation of the DICA must be seen as one option among others, a complementary mechanism which may prove useful under present circumstances.

Integration and Outward-Looking Policies

The progress achieved with respect to the CET and the Agreement with the EC—in contrast to the difficulties experienced in reaching agreement over payment mechanisms and stabilization issues—suggests that there is greater scope for a common approach on questions of aid and trade with the rest of the world than on regional debt and macro-economic adjustment policies. Equally, the link between peace and social justice is an issue which must figure on any future agenda of Central American cooperation.[26]

How far can there be a common approach to economic stabilization? Despite the urgent need for a coordinated regional stabilization program, the heterogeneity of government policies reduces the likelihood of agreement in this area. The influence wielded by the United States in organizations such as the International Monetary Fund, which plays a central role in the design of adjustment policies in Central America and the Caribbean, means that Nicaragua is effectively excluded from these discussions. The war effort in Nicaragua, financed by means of a fiscal deficit which in 1987 amounted to 25–30 percent of GDP, makes agreement on stabilization issues practically impossible. Nicaragua's resistance to external aggression should not obscure the need to implement some form of stabilization policy, probably drastic. A quote from Dudley Seers on stabilization in the USSR at the end of the First World War is instructive:

> After 1922, the direction of policy was completely reversed. The New Economic Policy then adopted would in many respects have gratified even the most doctrinaire member of the IMF staff. To balance the budget, taxes were increased, part of social expenditure was made the responsibility of local authorities, and government administrative staff were reduced by more than 50 percent. The increase in the money supply was halted, indeed, the government linked the rouble to gold; the real value of wages fell and the consequent strikes were repressed, often with violence; trade unions were brought under government control. Tax and price policies were manipulated to provide 'incentives' to peasants and traders. . . . Production recovered, inflation slowed down, and foreign payments were brought back into balance. The regime survived—but, not surprisingly, the result of such drastic version of what we would now call a 'stabilization' policy was a rapid increase in inequality and unemployment.[27]

One (admittedly small) step in the direction of developing a common approach to stabilization was the meeting held in San José in February 1986. Here, presidential delegates from four Central American countries (Nicaragua was not invited) met to propose themes for possible consideration at a presidential summit. The final communiqué refers to the need to achieve a common 'orientation' in stabilization policies rather than a joint set of policies. Other principles endorsed by the Meeting included the need for a common position vis-à-vis that of the multilateral financial institutions; the need to seek uniformity of criteria concerning the renegotiation and restructuring of foreign debt; the need to develop more uniform policies on purchases of petroleum and traditional exports, on the common external tariff, on regional economic and financial agreements, and on outstanding intra-Central American debt.

The themes identified are useful, but the political and exclusive nature of the initiative, even though it was not meant to include political and military topics, limits its scope. In this respect, the Caribbean Common Market (CARICOM) has accomplished a good deal more. A recent meeting of Caribbean heads of state based its discussions around the theme of integration on a document on structural adjustment prepared by a subregional organization (the Caribbean Development

Bank). In effect, heads of state agreed on the general orientation of their short- and long-term policies.[28]

A more promising area of cooperation in the financial area is that of strengthening of the *Banco Centroamericano de Integración Económica.* The BCIE, having gone through its worst financial crisis, it is now gradually regaining strength. Furthermore, countries outside the region are increasing their participation in BCIE and full membership of countries like Mexico, Venezuela and Argentina is imminent.

Another area of potential common interest is that of devising joint social programs. The regressive impact of stabilization programs, the painful consequences of military conflicts in the region, the tension between countries, and the disparate distribution of benefits generated by economic integration in the past; all have prompted the search for new forms of integration which would stress the social dimension. What stands out, in particular, is the need to meet the basic needs of low-income social sectors strongly affected by stabilization policies and military conflict. New possibilities for cooperation exist in areas such as refugee policy, low-income housing, health, rural development, food and nutrition and education.

It is true that the predominantly national character of social policies limits prospects for Central American cooperation in some of these areas. Cooperation in such fields as housing provision and rural development is generally restricted to exchanging experience and information ('horizontal' technical cooperation). In the area of projects, there is greater potential for cooperation if such projects generate joint benefits and require the establishment of joint institutions.[29]

Cooperation can include the formulation of joint proposals for obtaining finance such as occurred in the case of the ambitious regional health programme ('Health: The Bridge to Peace in Central America') or with the Food Aid Program, both supported by the EC. Other examples of projects which could have mutually beneficial effects are the joint purchase of medicines, the control of epidemics and diseases and the production and exchange of material in the fields of education and housing.

In general, one important implicit objective of such cooperation is to help reduce tension and promote peace by stimulating dialogue among all Central American countries. This is why the principle of according priority to projects in which all five nations of the region participate (or the five plus Panama) is vitally important. The recent initiative by the President Cerezo of Guatemala to promote the creation of a Central American Parliament falls within this context. Such a

Parliament, in addition to serving as a forum for discussion, might gradually extend its domain to include areas of regional social cooperation, thus helping to transcend the elitist character of the initial phase of Central American integration.

New initiatives in the area both of political and economic integration would be conducive to peace by strengthening the institutionalization of intra-Central American relations. The experience of Western Europe following the Second World War is of obvious relevance. Economic cooperation, by cementing interdependence, creates the material conditions for peace. The easing of political tensions helps this to become a self-sustaining process.

One area in which there is agreement is over the need to improve Central America's bargaining power in the world economy. If the region is become less vulnerable to price fluctuations for its primary exports, there must be greater integration of industry and agriculture. In addition to promoting economic development, this new approach towards integration seeks to increase the Central American countries' room for maneuver in carrying out joint negotiations, coordinating their industrial and foreign trade policies and promoting new forms of intra-regional trade.[30]

The region also has broadened its sphere of political and economic relations, largely as a result of the role of US foreign policy in the Central American crisis. Nicaragua enjoys preferential relations with Cuba and Eastern Europe and, in general, Western Europe, Latin America and Canada have shown greater interest in Central America. Given the divergence of interests among new foreign actors, one might have expected polarization to increase and the relative autonomy of local actors to decrease. However—certainly with respect to Latin American, Western European and Canadian actors and possibly with respect to the others—their presence has increased the scope for negotiating preferential agreements which, in turn, has created new opportunities for improving the region's position within the world economy.[31]

The gradual rise of a subregional export strategy implies the need to formulate coordinated export-promotion policies (which avoid potential 'incentive wars'),[32] as well as to push for efficient agro-industrial development. Such developments also might serve to strengthen the process of industrial reorientation, allowing firms currently supplying the regional market to export to the rest of the world. In time, a joint negotiating position may evolve in areas such as basic export products and multilateral trade negotiations within the GATT framework.

At present, the main instruments of industrial and foreign trade policy vary considerably from one country to another, ranging from sophisticated tax credit certificates in Costa Rica to the nationalization of foreign trade in Nicaragua. Nevertheless, the existence of the CET, of similar productive and resource bases, and of similar difficulties in obtaining access to foreign markets, together provides a solid foundation for cooperation.

In the short run, it is essential to promote non-traditional agricultural exports, support industrial restructuring and assist existing industries gradually to modify their production techniques and develop their marketing capacity.[33] In the long run, the importance attached by all the countries to agro-industry signifies possibilities for promoting backward linkages together with specialization at the subregional level, thus combining selective, efficient import-substitution with the growth of exports to the rest of the world. This process should be conducted within a stable, pragmatic and non-doctrinaire macroeconomic framework, setting relative prices in a manner which favors exports and efficient import-substitution, and accompanied by measures to encourage savings. At the same time, particularly in rural areas, it is necessary to encourage the reorganization of production along lines which help improve the distribution of income and attenuate poverty.[34]

Conclusions

The search for a stronger bargaining position within the world economy should not detract from the importance of reviving intra-regional trade. On the contrary, as has been noted repeatedly, such trade offers an essential medium for initiating and developing new export lines for the world market. There are a number of reasons why this is so.

A first reason is that intra-regional trade is important for nurturing the development of infant export industries. The markets of neighboring countries, in allowing preferential access and having similar demand structures, provide exporters with a learning period to produce more efficiently before exporting to third markets.[35] Equally, as a consequence of the economic crisis, numerous firms find themselves decapitalized. An increase in intra-regional exports would help them regain the financial stability necessary for exploiting extra-regional export opportunities.

Trading in the world market is a risky business. A buoyant regional market reduces the risk of depending exclusively on markets subject to exogenous shocks. It contributes to maintaining a more stable level of macroeconomic activity. Moreover, export diversification entails incurring fixed costs. From the point of view of the firm, sales in the regional market can help cover a high proportion of the fixed costs of production, allowing exports to be placed on the world market at their marginal cost.[36] In effect, higher-priced regional sales subsidize the extra-regional export drive. In addition, given the problem of gaining access to extra-regional markets, particularly in the new climate of world protectionism, the regional market can absorb products which otherwise would have no outlet.

Finally, a strong regional market can stimulate competition and enhance efficiency. Where trade is obstructed, there exists a tendency towards single-country import substitution, a form of ISI which is relatively inefficient in the region because of the size of single-country markets. Intra-regional trade, by contrast, can stimulate competition and promote specialization and efficiency. It constitutes the ideal bridge between the promotion of efficient import substitution and the development of exports. At the same time, it will be apparent from what has been said above about effective protection that a tariff and tax regime is required which does not discriminate against extra-regional manufacturing exports.

Under present circumstances, it would be unrealistic to attempt a global restructuring of the Central American Common Market. A more useful strategy consists of promoting gradual integration through specific projects. Of course there is a risk that if progress towards integration is too 'silent,' the goal might become purely symbolic and the process unsustainable.[37] Nevertheless, there are two general objectives shared by all Central American countries which can contribute to developing a more propitious 'climate of integration.'

One is to strengthen the position of Central America with the world economy. The other—the *sine qua non* of integration—is peace. The peace process would be enhanced greatly were the international community to provide 'peace incentives' (market access, financial aid) conditional upon greater intra-Central American cooperation. This implies granting special preferences to activities which involve greater national and regional integration or projects in which all five nations participate, giving priority to integration measures in the social arena and to the development of new agro-industrial activities. These goals may not be spectacular, but they constitute the common ground available for promoting integration.

TABLE 5.1 Central America: Intra-Central American Exports; 1970,
1975--1985; (US$ million FOB)

Year	Central America	Guatemala	El Salvador	Honduras	Nicaragua	Costa Rica
1970	286.3	102.4	73.8	18.0	46.1	46.1
1975	536.3	168.2	141.8	26.6	92.6	107.2
1976	649.2	189.0	176.1	35.7	117.8	130.7
1977	758.4	22.5	211.7	43.4	134.0	173.8
1978	826.7	256.0	233.6	49.2	146.3	178.7
1979	891.7	299.6	266.6	60.0	90.2	175.4
1980	1129.2	403.7	295.8	83.9	75.4	270.3
1981	936.8	355.5	206.5	65.9	70.9	238.0
1982	765.5	320.1	174.2	51.9	52.1	167.2
1983	766.6	308.7	164.9	61.3	33.5	198.2
1984	706.9	291.4	157.2	49.4	37.1	171.8
1985	538.2	227.9	106.2	29.8	21.3	153.0
1986	420.5	184.1	97.5	21.4	10.5	107.0

Note: CEPAL estimates of intra-regional exports for 1980--1986 are shown
in Chapter 2, Table 2.8; CEPAL's estimates for recent years are
lower than SIECA's, in part because of their different treatment of
transactions which do not go through the Central American Clearing House.

Source: SIECA, (1985b), Table 1; SIECA (1985c), Table 31; Cáceres and
Imendia (1987).

Notes

1. This chapter is based on, 'La Integración Económica Centroamericana: Nuevas Perspectivas a Partir de la Turbulencia,' *Occasional Paper Series,* Florida International University, March 1986.

2. See Bodenheimer (1974).

3. See CEPAL (1981a).

4. See Lizano (1982).

5. The 1980 figure was influenced strongly by the jump in Nicaraguan purchases from the region.

6. See Cohen and Rosenthal (1977).

7. See Hirschman (1977).

8. See SIECA (1984); Table 91; the author also has used SIECA estimates for 1985.

9. Data provided by the Secretariat of the Central American Monetary Council (CMCA), San José.

10. Data on debt (31 December 1986) provided by the Secretariat of the Central American Monetary Council (CMCA), San José.

11. The fall in income would reduce the demand for imports. The variations income, in turn, depend upon the prices of traditional export products. See Siri (1975).

12. The correlation coefficients are 0.8589 for Costa Rica and 0.6244 for Honduras, significant at the 99 percent and 90 percent confidence levels respectively (with eight observations).

13. The correlation coefficient is 0.5760, significant only at the 80 percent confidence level.

14. The first major exchange-rate adjustment was that undertaken by Costa Rica in early 1981. Successive devaluations of the colón in 1981 eliminated the country's traditional deficit with Guatemala and, in subsequent years up until 1985, Costa Rica enjoyed an overall surplus in its intra-regional trade account. Nevertheless, restrictive measures adopted by the country's trading partners partly neutralized the effect of an adjustment in the real exchange rate. The devaluation of the colón had relatively little impact on Costa Rica's trade balances with Nicaragua and Honduras because the latter resorted to various forms of non-tariff protection (NTP). The use of NTP measures spread rapidly given the reluctance of most countries to devalue in real terms or, in most cases, even nominally. For evidence on the important role of exchange rates on intra-regional trade see Checchi and Co. (1985); also Loehr (1986).

15. See SIECA (1984), Table 91, and the first table in the present chapter. On the stagnation of Nicaragua's industrial sector, see also Brundenius (1985).

16. In general, for all countries in the region, not only has IRT fallen but the tendency towards product diversification has been reversed. The eighty most important export products identified by SIECA accounted for 74 percent of El Salvador's IRT in 1977 and 85 percent in 1983. For Nicaragua, the corresponding figures are 75 and 97 percent. For the remaining countries the figures are as follows: Guatemala, 74 and 77 percent; Honduras, 88 and 82 percent; and Costa Rica, 75 and 83 percent. See SIECA (1985b), Tables 19–23.

17. One of the most important findings of this type of analysis is that there has been an erosion of the preferential trade-relationships which previously existed among the Central American countries. Thus, whereas an econometric study applied to intra-regional trade in 1978 showed the explanatory variable 'preferential trade-relationships' to be statistically significant, it was no longer statistically significant (and indeed had changed sign) when applied to 1984 data; see Fuentes (1986).

18. This situation was reversed in 1986, when Guatemala developed a trade surplus with Costa Rica after the effective devaluation of the Guatemalan quetzal.

19. See SIECA (1984), Table 91.

20. See Rosenthal (1983), p. 176.

21. See Hirschman (1977).

22. Information provided in the rest of this section is based on Fuentes (1986).

23. See *La Nación* of 21 October 1985, which states: "the World Bank will not stand by idly, but rather will insist that the tariff barrier continue to be lowered, is a fact that the public and private sectors take for granted and are now preparing to confront"(author's translation).

24. See, for example, CEPAL/CEMLA (1983).

25. Isaac Cohen warns against the obsession or "need for codification" in Central American economic integration; see Cohen (1982a).

26. See Castillo (1986).

27. See Seers (1983), p. 121.; also Griffith-Jones (1981), preface.

28. The reference is to the Nassau Declaration (1984); also see Demas (1984).

29. See Cohen (1981).

30. See CEPAL (1985).

31. On prospects for schemes similar to the Caribbean Basin Initiative supported by the EEC and members of ALADI, see Castillo (1985).

32. See Castillo (1985).

33. See AISA (1985).

34. See CEPAL (1985); also CEFSA (1983).

35. This is a variation on the infant industry argument and Linder's hypothesis to the effect that exporters need to produce first in a known domestic market before exporting. See Linder (1961), *An Essay on Trade and Transformation*; also Lizano (1982) for this argument applied to Costa Rica.

36. See Lizano (1982).

37. See commentary by Lara (1977) on the article by Cohen and Rosenthal (1977).

6

Central America's External Debt: Past Growth and Projected Burden

Rómulo Caballeros

Introduction

Although the countries of Central America have pursued relatively conservative policies with respect to external finance, the deteriorating terms of trade, increased burden of debt service and net outflow of private capital experienced in the 1980s have led to an unprecedented foreign exchange crisis. This situation has led to the proliferation of trade restrictions within the region which have contributed to the decline of the CACM.

The issues of terms of trade and capital flight are examined elsewhere in the book (see chapters 7 and 8 particularly). This chapter[1] examines the growth of Central America's external debt and the results of various debt renegotiations up to 1986. It projects debt over the period 1987–1994 and assesses the ability of the region to meet its external obligations. Broadly speaking, the argument advanced is that Central America's debt burden is extremely high, even by Latin American standards. Various reprogramming rounds have succeeded in deferring the problem for a time without solving it. Indeed, in some cases externally-imposed 'adjustment policies' have been so drastic as to actually undermine the future growth of the economy's productive base and, hence, of repayment capacity. Even assuming no increase in net indebtedness and a return to terms of trade prevailing in the mid–1970s, for the region to meet its obligations, the burden of debt service required in the late 1980s and early 1990s will be crippling.

Rómulo Caballeros is Head of the Development, International Trade and Statistics Section at ECLAC's Mexico City Office.

SECTION I

The Evolution of External Indebtedness

In 1970 the combined total external debts of the five Central American countries stood at US$ 1.35 billion, or US$ 88 per capita (see Tables 6.1 and 6.2). By 1986 this figure had grown to US$ 17.18 billion or US$ 729 per capita. In 1983 the average ratio of external debt to gross domestic product was 81 percent for the five Central American countries in contrast to 36 percent for Latin America as a whole (Table 6.3). The debt-to-GDP ratios in three countries (Nicaragua, Costa Rica and Honduras) were by far the highest in Latin America, and that of El Salvador was close to the highest (Venezuela and Chile). In the space of fifteen years, Central America has acquired an external debt burden which, relative to the region's productive capacity, is the heaviest in Latin America.

Examining the 1970 figures in Table 6.1 more closely, of the US$ 1.35 billion total, 48 percent consisted of loans contracted or guaranteed by the state and 52 percent of obligations to the private sector. About 60 percent of total publicly contracted debt was owed to the multilateral lending agencies (Table 6.4). External public debt service (interest and repayment of principal) represented 7 percent of the value of combined regional exports and 13 percent of combined public expenditure (Table 6.5). Central America's total foreign debt in 1970 was small but already significant.

By 1986, 95 percent (US$ 16.3 billion) of the US$ 17.2 billion total was publicly guaranteed. The breakdown of publicly guaranteed debt was approximately one-third multilateral, one-third bilateral and one-third private. For the region as a whole, debt service represented 39 percent of export earnings and 39 percent of public expenditure. Moreover, one must bear in mind that because the share of exports in GDP in Central America is about twice as high as for Latin America as a whole, comparisons with Latin America based on the debt service ratio (debt service as a percentage of total export earnings) are misleading.

How did this situation come about? Following the 1973–1974 oil crisis, the countries of the region turned in varying degrees to the international financial market in order to ensure themselves adequate levels of international liquidity. As it was impossible to obtain sufficient funds from official multilateral or bilateral sources, the bulk of new debt was contracted with private international banks. Accordingly, the share of commercial bank debt in the region's total external public debt increased from 36 percent in 1970 to 42 percent in 1979 and to almost 50 percent in 1982 (Table 6.2).

Three basic features distinguished this type of finance from that obtained traditionally from official sources. First, the loans did not have to be used to finance productive or developmental projects and thus were usually used to cover the trade deficit. Second, the agreed repayment periods were short, especially for those countries which had tended to experience recurrent deficits on current account. Lastly, most loans were contracted at variable interest rates based on those prevailing in the international market. At the time, it was difficult to foresee the level to which these rates would rise.

At the beginning of the 1980s, changes in international financial flows (caused, *inter alia*, by declining oil surpluses, the increase in the US fiscal deficit and the deregulation of the US banking system) swiftly produced spectacular interest rate rises in the international market. This led to a considerable increase in the interest payable on the external debt for all the countries and, in particular, for those which had opted for massive financing from external sources before the rules of the game were changed.

Within the region, a combination of growing financial instability and weakening economic performance led most governments to redouble their efforts to obtain foreign credit. Since the purchasing power of the region's exports was falling, the gap between commitments and repayment capacity grew.

However, from 1981 onwards, the growth rate of total external indebtedness slowed in all countries except Guatemala. The average increase for the area, which had been 18.5 percent between 1978 and 1981, fell to 17.8 percent for the three year period 1981–1983 and to 8 percent for 1983–1986 (Table 6.6). But these rates were still high given the weakening of other macroeconomic variables. Accordingly, over the period 1978–1986, the region's capacity to pay deteriorated to the point where all countries had to renegotiate their external commitments and some were forced to go to the IMF.

The slowdown in the growth of external debt was due in part to the decline in private sector overseas borrowing as foreign interest rates rose relative to domestic rates and businesses successfully turned their debts into public sector liabilities. By contrast, between 1978 and 1981, public sector external indebtedness continued to mount, particularly in Guatemala, El Salvador and Nicaragua. Although the rate of increase of public borrowing slowed in 1981–1983 as international credit dried up, the average rate for this period was still 20 percent.

By 1983 the per capita debt of Central America averaged US$ 729 (more than double the 1978 figure), and the figures for Costa Rica and Nicaragua were especially high (US$ 1,400 and US$ 1,700 respectively). Over the years 1978–1983 the ratio of debt to domestic product rose to 84 percent for the region. Nicaragua, Costa Rica and Honduras became the only three countries in Latin America where the ratio of external debt to GDP was greater than unity. From Table 6.3 it will be seen that the corresponding ratios for Argentina, Brazil and Mexico were 41 percent, 32 percent and 33 percent respectively.

Debt and Adjustment

Following the second oil price shock of 1979, as reserves fell and fiscal deficits mounted, governments were forced to choose between adjusting quickly to the new situation—in effect accepting a sharp decline in living standards with the political and social consequences this implied—and postponing adjustment by recurring to foreign borrowing. Not surprisingly, most governments chose the latter course. Given the social and political tensions of the region, nobody was keen to accept IMF-style solutions.

As a result, external borrowing became the central pillar of economic policy; it served as the basic support for savings, it financed practically all public investment and covered the fiscal deficit, as well as providing international liquidity for the external sector.

As the cost of credit rose sharply after 1980, the burden of debt service became onerous. At the same time it must be recalled that credit terms had been hardening steadily throughout the 1970s as can be seen in Tables 6.7 and 6.8. For example, in 1970 interest payments accounted for 29 percent of the external debt service for the whole region; by 1978 this figure had risen to 48 percent (Table 6.8). Moreover the structure of debt worsened (Table 6.7). The deteriorating structure of debt reflected the relatively short maturity dates of the increased proportion of commercial obligations contracted. In effect, the debt problem was not something which suddenly emerged in the early 1980s. Rather, it was a problem which had grown throughout the 1970s. Underlying the crisis of the early 1980s is the coincidence of three factors: the increased demand for credit, the higher cost of credit and the sharply diminished repayment capacity of borrowers.

Differences between the Central American Countries

At the beginning of the present decade, the two countries of the region which had traditionally been most conservative in matters of finance, Guatemala and El Salvador, owed relatively little to the international commercial banks (Table 6.4). In El Salvador, commercial borrowing declined further in the early 1980s, in part because banks were reluctant to lend and in part because greatly increased flows of official external aid and remittances from nationals living abroad made such borrowing unnecessary.

By contrast, Guatemala increased its commercial borrowing and, from 1984 onward it did so at an accelerating rate such that by 1986, commercial obligations accounted for 42 percent of its external public debt.

At first, Honduras too was reluctant to turn to the commercial market, but this changed largely because the government's monetary policy forced the country's private banks to look abroad to meet domestic credit demand. Accordingly, by the end of 1982, foreign commercial debt amounted to 35 percent of the total and, compared to 1970, the average repayment period had fallen by a third and the interest rate had more than doubled Table 6.6).

After 1979, Nicaragua attempted to diversify the structure of its borrowing and increase its use of official development assistance. Official aid was particularly abundant over the period 1980–1982 as the government sought assistance in rebuilding an economy severely damaged by war. Paradoxically, though, Nicaragua's overseas commercial debt rose as a proportion of total debt. This was because, upon coming to power, the new government chose to honor almost all obligations of the Somoza regime of which privately contracted commercial debt represented just over half. Hence, in 1982, Nicaragua's obligations to the international banking community amounted to 52 percent of its total external debt. However, by 1986, this proportion had fallen significantly (Table 6.4).

Of the five republics, Costa Rica became most heavily indebted to the commercial banks. With the onset of the crisis at the beginning of the decade, the government increased its proportion of overseas commercial borrowing in order to maintain historical levels of consumption and investment. It achieved its goals in the short term, but by mid–1981 it found itself in serious balance of payments difficulties and fell behind in its debt service payments, the consequences of which are discussed below. By 1984 Costa Rica's foreign commercial liabilities accounted for 56 percent of its total liabilities and for 36 percent of all Central American commercial debt (Table 6.4).

In summary, at the end of 1986, 95 percent of the total external debt of Central America consisted of public sector obligations (Table 6.1). Nicaragua with US$ 5.7 billion and Costa Rica with US$ 3.74 billion accounted for more than half the region's total external debt. El Salvador's debt (US$ 2.1 billion) was the smallest while the figures for Guatemala and Honduras were US$ 2.64 and US$ 2.93 billion respectively.

A word of caution about interpreting debt service obligations. As debt has mounted and repayment capacity has been squeezed in the 1980s, the gap between debt service obligations and payments has grown. Measured in terms of debt service actually paid, in 1986 Central America as a whole allocated 39 percent of its export receipts to principal and interest repayment (Table 6.5). The highest debt service figures (48 percent in both cases) were those of El Salvador and Costa Rica. El Salvador honored its obligations fully (although it also enjoyed very high levels of aid). Costa Rica, while making strenuous efforts, still continued to accumulate arrears. For Guatemala the figure exceeded 30 percent, while Nicaragua could only make payments representing 13 percent of its exports (although one must bear in mind that Nicaragua's absolute debt burden was the highest of the region).

SECTION II

Debt Renegotiation: The Creditors

As the foreign trade balance of the Central American countries deteriorated after 1979, the flight of capital assumed alarming proportions.[2] Net reserves (the difference between Central Bank gold and dollar assets and liabilities) were falling and, in some cases, turned negative. As some countries were quite unable to meet their external debt commitments, delays occurred in the repayment of principal and even in the payment of interest to the point where the authorities were compelled to enter negotiations. Most negotiations took place in order to reprogram payments due to the international commercial banks although, in some cases, negotiations were also held with bilateral and multilateral agencies.

Commercial debt negotiations are usually conducted by the national authorities and *ad hoc* banking committees appointed by the lending banks in the case of private sources or, in the case of official debt, with the Club of Paris which comprises the main creditor governments of the OECD countries. Of course, any member country of the IMF is entitled to draw up to a particular amount with that body to see it through temporary balance of payments problems. Beyond that limit (which is in practice quite small), drawing rights are no longer automatic and further IMF loans must be negotiated. The importance of negotiating with the Fund lies not so much in obtaining further funds as in restoring a country's credit rating which enables it to borrow once more on the commercial market.

The IMF Agreements

A standby loan agreement with the IMF involves signing a letter of intent according to which the country undertakes to adopt an adjustment policy and meet certain concrete targets with respect to specific macroeconomic variables, so as to meet the (usually quarterly) payments agreed. 'Conditionality,' or the imposition of lending conditions intended to correct fundamental imbalances in the economy, is applicable both to the financial support from the Fund and to the use of the resources obtained through renegotiation.[3]

Broadly speaking, 'adjustment' consists of two sets of related measures designed to restore external balance. First, relative prices must be got right including, in particular, correcting for an overvalued exchange rate and removing protective measures. This encourages resources to be switched from home to export production. Second, to help boost savings and investment, it is necessary to cut aggregate demand by means of some appropriate mix of fiscal and monetary measures. It is particularly important to cut the central government deficit since government expenditure is considered to 'crowd out' private saving.

The arguments against this position have been summarized elsewhere including in a recent publication by CEPAL.[4] It will suffice to say that, while the counter-argument does not reject the need for financial discipline, it does emphasize the fact that excessive adjustment can seriously compromise a country's long term development prospects.

In the case of Central America, three countries concluded separate standby loan agreements over the period 1982–1986: Honduras in November 1982, Costa Rica one month later, and Guatemala at the end of August 1983. These agreements included imposing maximum limits on the growth of domestic monetary assets, domestic credit, the public sector deficit and central government current expenditure . The agreements also required central government to increase current revenue, to raise interest rates to positive real levels, to raise charges for public utilities and to set specific levels for net external assets. In the case of Costa Rica and Guatemala the agreements stipulated that arrears in the payment of principal and interest on loans should be settled, and that there should be a devaluation of the real exchange rate. Costa Rica was further required to cut wages and salaries in real terms and conform to specific levels of external public borrowing.

The terms imposed by the IMF affect almost every aspect of domestic economic policy. In the case of Costa Rica, the terms imposed by the Fund included the elimination of 5,000 public jobs, reduction of the fiscal deficit to less than 3 percent of GDP, the elimination of the exchange losses of the Central Bank and the slowing down of money wage increases. Honduras also held talks with the Fund in 1986 with a view to signing a standby loan agreement; the discussion focused on the reduction of the fiscal deficit and exchange rate adjustment. In the case of Guatemala, the most controversial topics were exchange rate unification, the elimination of the losses of the Central Bank and the privatization of a number of public enterprises.

For a variety of reasons the three countries in question had difficulty in meeting some of these terms and the agreements were therefore suspended before the end of the period originally agreed. In early 1987 these countries were still at different stages of negotiating new IMF agreements.

Agreements with the Commercial Banks

Nicaragua

The uprising which took place against Somoza in 1978–1979 precipitated a serious financial crisis. The new government was keen to maintain its standing in the international financial market and, in consequence, honored virtually the whole of the debt inherited from the Somoza regime including arrears. However, given the war damage sustained by the country's economy and the dislocation of the export sector, it was clear that obligations would need to be rescheduled pending economic reconstruction.

Accordingly, after fairly broad financial and economic assistance had been obtained in the first year, an initial understanding was reached with the international banks at the end of 1980. The banks undertook, without prior agreement with the IMF,[5] to renegotiate US$ 390 million—representing principal already due or payable between 1979 and 1982—with a grace period of five years, a repayment period of seven years (with half-yearly installments) and a variable interest rate with a surcharge of between 0.75 and 1.5 percent above LIBOR (London Inter-Bank Rate), but subject to a ceiling of 7 percent. The difference between the rate agreed and the rate paid would be capitalized and repayment would begin in 1985.

At the same time Nicaragua attempted a global renegotiation of its bilateral debt with the Club of Paris. However, the lack of a normal agreement with the IMF made an overall settlement difficult and in the end bilateral agreements were reached with most of the creditor governments.

During a second round of talks at the end of 1982, the total commitments of the publicly-owned banking system were renegotiated as were those of about 90 modern enterprises—both previously owned mainly by Somoza—which together amounted to a little over US$ 250 million. The terms were similar to those agreed in the earlier negotiation.

A further US$ 100 million in private obligations were the subject of special negotiations on a case-by-case basis or were covered with dollar-denominated five-year certificates of deposit bearing an annual interest rate of 7 percent.

However, in the wake of the renewed economic dislocation brought about by the 'contra' war, it proved impossible for Nicaragua fully to honor its commitments. While continuing to pay these in part, the government has been involved in further rounds of negotiations with its creditors on an almost permanent basis since 1983.

Costa Rica

As a result of the country's high level of foreign debt commitments and its critical domestic economic situation, in September 1981, the government and the Central Bank notified their creditors, both official and banking, that Costa Rica could not continue to service its entire debt.[6] Up to mid–1982 both the repayment of principal and the payment of interest on part of the outstanding foreign debt were declared in arrears, including the private debt consisting of matured liabilities for which the debtors had requested the necessary foreign exchange. In 1981 public debt commitments amounted to US$ 61 million of principal and US$ 121 million of unpaid interest. In June 1982 the total arrears in interest payments was US$ 240 million and the arrears on repayment of principal amounted to US$ 520 million. A further US$ 300 million was to fall due in the second half of 1982 and, a further US$ 600 million was to fall due in 1983.

It was clear that most obligations to private creditors which were coming to maturity would need to be restructured, including those falling due in 1982 and 1983. Negotiations to this end were set in motion in the second half of 1982.

At the end of 1982, a new standby loan agreement was agreed with the IMF which included a loan of a little under US$ 100 million, and a second line of credit of US$ 20 million was established to offset fluctuations in export earning.

Agreements were then reached with the majority of the unilateral creditors (Club of Paris) to reprogram just under US$ 140 million of principal over a period of five years, with five years of grace and half- yearly payments beginning in September 1987.

In 1981 a coordinating committee drawn from 12 of the 170 creditor banks had been set up to deal with the commercial debt outstanding.[7] The negotiations moved slowly but significant results began to emerge in the second half of 1982, once the initial terms of reference had been established, and even more so when the standby loan agreement was concluded with the IMF. This first stage was particularly difficult because Costa Rica was one of the first Latin American countries to fall behind in its payments.

Finally, in December 1983, a first reprogramming agreement was concluded which covered not only the accumulated arrears of 1981 and 1982 but also payments due in 1983 and 1984. Quite exceptionally, four years' commitments had been renegotiated. The total amount negotiated was US$ 617 million, and the repayment schedule was in two stages. Of the US$ 475 million covered by 'Stage I,' 95 percent was restructured over a period of eight and a half years beginning in January 1983. The agreement included a four-year grace period (1983–1986) during which only the interest would be paid. The remaining 5 percent was to be paid on 31 January 1984. 'Stage II' (US$ 142 million) provided for a repayment period of seven and a half years beginning in January 1984, also with a four-year grace period.

With respect to operating costs, the margins agreed with the banks for the restructured portion were 2.25 percent above LIBOR or 2.125 percent above the United States prime rate. In addition, the charges for deferred payments and refinancing were set at 0.25 and 1.0 percent respectively.

Lastly, in order to bring the payment of interest up to date, Costa Rica obtained a revolving commercial import credit equivalent to 50 percent of total current interest and matured interest for a term of three years and at a rate of 1.75 percent above LIBOR.

In mid–1986 various problems re-emerged with regard to meeting foreign commitments. The authorities met with a syndicate representing 150 commercial banks with a view to renegotiating US$ 1.6 billion. The conditions proposed by Costa Rica included repayment over 25 years with a seven-year grace period, interest to be set below the US prime rate and interest payments limited to US$ 5 million a month until the US$ 30 million in interest arrears had been cleared. These negotiations were not in fact held because, before they would consider the proposal, the commercial banks required that Costa Rica should sign a new standby loan agreement with the IMF.

Honduras

In Honduras, too, by 1982 the pressure of external debt service on the meager supply of foreign exchange had become a problem, although one less serious than in the cases described above. Accordingly, talks with representatives of the commercial banks were initiated with a view to restructuring part of the principal due.

The negotiations continued well into 1983, at which point payments due in 1984 were also included, so that the amount being negotiated totalled just under US$ 125 million. In the middle of that year an agreement was reached in principle under which US$ 123 million of the Honduran debt was restructured over seven year, including a three-year grace period, at a variable interest rate 2.375 percent above LIBOR or 2.25 percent above the US prime rate, plus commissions of 0.375 percent for deferred payment and 1 percent for refinancing. However, the agreement remained pending owing, on the one hand, to disagreements about the amount of additional credit to be included in the package and, on the other, the insistence by the banks that negotiations on a standby loan agreement with the IMF be concluded.

In the event, Honduras acted as if the agreement reached in principle was in fact binding and adhered to the new schedule. By the end of 1983 it had paid off interest arrears on its foreign debt.

The lengthy process of renegotiation of the debt with international private banks was resumed in 1986. The agreement was to cover an amount of US $218 million and, in principle, would meet the payments falling due between 1987 and 1989. The Honduran authorities proposed the renegotiation of 100 percent of these amounts, a term of 16 years for repayment of the principal, three years grace and interest set at LIBOR without any surcharge. The Coordinating Committee of the Creditor Banks proposed the immediate payment of 10 percent and, for the remaining 90 percent, a term of 14 years, including a three year grace period, and interest set at LIBOR plus 1.75 percent. Negotiations were still underway at the end of 1986.

Guatemala

Although up until 1986 Guatemala had generally been able to meet its external commitments, the amounts due on recent loans contracted by the Central Bank and certain temporary arrears problems obliged the authorities to seek limited reprogramming on a case by case basis. During 1986 they managed to renegotiate US$ 202 million of payments due in 1986 and 1987 owed to three creditors (one private international financier, the Bank of Mexico and the Investment Fund of Venezuela). The terms varied in each case, but they consisted basically of longer repayment periods.

SECTION III
Forecasting the Debt Burden, 1987–1994

The region's payment capacity over the next eight years (1987–1994) will be determined in part by the extent to which the international economy recovers and in part by the effort it makes to achieve a significant surplus on current account as well as whether the international community responds to that effort. The estimates presented below may provide an useful benchmark in assessing that effort and the response of the international community (Tables 6.9, 6.10 and 6.11).

In forecasting repayments (Table 6.9), only existing debt has been taken into account. Average terms assumed are those prevailing in 1986, taking into account the conditions obtained by Costa Rica and Nicaragua. Repayment capacity is estimated on the assumption that, by 1994, export volumes and prices will have reached the highest level recorded between 1970 and 1985 (Table 6.10). In short, our assumptions are such that it is difficult to argue that we have overestimated the likely future burden of debt service.

On the basis of these forecasts it is clear that for all Central American countries, if debt schedules were to be met, the remaining years of this decade would be extremely difficult. Obviously, the burden would increase if any new external commitments were contracted falling due within this period or if exports failed to recover in line with our assumptions. The forecasts indicate that Nicaragua and Costa Rica would have the most acute difficulties. Problems would be more manageable for Honduras and El Salvador, but would arise sooner. Guatemala would also have to cope with short term strains, although less severe than those arising in the other countries.

In absolute terms, and assuming that 1986 interest rates prevailed, between 1987 and 1994 the region would have to pay out just under US$ 15 billion in principal and interest payments on existing external public debt, an amount almost as great as existing public debt. Annual repayments would range between US$ 2.7 and US$ 1.1 billion. If exports performed as forecast, the debt service ratio would exceed 40 percent for the period 1987–1989 and would exceed 30 percent in the following two years (Table 6.11).

Even if no account is taken of service of any debt contracted from 1987 onwards, Nicaragua, the region's most heavily indebted country, would find itself in an extremely difficult position. To service its 1986 commitments, it would need to pay somewhat more than US$ 4 billion (26 percent of the external payments of the whole region) in annual amounts equivalent to more than twice the country's assumed export earnings in 1988 and more than 100 percent of assumed earnings at the end of the decade.

Costa Rica would have to pay about US$ 4 billion (27 percent of the region's total) and this would be most difficult since the annual commitment would represent about 48 percent of exports earnings for the period 1987–1989 and more than 32 percent on average up to 1992.

Such prolonged efforts of this kind are quite incompatible with these countries' capacity to respond, so that even given broad access to new flows of capital, it seems inevitable that in the short term they will have to begin a new round of negotiations to enable them to spread their present obligations over a much longer period and, above all, to ensure that new borrowing does not increase the burden of repayment in the present decade.

Of course the situation could turn out to be even more serious if the effects of the international economic recovery on the Central American economy were delayed or weaker than expected, or if interest rates were to start rising again, as might be the case if the US budget deficit were to continue to rise. Equally, the burden of Central America's high defense expenditure should not be forgotten, for it has eroded—directly and indirectly—the repayment capacity of some governments and forced them to borrow more from abroad. If this situation were to persist, the prospects would be even more gloomy.

In summary, even in relation to present commitments, it is unlikely that the region will be able to meet its obligation even if one makes optimistic assumptions about the recovery of export capacity and world prices. Indeed, it is probable that the region will need to contract further debt and that the terms of new debt will be less favorable than at present, thus worsening the structure of debt.

It must also be remembered that the countries with the greatest current difficulties will have to resort to costly and lengthy renegotiations which will mean further deterioration in their foreign commitments while providing them only temporary relief. So far, negotiations have not succeeded in bringing debt into line with the countries' real repayment capacities. Negotiations have generally involved a considerable increase in expenditure by way of banking commissions and risk surcharges on LIBOR. As a general rule, the agreed repayment periods have been too short to enable sustained economic recovery and modernization to boost repayment capacity. This has led to further reprogramming of the debt at even higher costs.

Conclusions

In the first half of the 1980s, the Central American economies have had to cope with serious external financial imbalances caused by increased debt service under conditions of stagnant export earnings. Where debt is measured in relation to GDP, Central America's debt burden is about twice the average for Latin America as a whole and far higher than that of the largest debtor countries. Virtually the whole of the region's debt is public (or publicly guaranteed). About two-thirds of this has come from official sources and the rest from commercial banks although, for Costa Rica and Nicaragua, the share of commercial debt is higher.

The debt problem is not new. Central American indebtedness grew throughout the 1970s, particularly after the first oil crisis. Because much new borrowing was from the international commercial banks, terms were harder than on earlier debt contracted with the multilateral agencies. This led to a deterioration in the structure of debt. The second oil crisis was followed in the early 1980s by falling commodity prices; together, these events produced a serious decline in the region's repayment capacity. To mitigate the effects of recession, most countries of the region borrowed heavily. The sharp rise in world interest rates which followed greatly exacerbated the problem. Moreover, as political instability in the region grew, the flight of capital from the region accelerated. Governments found themselves covering not only their own budgetary requirements, but refinancing the private sector.

Starting in 1982, most countries found it necessary to negotiate with commercial creditors in order to restructure their payment obligations. El Salvador, which enjoyed high levels of official assistance, was the exception. Also, Costa Rica and Honduras (and more recently Guatemala) initiated talks with the IMF. Private creditors generally required the Fund's seal of approval to carry on restructuring. Successive IMF programs have been negotiated with Costa Rica, although with some difficulty. IMF 'conditionality,' in practice, has meant severe belt tightening. In early 1987, Honduras and Guatemala, although talking with the Fund, had still not signed letters of intent. Nicaragua, exceptionally, managed to negotiate with the commercial banks without first going to the Fund.

The repayment projections presented in this chapter suggest that it is extremely unlikely that the region can meet even its 1986 level of commitments unless further debt renegotiation is undertaken between now and the end of the decade. The projections incorporate 'best scenario' assumptions, the most important ones being that export prices and volumes will recover, interest rates will not rise and no new obligations will be incurred. Even on these assumptions, the total outflow of resources required to service debt until 1994 is of the order of US$ 15 billion, or nearly as much as the current regional debt. Average debt service in the next few years would run at about 45 percent of export earnings and, in the case of Nicaragua, would exceed export earnings.

In the past, even where debt renegotiation has eased the pressures of debt service on the external balance, results have generally proved unsatisfactory. Firstly, renegotiation has meant an increase in the surcharges on the base rates to cover the costs arrears and the perceived increase in risk of default. A further percentage usually has been applied for 'deferment' and 'refinancing' charges, and the banks have charged other commissions for arranging the commitment of funds, opening of letters of credit, and legal fees. More important, the repayment periods required have not generally been compatible with the time required for genuine recovery measures to take effect. In practice, this has involved successive rounds of debt renegotiation at increased cost.

As for stabilization policy, since per capita income levels have already fallen sharply in the region, it is difficult to see what scope remains for further belt tightening. Adjustment policies may be necessary but they take time. Resources cannot be switched quickly from the domestic to the overseas market. The required cut in domestic demand may be so severe as to deter new investment, thus further jeopardizing future repayment capacity. There is some evidence to suggest that the successful development of new export lines requires, *inter alia*, a buoyant home market.

Bearing in mind the challenges which Central America will have to face over the next five years, caution will be required both with respect to renegotiating existing debt and contracting new commitments. As concerns renegotiation, it will be necessary to agree that, for a time, arrears will be inevitable so as to pre-empt the need to begin a new reprogramming process. Debtor countries might also attempt multilateral negotiations to eliminate some of the additional costs resulting from the current arrears.

The international community will need to show greater understanding of the region's economic problems which stem not from one crisis but from three interrelated crises: that of world trade and payments, that of regional trade and payments and that of the region's social and political structures. The negotiating position of the Central American countries will be strengthened to the extent that they devise joint proposals and responses. In this connection, resolving the crisis of the Central America Common Market warrants high priority.

Perhaps most important, though, more efficient use will need to be made of external resources. Commercial borrowing will need to be used strictly for the financing of highly profitable activities which have a direct effect on the generation of foreign exchange, and the gestation periods of such activities will need to be consistent with loan repayment periods. This means that the share of official development assistance will probably grow once more, and it will therefore be necessary to strengthen development project planning capacity. Moreover, the total net inflow of external resources will probably be considerably smaller than in the past. In summary, the region will need to revert to the basic principle that external resources are a complement to and not a substitute for national development efforts.

TABLE 6.1   Central America: Balance of Total Debt Disbursed by Debtor, 1970--1986

	1970	1975	1980	1981	1982	1983	1984	1985	1986
	(millions of US dollars)								
Central America	1349	3390	7651	9834	11962	13655	15106	16267	17177
public	648	1863	6387	8582	10548	12578	14118	15429	16257
private	701	1527	1264	1252	1414	1077	988	838	920
Costa Rica	429	1032	2209	2687	3188	3532	3752	3742	3739
public	134	421	1797	2315	2807	3184	3419	3425	3432
private	295	611	412	372	381	348	332	317	307
El Salvador	142	502	1176	1608	1808	2023	2095	2162	2093
public	117	323	1030	1391	1615	1839	1909	1982	1927
private	25	179	146	217	193	184	186	180	166
Guatemala	281	465	1053	1385	1841	2149	2505	2624	2641
public	152	255	764	1148	1435	2000	2387	2548	2470
private	129	210	289	237	406	149	118	76	171
Honduras	183	502	1388	1588	1986	2162	2392	2803	2931
public	90	264	971	1162	1552	1766	2041	2538	2655
private	93	238	417	426	434	396	351	265	276
Nicaragua*	314	889	1825	2566	3139	3789	4362	4936	5773
public	155	600	1825	2566	3139	3789	4362	4936	5773
private	159	289	-	-	-	-	-	-	-
	(percentages)								
Central America	100.0	100.0	100.0	100.0	100.0	100.0	100.0	100.0	100.0
public	48.0	55.0	83.5	87.3	88.2	92.1	93.5	94.8	94.6
private	52.0	45.0	16.5	12.7	11.8	7.9	6.5	5.2	5.4
Costa Rica	100.0	100.0	100.0	100.0	100.0	100.0	100.0	100.0	100.0
public	31.2	40.8	81.3	86.2	88.0	90.1	91.1	91.5	91.8
private	68.8	59.2	18.7	13.8	12.0	9.9	8.9	8.5	8.2
El Salvador	100.0	100.0	100.0	100.0	100.0	100.0	100.0	100.0	100.0
public	82.4	64.3	87.6	86.5	89.3	90.9	91.1	91.7	90.1
private	17.6	35.7	12.4	13.5	10.7	9.1	8.9	8.3	9.9
Guatemala	100.0	100.0	100.0	100.0	100.0	100.0	100.0	100.0	100.0
public	54.1	54.8	72.6	82.9	77.9	93.1	95.3	97.1	93.5
private	45.9	45.2	27.4	17.1	22.1	6.9	4.7	2.9	6.5
Honduras	100.0	100.0	100.0	100.0	100.0	100.0	100.0	100.0	100.0
public	49.2	52.6	70.0	73.2	78.1	81.7	85.3	90.5	90.6
private	50.8	47.4	30.0	26.8	21.9	18.3	14.7	9.5	9.4
Nicaragua	100.0	100.0	100.0	10.0	100.0	100.0	100.0	100.0	100.0
public	49.4	67.5	100.0	10.0	100.0	100.0	100.0	100.0	100.0
private	50.6	32.5							

Note: *Refers to the external public debt from 1980.

Source: ECLAC based on World Bank figures, the Bank for International Settlements and the International Monetary Fund.

TABLE 6.2   Central America: Ratios of Total External Debt to Population a\,
Product and Exports: 1970--1986

	1970	1975	1980	1981	1982	1983	1984	1985	1986
Per capita external debt \b:				(dollars)					
Central America	88	190	379	475	563	626	675	708	729
Costa Rica	248	525	969	1147	1325	1430	1480	1439	1404
El Salvador	40	121	260	351	391	433	444	453	434
Guatemala	52	74	152	195	252	286	324	330	322
Honduras	69	162	376	416	502	528	565	641	650
Nicaragua	153	369	659	897	1062	1239	1379	1508	1705
Ratio to GDP:				(percentages)					
Central America	24.9	33.8	37.2	53.7	67.8	74.0	77.0	89.2	83.6
Costa Rica	43.5	52.6	49.3	99.7	130.6	113.2	101.8	98.0	87.8
El Salvador	13.8	27.5	33.0	50.2	58.5	61.8	61.1	68.5	53.2
Guatemala	14.8	12.8	13.4	17.7	24.3	28.0	32.8	42.0	37.0
Honduras	25.3	48.1	54.6	60.1	75.1	84.2	91.8	103.1	100.4
Nicaragua	40.4	56.4	87.7	125.8	166.0	207.2	193.7	215.6	252.6
Ratio to exports of goods and services:									
Central America	104.4	122.7	137.1	197.4	270.0	306.9	324.0	364.0	359.8
Costa Rica	154.9	173.1	184.4	228.7	285.7	311.7	294.3	306.5	271.9
El Salvador	55.5	84.6	96.8	174.0	219.7	231.7	234.3	253.2	235.2
Guatemala	80.4	59.4	60.9	95.8	144.1	183.4	203.3	225.8	216.7
Honduras	93.1	145.7	147.3	179.6	258.9	269.9	287.5	313.5	264.6
Nicaragua	147.3	199.0	369.4	464.0	702.2	804.5	1014.4	1460.4	1977.1

Notes: a\ From 1979 these are preliminary population figures estimated by the
Ministry of Planning (MIPLAN) which differ from the CELADE estimates.
     b\ At current prices.

Source: ECLAC, based on World Bank and official figures.

TABLE 6.3   Latin America; Total External Debt and its Ratio to
            1983 GDP and Exports

	Total Debt (US$ bn)	Debt/ GDP	Debt/ Exports	Debt Service/ Exports
Latin America:	311.6	35.7	282.0	–
Central America:	13.6	80.9	347.9	36.7
Costa Rica \b	3.5	139.4	409.0	52.5
El Salvador \b	2.0	66.4	235.6	59.5
Guatemala \b	2.1	29.9	195.6	22.2
Honduras \b	2.2	100.6	340.4	19.7
Nicaragua \b	3.8	184.9	850.5	21.9
Oil Exporting:	134.5	38.6	243.0	–
Bolivia \c	2.7	58.4	277.0	30.8
Ecuador \d	6.2	43.5	236.0	64.0
Mexico \b	85.0	33.0	270.0	44.3
Peru \d	10.6	40.8	238.0	26.3
Venezuela \d	30.0	61.8	134.0	13.5
Non-Oil Exporting:	165.1	33.7	322.0	–
Argentina \b	42.0	41.4	365.0	53.0 \e
Brazil \d	83.0	31.6	345.0	72.6 \f
Colombia \b	10.3	17.4	230.0	20.8
Chile \b	17.6	60.2	317.0	58.6
Guyana \d	0.8	–	–	–
Haiti \d	0.8	40.9	280.0	8.2
Panama \c	3.1	49.0	–	26.3
Paraguay \d	1.3	26.1	224.0	25.0 \f
Dominican Rep. \b	2.0	24.4	181.0	49.3 \f
Uruguay \b	4.2	29.5	193.0	41.5 \f

NOTES: a/ Preliminary figures.
       b/ Total public and private external debt.
       c/ Public debt.
       d/ Includes officially guaranteed public and private debt plus non-guaranteed long- and short-term debt with financial institutions which report to the Bank for International Settlements.
       e/ Interest on total external debt.
       f/ Service of the total external debt.

Source: For Central America, ECLAC based on official and World Bank figures; for other countries: CEPAL, Políticas de ajuste y renegociación de la deuda externa, (E/CEPAL/G.1299), Santiago de Chile, 1984.

TABLE 6.4A Central America: Value of External Public Debt by Source, 1970--1986

	1970	1975	1980	1981	1982	1983	1984	1985	1986
				(millions of US dollars)					
Central America	648	1863	6387	8582	10548	12578	14118	15429	16257
Official Sources	416	1013	3336	4559	5381	7734	8808	10179	10731
multilateral	251	591	1890	2437	2764	3453	4056	4932	5005
bilateral	165	422	1446	2122	2617	4281	5752	5247	5726
Private Sources	232	850	3051	4023	5167	4844	5310	5250	5526
Costa Rica	134	421	1797	2315	2807	3184	3419	3425	3432
Official Sources	96	241	658	903	1081	1379	1491	1654	1613
multilateral	57	140	364	468	511	529	609	959	927
bilateral	39	101	294	435	570	850	882	695	686
Private Sources	38	180	1139	1412	1726	1805	1928	1771	1819
El Salvador*	117	323	1030	1391	1615	1839	1909	1982	1927
Official Sources	70	145	523	716	822	1539	1642	1764	1727
multilateral	41	78	300	385	431	704	771	823	858
bilateral	29	67	223	331	391	835	871	941	869
Private Sources	47	178	507	675	793	300	267	218	200
Guatemala*	152	255	764	1148	1435	2000	2387	2548	2470
Official Sources	54	129	534	729	1006	*1296	1406	1511	1428
multilateral	33	75	350	427	522	644	835	966	981
bilateral	21	54	184	302	484	652	571	545	447
Private Sources	98	126	230	419	429	704	981	1037	1042
Honduras	90	264	971	1162	1552	1766	2041	2538	2655
Official Sources	86	244	618	769	1009	1302	1565	1954	2044
multilateral	62	163	417	503	660	818	1049	1345	1407
bilateral	24	81	201	266	439	484	516	609	637
Private Sources	4	20	353	393	543	464	476	584	611
Nicaragua	155	600	1825	2566	3139	3789	4362	4936	5773
Official Sources	110	254	1003	1442	1463	2218	2704	3296	3919
multilateral	58	135	459	654	640	758	792	839	832
bilateral	52	119	544	788	823	1460	1912	2457	3087
Private Sources	45	346	822	1124	1676	1571	1658	1640	1854

Note and Source: See Table 6.4B.

Table 6.4B Central America: Percentage Composition of External Public Debt
by Source, 1970--1986

	1970	1975	1980	1981	1982	1983	1984	1985	1986
					(percentages)				
Central America	100.0	100.0	100.0	100.0	100.0	100.0	100.0	100.0	100.0
Official Sources	64.2	54.4	52.2	53.1	51.0	61.5	62.4	66.0	66.0
multilateral	38.7	31.7	29.6	28.4	26.2	27.5	28.7	32.0	30.8
bilateral	25.5	22.7	22.6	24.7	24.8	34.0	33.7	34.0	35.2
Private Sources	35.8	45.6	47.8	46.9	49.0	38.5	37.6	34.0	34.0
Costa Rica	100.0	100.0	100.0	100.0	100.0	100.0	100.0	99.8	100.0
Official Sources	71.6	57.3	36.6	39.0	38.5	43.3	43.6	48.3	47.0
multilateral	42.5	33.3	20.3	20.2	18.2	16.6	17.8	28.0	27.0
bilateral	29.1	24.0	16.3	18.8	20.3	26.7	25.8	20.3	20.0
Private Sources	28.4	42.7	63.4	61.0	61.5	56.7	56.4	51.5	53.0
El Salvador	100.0	100.0	100.0	100.0	100.0	100.0	100.0	100.0	100.0
Official Sources	59.8	44.9	50.8	51.5	50.9	83.7	86.0	89.0	89.6
multilateral	35.0	24.1	29.2	27.7	26.7	38.3	40.4	41.5	44.5
bilateral	24.8	20.8	21.6	23.8	24.2	45.4	45.6	47.5	45.1
Private Sources	40.2	55.1	49.2	48.5	49.1	16.3	14.0	11.0	10.4
Guatemala	100.0	100.0	100.0	100.0	100.0	97.0	100.0	100.0	100.0
Official Sources	35.5	50.6	69.9	63.5	70.1	64.8	58.9	59.3	57.8
multilateral	21.7	29.4	45.8	37.2	36.4	32.2	35.0	37.9	39.7
bilateral	13.8	21.2	24.1	26.3	33.7	32.6	23.9	21.4	18.1
Private Sources	64.5	49.4	30.1	36.5	29.9	32.2	41.1	40.7	42.2
Honduras	100.0	100.0	100.0	100.0	100.0	100.0	100.0	100.0	100.0
Official Sources	95.6	92.4	63.7	66.2	65.0	73.7	76.7	77.0	77.0
multilateral	68.9	61.7	43.0	43.3	42.5	46.3	51.4	53.0	53.0
bilateral	26.7	30.7	20.7	22.9	22.5	27.4	25.3	24.0	24.0
Private Sources	4.4	7.6	36.3	33.8	35.0	26.3	23.3	23.0	23.0
Nicaragua	100.0	100.0	100.0	100.0	100.0	100.0	100.0	99.0	100.0
Official Sources	71.0	52.7	55.0	56.2	46.6	58.5	62.0	66.8	67.9
multilateral	37.4	27.5	25.2	25.5	20.4	20.0	18.2	17.0	14.4
bilateral	33.6	25.2	29.8	30.7	26.2	38.5	43.8	49.8	53.5
Private Sources	29.0	47.3	45.0	43.8	53.4	41.5	38.0	32.2	32.1

Note: *Includes Central Bank debt.

Source: ECLAC: for 1970--1982, based on figures of the World Bank, the Bank
for International Settlements and the International Monetary Fund; for 1983--
1986, preliminary estimates based on official data.

TABLE 6.5   Central America: Burden of External Public Debt Service, 1970--1986

	1970	1975	1978	1980	1981	1982	1983	1984	1985	1986
As a percentage of Exports of Goods and Services										
Central America	7.4	9.6	10.6	12.0	23.4	36.7	36.7	35.6	36.2	39.4
Costa Rica	10.1	10.7	18.1	21.5	35.6	67.0	52.5	51.0	52.3	48.6
El Salvador	4.7	16.5	9.9	11.4	32.6	27.1	59.9	40.7	29.9	48.0
Guatemala	7.4	3.8	3.9	3.5	8.8	17.3	22.2	29.2	31.2	31.7
Honduras	2.5	4.6	9.5	10.8	14.6	30.1	19.7	25.0	33.1	36.1
Nicaragua	11.3	12.5	14.3	22.3	34.7	45.4	21.9	18.4	20.1	13.0
As a percentage of Public Expenditure										
Central America*	12.8	16.3	16.7	16.9	31.2	46.6	38.9	35.6	36.4	38.7
Costa Rica	16.8	14.7	21.3	26.4	89.5	183.3	89.1	91.9	90.5	80.9
El Salvador	8.6	28.6	15.1	22.6	46.7	36.7	73.6	55.2	47.2	58.0
Guatemala	13.2	8.1	7.2	5.0	9.4	17.6	23.7	30.5	30.6	17.0
Honduras	3.8	7.4	15.9	18.7	22.0	37.9	23.4	26.7	36.4	43.1
Nicaragua	22.4	22.0	27.2	17.3	27.4	27.4	9.2	5.9	5.3	3.4

Note: *From 1980 onwards, public expenditure refers to central government only.

Source: ECLAC; see also Table 6.8.

TABLE 6.6   Central America: Average Growth Rate of External Debt, 1970--1986

	1970--73	1973--78	1978--81	1981--83	1983--86
			Total Debt		
Central America	12.7	25.1	18.5	17.8	8.0
Costa Rica	18.2	21.4	12.8	14.6	1.9
El Salvador	8.0	40.7	17.7	12.2	1.1
Guatemala	4.8	20.5	19.0	24.6	7.1
Honduras	11.8	30.8	17.5	16.7	10.7
Nicaragua	14.0	21.9	27.1	21.5	15.1
			Public Debt		
Central America	17.3	29.2	31.5	21.1	8.9
Costa Rica	22.9	34.9	27.7	17.3	2.5
El Salvador	8.6	27.8	39.5	15.0	2.6
Guatemala	5.8	21.9	33.3	32.0	1.6
Honduras	14.2	39.0	18.6	23.3	14.6
Nicaragua*	29.2	23.8	38.3	21.5	15.1
			Private Debt		
Central America	21.6	31.2	-16.3	-7.3	-5.1
Costa Rica	35.7	44.4	-21.1	-3.3	-4.1
El Salvador	5.4	29.3	-22.9	-7.9	-3.4
Guatemala	-1.4	14.9	-11.0	-20.7	4.7
Honduras	7.7	112.2	14.5	-3.6	-11.3
Nicaragua	55.1	20.3	-	-	-

Note: *From 1981 onwards, figures refer to official public debt.

Source: ECLAC based on official figures.

TABLE 6.7   Central America: Average Terms of External Public Debt,*
            1970--1982

	1970	1975	1978	1980	1982
Costa Rica					
Interest rate	5.6	7.9	8.6	10.9	14.7
Total Term	28.0	17.1	15.3	12.6	6.5
Grace Period	6.0	4.2	5.5	4.6	2.0
Subsidy Element	-	13.1	10.1	0.7	-
El Salvador					
Interest rate	4.7	6.3	6.0	3.4	8.7
Total Term	23.0	17.4	23.6	27.3	13.0
Grace Period	6.0	5.7	6.5	8.1	3.0
Subsidy Element	-	27.2	29.5	50.1	-
Guatemala					
Interest rate	5.2	7.0	6.1	7.9	9.3
Total Term	26.0	18.1	21.3	17.8	13.0
Grace Period	6.0	6.3	6.4	4.6	4.0
Subsidy Element	-	21.0	28.4	13.2	-
Honduras					
Interest rate	4.1	5.9	7.7	7.0	10.0
Total Term	30.0	19.4	16.0	23.8	19.0
Grace Period	7.0	5.5	5.5	6.5	4.4
Subsidy Element	-	25.4	15.9	25.8	-
Nicaragua					
Interest rate	7.1	7.3	6.4	4.1	9.0
Total Term	18.0	17.8	17.3	25.7	10.0
Grace Period	4.0	4.7	6.1	6.6	6.0
Subsidy Element	-	20.2	26.2	41.5	-

Note: *Refers to the average terms of new loans signed in the years
indicated.

Source: ECLAC based on World Bank and Inter-American Development Bank
figures.

TABLE 6.8   Central America: Service of the External Public Debt, by Component, 1970--1986

	1970	1975	1978	1980	1981	1982	1983	1984	1985	1986
				(millions of US dollars)						
Central America	95	264	491	669	1168	1626	1635	1661	1620	1848
principal	67	158	256	235	569	798	931	996	987	1167
interest	28	106	235	434	599	828	704	665	633	681
Costa Rica	28	64	182	258	419	748	595	650	638	668
principal	21	41	113	80	126	350	247	336	358	392
interest	7	23	69	178	293	398	348	314	280	276
El Salvador*	12	98	91	139	301	223	519	364	255	427
principal	6	75	42	67	234	130	397	269	189	330
interest	6	23	49	72	67	93	122	95	66	97
Guatemala*	26	30	50	60	127	221	260	360	363	355
principal	20	16	15	18	77	149	175	235	220	195
interest	6	14	35	42	50	72	85	125	143	160
Honduras	5	16	65	102	129	231	158	208	296	360
principal	3	6	34	48	61	110	72	128	197	237
interest	2	10	31	54	68	121	86	80	99	123
Nicaragua	24	56	103	110	192	203	103	79	68	38
principal	17	20	52	22	71	59	40	28	23	13
interest	7	36	51	88	121	144	63	51	45	25
				(percentages)						
Central America	100.0	100.0	100.0	100.0	100.0	100.0	100.0	100.0	100.0	100.0
principal	70.5	59.8	52.1	35.1	48.7	49.1	56.9	60.0	60.9	63.1
interest	29.5	40.2	47.9	64.9	51.3	50.9	43.1	40.0	39.1	36.9
Costa Rica	100.0	100.0	100.0	100.0	100.0	100.0	100.0	100.0	100.0	100.0
principal	75.0	64.1	62.1	31.0	30.1	46.8	41.5	51.7	56.1	58.7
interest	25.0	35.9	37.9	69.0	69.9	53.2	58.5	48.3	43.9	41.3
El Salvador	100.0	100.0	100.0	100.0	100.0	100.0	100.0	100.0	100.0	100.0
principal	50.0	76.5	46.2	48.2	77.7	58.3	76.5	73.9	74.1	77.3
interest	50.0	23.5	53.8	51.8	22.3	41.7	23.5	26.1	25.9	22.7
Guatemala	100.0	100.0	100.0	100.0	90.0	100.0	100.0	100.0	100.0	100.0
principal	76.9	53.3	30.0	30.0	60.6	67.4	67.3	65.3	60.6	54.9
interest	23.1	46.7	70.0	70.0	29.4	32.6	32.7	34.7	39.4	45.1
Honduras	100.0	100.0	100.0	100.0	100.0	100.0	100.0	100.0	100.0	100.0
principal	60.0	37.5	52.3	47.1	47.3	47.6	45.6	61.5	66.6	65.8
interest	40.0	62.5	47.7	52.9	52.7	52.4	54.4	38.5	33.4	34.2
Nicaragua	100.0	100.0	100.0	100.0	100.0	100.0	100.0	100.0	100.0	100.0
principal	70.8	35.7	50.5	20.0	37.0	29.1	38.8	35.4	33.8	34.2
interest	29.2	64.3	49.5	80.0	63.0	70.9	61.2	64.6	66.2	65.8

Note: *Includes Central Bank debt.

Source: ECLAC: for 1970--1982, based on figures of the World Bank, the Bank for International Settlements and the International Monetary Fund; for 1983--1986, preliminary estimates based on official data.

TABLE 6.9   Central America: Forecast of Public Debt Service on Loans
Outstanding at the End of 1986 (millions of US dollars)

	Total 1987--94	1987	1988	1989	1990	1991	1992	1993	1994
Central America	15233	2287	2713	2200	2050	1853	1653	1341	1136
principal	10208	1399	1827	1422	1366	1267	1165	954	808
interest	5025	888	886	778	684	586	488	387	328
Costa Rica	4217	678	748	705	655	526	465	300	140
principal	2929	387	495	486	477	389	366	237	92
interest	1288	291	253	219	178	137	99	63	48
El Salvador	1715	353	254	245	201	196	164	157	145
principal	1158	258	168	166	130	131	104	102	99
interest	557	95	86	79	71	65	60	55	46
Guatemala	2828	487	668	357	316	293	254	232	221
principal	1963	320	520	241	210	196	167	155	154
interest	865	167	148	116	106	97	87	77	67
Honduras	2415	320	336	337	327	310	276	263	246
principal	1402	178	189	193	191	184	161	157	149
interest	1013	142	147	144	136	126	115	106	97
Nicaragua	4068	449	707	556	551	528	494	399	384
principal	2756	256	455	336	358	367	367	399	384
interest	1312	193	252	220	193	161	127	96	70

Source: ECLAC based on World Bank figures.

TABLE 6.10   Forecast Growth of Exports of Goods and Services, 1987--1994
(millions of US dollars)

	Average Annual Rate (1978--1994)	1987	1988	1989	1990	1991	1992	1993	1994
Central America	5.3	5023	5285	5563	5856	6165	6491	6838	7205
Costa Rica	4.2	1433	1493	1556	1621	1689	1760	1834	1911
El Salvador	6.0	943	1000	1060	1124	1191	1262	1338	1419
Guatemala	4.8	1278	1339	1403	1470	1541	1615	1693	1774
Honduras	5.0	1048	1100	1155	1213	1274	1337	1404	1475
Nicaragua	10.0	321	353	389	428	470	517	569	626

Source: ECLAC.

TABLE 6.11   Central America: Forecast Debts Service Ratios, 1987--1994

	1987	1988	1989	1990	1991	1992	1993	1994
Central America	45.5	51.3	39.5	35.0	30.1	25.5	19.8	15.8
Costa Rica	47.3	52.5	45.3	40.4	31.1	26.4	16.4	7.3
El Salvador	37.4	25.4	23.1	17.9	16.5	13.0	11.7	9.7
Guatemala	38.1	49.9	25.4	21.5	19.0	15.7	13.7	12.5
Honduras	30.5	30.5	29.2	27.0	24.3	20.6	18.7	16.7
Nicaragua	139.9	200.3	142.9	128.7	112.3	95.6	70.1	61.3

Source: ECLAC (based on Tables 6.9 and 6.10).

Notes

1. The present chapter is an amended version of a piece published in the August, 1987 issue of *CEPAL Review*. The editors of the present work wish to thank ECLAC for permission to use the relevant sections of the article. See Caballeros (1987).

2. Although there is no official information for individual countries, the approximate amount of the flight of capital from Central America for the period 1980–1986 is believed by CEPAL to exceed US$ 4.5 billion. This estimate is based on a comparison of the results of the analysis of the balance of payments and the total amounts of the external debt according to exchange control records. Other estimates given in this book include those in the chapter by Weeks and that by FitzGerald and Croes.

3. Although there are no formal requirements in this respect, it has gradually become established practice that the signature of the required agreement means more than just receiving financial aid from the IMF; an IMF agreement has become almost essential for obtaining aid from the rest of the international financial community.

4. See CEPAL (1987c).

5. Nicaragua did not accept the involvement of the IMF in its agreements and, although it continued to meet its existing commitments to the Fund, it succeeded, exceptionally, in negotiating without it. For a fuller account of the Nicaraguan debt renegotiations, see Weinert (1983).

6. See República de Costa Rica (1983), *Convenio de Crédito Revolutivo suscrito entre el Banco Central de Costa Rica, la República de Costa Rica y los Bancos Acreedores*, San José, 24 November 1983, mimeo.

7. The Committee was chaired by the Bank of America and included representatives from: Bank of Montreal, Bankers Trust Company, Citibank, Deutsche-Sudamerikanische Bank, Industrial Bank of Japan, Lloyds Bank International, Marine Midland Bank, Royal Bank of Canada, Security Pacific National Bank and Wells Fargo Bank.

7

The Regional Monetary System and Economic Recovery

E.V.K. FitzGerald and Edwin Croes

Introduction

This chapter deals with the issue of trade finance and the Central American monetary system which, we shall argue, is one of the major problems that will need to be resolved if economic recovery is to take place in Central America once armed conflict has terminated and external pressures reduced to a level that might be regarded as normal for the Third World. The financing of foreign trade is crucial because half of the material product of the region is exported, and the 'working capital' (i.e. reserves) which is essential for these transactions and which forms the basis for the monetary system, have been drained off by capital flight and debt payments. This aspect of reconstruction has been generally overlooked in discussion of the financial problems of the area which have tended to concentrate on capital transfers and indebtedness (see Chapter 6 by Caballeros) and on the current trade account and commercial policy (see Chapter 4 by Bulmer-Thomas).

In order to understand the present situation, the inner logic of the Central American monetary system for the 1960–1980 period is dealt with first, particular attention being given to the apparent success of the system. Monetary integration and fixed parities are held to have contributed to stable and rapid growth in the region. However, more detailed examination reveals that all the economies of the region were on a 'dollar standard' due to their open economies, while their macroeconomic stability is attributable not so much to skillful monetary management but rather the nature of the agro-export model

E.V.K. FitzGerald is Professor of Economics at the Institute of Social Studies, The Hague, where Edwin Croes is currently a Visiting Research Fellow.

itself. After 1980, the regional trade crisis rapidly led to a breakdown of the monetary system. But this crisis is explained by factors external to the region, and the recovery of exports is hampered by the lack of hard-currency liquidity.

We shall argue that a new source of trade finance is absolutely crucial for the reactivation of these agro-export economies without which new investment lending or commercial policies will not be able to take effect. In consequence, monetary reform on a regional scale is necessary; we sketch how this might be done through a debt-equity swap and the creation of new regional financial instruments. This is conceptually and administratively feasible so long as there is determined support from multilateral and bilateral aid agencies.

Financial Integration in Central America, 1960–1980

An important aspect of economic integration in Central America has always been monetary unification, as a complement to trade integration through the customs union, and the eventual industrial integration through the allocation of manufacturing plant between the five members to serve the whole region.[1] Attempts were made by the five central banks to establish a regional payments system as early as 1952, but only in 1961 was the Central American Clearing House (*Cámara de Compensación Centroamericana*, CCC) set up. The integration of the intra-regional monetary operations of the five Central Banks[2] through the *Consejo Monetario Centroamericano*, CMCA (Central American Monetary Council), was achieved by 1964. In subsequent years, a project to discuss a stabilization fund in extra-regional currencies was endorsed in several inter-governmental meetings. The scheme was to be based on the partial pooling of foreign exchange reserves in the area, but made little progress due to the difficulty of obtaining assistance (e.g. from the IMF) to finance its operations.

In effect the *peso centroamericano* was set up as the unit for transactions among the five republics, for loans from the *Banco Centroamericano de Integración Económica*, (BCIE) and for reserves of each others' currencies held by their Central Banks. Until the breakdown of the regional economy in 1980, the five currencies were pegged to the *peso centroamericano* for nearly twenty years without substantial variations, while complete convertibility between the five was maintained. The *peso centroamericano* in turn was stable with respect to the US dollar in marked contrast to the experience of the rest of Latin America.

Visible and invisible transactions between the five republics were carried out by importers paying their own currency, which the exporters exchanged at their own central bank for their own national currency. The central banks then cleared any resulting net excess monetary balances every six months among themselves through the Central American Clearing House, the debtor banks in effect repurchasing their own currencies in dollars. The Central Banks did not use member currency balances for open market operations; they acted in effect as 'purchasers of last resort' and there was no net pressure on exchange rate which remained stable.

There is no doubt that the existence of this common currency area and the clearing facilities helped stimulate trade, particularly in locally produced manufactures but also in food products among the five republics. At first sight, it might appear that this was a very advanced monetary union, far more so than even the European Monetary System, let alone the Andean Pact which had hardly contemplated such a scheme. However, in reality, this harmony was more apparent than real for two reasons.

First, at the institutional level, the various regional bodies concerned with trade and finance did not in fact form a coordinated system. Second, more importantly, mutual monetary relations were maintained in practice by certain features of the economic structures of the member republics. In consequence, once the five economies began to run into serious production difficulties in the 1980s, the monetary system broke down despite major injections of funds into the region. In order to suggest how this relatively high degree of financial integration with its accompanying benefits for regional trade might be revived, it is necessary to see how it actually worked.

At the institutional level, the *peso centroamericano* was never more than a unit of account. It could not be used for commerce with other currency blocs (with which the greater part of the trade of the region was conducted), and no mechanism had been devised by which it could be used in order to refinance on a longer term basis the short-term balances of the Clearing House. The CMCA provided a valuable statistical and training service to the five central banks, but did not really manage to act as coordinator of these banks' own domestic monetary policies. Nor did it regulate the flows of capital into (and out of) the region, which were the main determinant of the monetary base.

The development of related regional institutions was not conducive to greater financial integration. The successful process of constructing a common tariff system (which has continued to the present despite much political tension), coordinated by the Central American Secretariat for Economic Integration (SIECA), was not accompanied by a common approach to the financing of extra-regional trade. The parallel process of establishing 'integration industries' (plant to serve the whole region) was not accompanied by a common approach to foreign investment legislation or the regulation of technology transfer. The Central American Bank for Economic Integration (BCIE) was established in 1963 and rapidly built up a large loan portfolio, particularly for modern industrial and agro-industrial projects. The Bank's capital was subscribed by the five republics, but there was also an important external component, first from the USAID and later from the Inter-American Development Bank, and to a lesser extent the IBRD. Most major infrastructure projects in Central America were directly financed by the IDB and the IBRD. However, these multilateral institutions (let alone the IMF) did not coordinate their operations with the BCIE, which would have enormously strengthened the financial and monetary integration of the region.

Moreover, this considerable accumulation effort carried out by regional and multilateral institutions was never integrated into the regional monetary system in terms of the creation of common reserves, budgetary coordination or interest rate policy. Nor, apparently, was any joint effort made to negotiate trade credit for the region; each country's banking system raised commercial credit from the financial centers in their principle export markets. Of course, a truly integrated monetary system would have required central control of (or at least agreement on common criteria governing) money supply, debt management by governments and the regulation of private banks. Although this would not have been an easy task, neither would it have been infeasible—given the common attitude of the central banks on these topics—had external financial institutions supported such a process.

In fact, the apparently high degree of monetary 'integration' was based on the fact that each of the Central American currencies was itself freely convertible with the US dollar at a fixed exchange rate throughout this period. In effect the region remained on a Dollar Standard despite the fact that the dollar itself was fluctuating with respect to other major currencies. Thus the Central American monetary system was effectively passive and did not have to deal with any realignment of the five parities or major reserve imbalances between the five republics.

Fixed parities and full convertibility were in turn due to a series of characteristics of the individual Central American economies that underlie their extraordinary macroeconomic stability.[3] Economic growth had been based on dynamic export sectors, themselves constructed from relatively modernized agro-business firms with cheap labor and high profit rates.[4] Domestic wage-goods demand and industrial input requirements were not so large as to force a structural trade deficit as occurred elsewhere in Latin America. Even when prices turned down in commodity cycles, the fall in export revenue was automatically translated into reduced expenditure by the export sector which in turn reduced imports and GDP.

Unlike elsewhere in Latin America, a high degree of confidence among capitalists ensured that capital flight was not excessive while the modest participation of the state in direct investment was amply covered by foreign bilateral or multilateral aid on generous financial terms, if not without political conditionality. Thus, before 1980, the burden of external debt was relatively small. Fiscal policy was neutral as tax revenues were largely derived from trade. If revenue varied, so did government expenditure, due to a tradition of balanced budgets. Central banks enjoyed a considerable degree of autonomy and could resist attempts by finance ministries to issue more than a minimum of treasury bonds which, in the absence of local capital markets, would automatically have lead to either inorganic fiduciary issue or credit cuts to the private sector. Domestic credit was, however, closely linked to the working capital requirements of the agro-exporting and industrial sectors and thus closely[5] followed external trade patterns.

In consequence, although credit money supply adjusted more or less automatically to changes in the external reserve position, it was mainly demand-determined and out of the hands of the monetary authorities. Aggregate demand was determined by exports, either directly or indirectly through import availability. World prices relatives were reflected automatically within the Central American economies due to comparatively low tariff barriers. In a real sense, the Central American governments neither had nor needed, any active macroeconomic policy at all.[6]

In any case, generally conservative governments saw no need to change the pattern of resource allocation and the model of agro-industrial growth and limited manufacturing expansion.[7] Inflation remained low and roughly equal to that of the US economy itself which, with dollar convertibility, meant that middle class support could be maintained on economic if not on political grounds.

These conditions would have been sufficient to guarantee a certain monetary stability and make the region an almost perfect example of the theory of the monetary approach to the balance of payments, albeit for structural reasons rather than as the result of financial rectitude. However, there was another important factor in the financial system which not only underpinned convertibility but also allowed these export economies to function at all. Agro-export production follows a clearly defined cycle over the year, and is based more on the use of working capital for wages, fertilizers, machinery repairs, etc. than on fixed capital as such.

Specifically, the system worked more or less as follows. Farmers must purchase inputs and spend on wages for much of the year before receiving cash income at harvest time which, if left to market forces alone, would bankrupt farmers and cause enormous monetary fluctuations. Thus, in practice, Central American banks extend production credit over the cycle to be recovered from export receipts. At the national level, there is a similar cycle of exports and imports over the year. This traditionally was financed by 'pre-export' credit from foreign banks, secured by export receipts and repaid once the cycle was complete only to be renewed once more.

Technically, this allowed the domestic money supply to vary throughout the year on the sound basis of fresh international reserves at the Central Bank. Even for industrial exports, a similar pattern emerges due to the high import-intensity of manufacturing. Such trade credit was probably far more important than direct foreign investment or long-term commercial bank credit in ensuring continued agro-industrial expansion during the period.

In sum, it was not monetary integration at the regional level which ensured mutual convertibility with the dollar, nor monetary policy which ensured stable parities, but rather the nature of the agro-export system which guaranteed them both. To argue that this system was technically effective is not to suggest that it was socially desirable or capable of sustaining balanced economic development. However, it was an essential part of the regional export model, and any alternative strategy would certainly have to contain an equivalent method of flexible trade finance since at least half of the material product of the region will continue to be exported among the five republics and to the outside world.

The Crisis of the 1980s

At the end of the 1970s, the Central American economies entered sustained crisis, in part because of changes in the world economy (particularly higher energy and producer goods prices, and declining markets for traditional exports such as sugar and cotton) but also because of political events born in considerable part of the social consequences of the previous economic growth model.[8] In addition, the dollar itself had become unstable and decreasingly effective as a currency standard.

The first reaction of the five republics to the opening balance of payments deficits with the outside world was radically distinct from the monetary tradition of the region. All tried to maintain their levels of production and income by expansive macroeconomic policies, increased official indebtedness (indicated in Table 7.5) and forms of import control.[9] Not surprisingly the results were highly inflationary; capital flight (which in Nicaragua had already occurred in 1978–1979) drained away reserves and the military-political situation depressed business confidence and even affected export production capacity.

Between 1980 and 1986 the total indebtedness of the region rose fourfold from US$ 6.4 billion to US$ 17.9 billion. Some two-thirds of this debt is in the form of obligations to governments or multilateral institutions (particularly the IBRD and the IDB), which has placed Central America in a very different situation from the rest of Latin America. On the one hand, interest rates and repayment schedules are more generous; but on the other, the political conditions are quite binding.

From 1983 all the five republics applied strong deflationary measures, combined with continued import controls, even on regional trade itself. Intra-regional trade contracted even more rapidly than extra-regional trade, as Tables 7.1 and 7.2 indicate. The accumulated imbalances in the Clearing House could not be cancelled as before by dollar payments between the Central Banks; the imbalances were larger and the reserves smaller (see Table 7.3 and Appendix B) because of capital flight and debt service. Official estimates put this flight at US$ 4.5 billion over the period 1979–1985,[10] although the figures in Table 7.4 indicate a somewhat lower figure. Combined with debt service, this gives a total outflow in liquid hard currency from the region of US$ 15.2 billion, equivalent to approximately three-and-a-half years' exports.

In consequence, these balances had to be converted into official inter-government debt, mainly to the disadvantage of Costa Rica which emerged as a major lender to its partners. It should be noted however, that this in itself was a step forward in the financial development of the regional system. As there was no way of collectively refinancing this debt in the form of long-term securities, creditor governments subsequently insisted on part of current transactions being conducted in dollars so as to avoid recurrent deficits, and thus the system effectively returned to bilateral clearing. In this way, much of the trade-creating capacity of the regional monetary system was lost.

Even more seriously, the system of short-term trade finance broke down as international commercial banks became more wary of Latin American lending in general, and of Central America in particular. The effective use of trade credit to finance capital flight by private sector recipients (who could effectively take out dollar credits and then leave the country) left local commercial banks (and by implication their governments) with an increasing commercial debt, making it far more difficult to keep the previous 'revolving' system going. To some extent this was offset by the short-term finance of imports by supplier credits against export commodities but, in reality, the system amounted to little more than barter.

In the midst of this banking sclerosis, the Central American business sector did more than the governments themselves to keep trade going among the five republics. At the commercial level, businesses began to use barter deals, not because of the lack of a monetary equivalent (after all the dollar is the universal unit of account) but rather in order to avoid transactions having to pass through the banking system and thus getting tied up in the Clearing House. At the monetary level, businesses developed a wide 'parallel market' in the currencies of the member countries, which rapidly established flexible and unified mutual exchange rates quite different from those officially recognized. These parallel rates were, needless to say, all related to the dollar, which was itself increasingly circulating inside the region as a store of value at 'street level.'

Some official attempts have been made to adapt to this new reality, particularly the creation of negotiable commercial bills (DICAs) which effectively allow exporters within the region to re-sell their receipts to importers at a market-clearing rate, which if and when it becomes more widespread will effectively allow for flexible exchange rates between the five currencies determined by the market. In the long run, this may turn out to be not just a temporary expedient to avoid the thorny issue of the pending debts within the Clearing House, but rather a realistic way of managing the Central American monetary system in a situation where the member governments follow different macroeconomic policies.[11]

Unfortunately, the role of the CMCA (*Consejo Monetario Centroamericano*) has been reduced in the 1980s to that of little more than a statistical bureau struggling to survive. Even the BCIE has cut its lending operations to a minimum, undermined by the lack of multilateral support and the Nicaraguan moratorium; indeed it is hard put to meet its own payroll. It is notable that the US Government, which has poured enormous sums of money into the region since 1980, has not seen fit to use the Central American institutions to do this. On the contrary, Washington has undermined integration attempts and attempted to exclude Nicaragua from all regional fora.

These political pressures apart, it is clear that the economic model of Central America has changed fundamentally and will not return to its old mold. On the one hand, any future reconstruction will require a broader development base than the old agro-export model in the sense both of new export branches and of a greater commitment to employment creation and social welfare. This implies more active fiscal and monetary policies, and the development of trade relations with new markets for more processed products. At the same time, the five members will probably have different trade relations with the outside world, and various domestic institutional models. These will require more flexible parity and reserve policies on the part of Central Banks.

The two main views of foreign assistance to date have neglected this issue. It has been suggested that highest priority be given to food security and the basic needs of the population.[12] But in the long run, to be self-sustaining, this effort must incorporate renewed trade among the five republics in precisely these essential goods and services; also stable export markets are required to enable the relevant imports to be guaranteed. On the other hand, it is argued that massive infrastructure investments must be made and industry modernized.[13] But to finance these loans new export markets (or efficient import-substitution lines) must be established, or else the debt problem will never be overcome.

Nonetheless, any proposal for reconstruction must be a regional one if only because the individual economies are too small to support the sustained industrialization necessary for success in basic needs provision, agricultural modernization, and competitive manufactured exports. Such a regional economy, whatever its nature, will require a regional monetary system. This will be crucial in order to provide the commercial liquidity to get trade going again, and from which business confidence and investment will spring. Injections of long-term public loan capital, however large, cannot replace this function.

Elements of a Possible Solution

The following proposal for restoring trade liquidity to Central America is not entirely new, nor is it excessively ambitious. From the point of view of those asked to finance it, the true opportunity cost is much less than it might seem at first sight. In addition to the economic benefits of reviving intra-regional and extra-regional trade, the impulse given by a revived monetary system to cooperation among governments would presumably have beneficial political consequences as well.

The restoration of trade finance necessary for the recovery of what might be termed the 'simple reproduction' of the productive apparatus (i.e. aiming to raise exports to a level where they can finance operational imports and debt servicing with a reasonable reserve position) is essential because around half of the material product of Central America is exported, and depressed trade is the major cause of macroeconomic stagnation (and thus the potential means of relieving poverty) in the region. The constraint on private and public investment in the region is not savings as such and indeed rates of profit are high by any standards. Rather, what is required is a buoyant export situation and a broad regional market.

Commercial banks cannot realistically be expected to renew lending to individual producers, private banks or even governments in the region in view of the sovereign risk involved and the present situation in world financial markets. Thus an alternative system of trade finance must be established by the five governments and those aid agencies concerned for economic recovery in the region.

We shall not deal with the potential recovery of Central American exports here. For our purposes it is enough to point out that the establishment of new export branches or the opening up of new markets will require considerable working capital, to enable distribution networks to be set up, packing plants to be refurbished and new products developed. On even the most conservative estimate, regional exports would have to rise from their current (1986) level of US$ 4.2 billion to at least US$ 5.9 billion in order to restore stability and certain liquidity,[14] with a proportionate need for fresh trade finance.

The recapitalization of foreign and regional trade could best be financed by an inter-governmental regional institution (bank or fund), thus avoiding the sovereign risk element from the point of view of the outside world and helping to resolve differences among the five central banks. The BCIE and the CMCA could form the basis for such a Fund. Alternatively a Central American trade bank could be set up along the lines of the BLADEX. Such a Fund could be responsible initially for three tasks:

1. the pre-financing of traditional export crops such as coffee, cotton, bananas and sugar, linked to the import of their respective inputs, and secured by forward contracts on the products, to be cleared on a yearly basis;
2. loans on a medium term basis (one or two years) for the litation of export industries (plant retooling and restoring inventories of raw materials), to be paid from export receipts;
3. the finance of trade among the republics, allowing uncleared balances in the Clearing House to be carried (for up to three years) until the respective governments can implement the corresponding policies to generate compensating exports.

The initial capital of such a Fund could be made up in the following way. The existing debts of Central American governments to the governments and banks of the industrialized countries (currently amounting to some US$ 10 billion, of which US$ 2.0 to 2.5 billion is owed to Western Europe—see Table 7.6 and Appendix A) could be exchanged for equity capital in the Fund, the Fund later renegotiating with the five republics a new and more extended payments schedule, partly in dollars and partly in local currency. The equity holders (who could enjoy voting rights to be negotiated) would receive income at some future date depending upon the profitability of the bank.

From the point of view of the creditor governments involved, this would be a considerable step forward, for they not only have a political interest in the stabilization of the region, but also a natural concern that the present situation of virtual subsidy be overcome. In any case official creditors are extremely unlikely to have their obligations paid in full under the present arrangements, so this scheme would represent an improvement in financial terms as well.

From the point of view of the Central American governments, they would not only be relieved of part of their presently crushing debt service obligations, but their producers would be in receipt of fresh export credit. It might be thought that the distinct development strategies of the five republics, even in the event of political reconciliation within the region, would make regional monetary cooperation between them almost impossible. There are a number of reasons for thinking otherwise, however. First, the crisis itself has resulted in all the Central Banks imposing some form of exchange control, and they now have considerable experience in managing such controls. None of the five would press for a return to the old open system. Second, there is now broad agreement among economists in the region, whatever their ideology, on the need to base development strategies on a healthy foreign trade sector, working at international price levels with realistic exchange rates, combined with macroeconomic stability and low rates of inflation. Third, throughout the regional crisis the integration institutions have gone on operating and there is considerable enthusiasm for their reactivation on the part of all five governments. Fourth, there is the considerable attraction of access to international credit and relief of the debt burden; which are probably only negotiable on a regional basis.

This scheme could start with the European governments and Canada converting their part of the debt into capitalization of the Fund. This would be the best place to start, because it would not involve the political implications of the USA taking the first step. The IBRD and the IDB might follow, as this would establish an interesting precedent for other regional country groupings. Finally, in this initial stage, Mexico and Venezuela (who are major creditors due to the San José oil supply agreements and who have little realistic expectation of recovering the outstanding amounts) could be encouraged to join as part of their own debt renegotiations with multilateral financial institutions. In a subsequent stage, the US administration could find itself obliged to take part in view of the example set by other governments, and there is no reason why the socialist creditors of Nicaragua should not be included as well. Initiation of the scheme should not, however, be made conditional on the participation of these two parties.

Even if only a part of these arrangements comes into operation, it would immediately give the fund a current income stream of considerable proportions, in view of the fact that the present debt service of the region is of the order of US$ 1.8 billion a year. The immediate liquidity available to the Fund could be increased by issuing bonds on international financial markets, backed by the guarantees of the extra-regional equity holders, including the multilateral agencies themselves. The servicing of these loans would be met from the income stream of the Fund. It is important to note that no 'moratorium' or 'debt pardon' would be involved, so that the international banking community should not be opposed to the scheme either.

The next logical step might by to buy up the now heavily discounted Central American debt held by the commercial banks, which could probably exchanged for dollar denominated bonds (duly underwritten by the IBRD) for a fraction of their face value. At current (early 1988) valuations this could be as little as 10 percent. Once again, the income stream of eventual interest payments could be directed into the Fund's own resources.

Another possibility would be for the Fund to issue special

certificates of deposit in order to attract the flight-capital of Central American businesses themselves, either bringing it back into the region or preventing it from leaving in the first place. This would require special legislation in the five republics in order to guarantee anonymity and possibly tax relief, but the Mexican experience indicates that this can be quite effective.

Once established, the Fund could explore further activities designed to strengthen its role as financial intermediary and improve the Central American trade position. For instance, it could help negotiate collective sales of export products or joint purchases of essential imports, thus increasing the bargaining power of the region. In the longer run, it might be possible to establish the *peso centroamericano* as a true currency; although this would involve a very high degree of fiscal coordination among the five republics and the requisite powers to the Fund to act as a central bank for the region as a whole.

This proposal may seem not only somewhat hypothetical, although we have tried to show that in both technical and institutional terms it could be feasible, but also somewhat irrelevant to the real geopolitical problems of the region. To this concern there are two concluding points we would like to make. The first is that without economic recovery (for which monetary reactivation is a necessary condition) there is little chance of democratization in the longer run, for the region will be forced into either aid dependency or repressive subsistence. What sort of economic model is adopted will of course define its social content, but any model must have a substantial foreign trade component which will require financing.[15] The second is that economic integration with strong support from Europe and Latin America would reduce the capacity of Washington to exert pressure on individual governments in the region, particularly Nicaragua at present, but hopefully others in the future which will make genuine efforts to overcome poverty and establish national sovereignty.

152

TABLE 7.1   Central America: Intra- and Extra-regional Exports, 1978--1986
            (Index, 1978=100)

Country	1978	1979	1980	1981	1982	1983	1984	1985	1986
To the Region	100	103	131	109	89	89	83	57	43
Costa Rica	100	98	151	133	93	111	108	81	55
El Salvador	100	114	126	88	74	71	67	41	40
Guatemala	100	118	158	139	125	121	112	80	58
Honduras	100	122	171	135	106	124	98	41	39
Nicaragua	100	62	51	49	36	23	26	16	8
To the Rest of the World	100	119	119	111	100	95	102	107	121

Source: G. Rosenthal (1986), Centroamérica: Crisis Política y su Impacto
sobre el Proceso de Integración Económica.

TABLE 7.2   Central America: Transactions through the Central American
            Clearing House, 1978--1985 (millions of US dollars and
            percentages)

Item	1978	1979	1980	1981	1982	1983	1984	1985
Total Amount (US$ millions)	971	1037	1256	979	644	579	506	395
Percentage of Registered Trade(%)	110	117	114	101	81	71	70	69

Source: SIECA, Reactivación del Mercado Común Centroamericano, julio de
         1986.

TABLE 7.3   Central America: International Reserve Position (millions of US dollars)

Year	Gross International Reserves					International Liabilities				Net Reserves*
	Foreign Exchange	SDRs	IMF	Gold	Total	Commer. Banks	Central Banks	Others	Total	Total
1975	615.1	32.5	10.5	44.8	702.9	214.3	308.1	61.4	583.8	119.1
1976	1008.3	26.5	13.9	44.7	1093.4	249.8	359.8	75.2	684.8	408.6
1977	1338.5	39.1	21.2	55.9	1454.7	376.6	414.2	96.8	887.6	567.1
1978	1353.8	38.4	46.4	60.0	1498.6	422.2	637.3	108.2	1167.7	330.9
1979	1208.0	57.7	47.7	81.2	1394.6	448.9	768.0	127.1	1344.0	50.6
Average 1975–1979	1104.7	38.8	27.9	57.3	1228.8	342.4	497.5	93.7	933.6	295.3
1980	831.9	22.7	27.7	99.7	982.0	506.7	1637.8	127.2	2271.7	-1289.7
1981	551.4	4.4	9.7	53.0	618.5	330.9	2373.8	213.6	2918.3	-2299.8
1982	725.6	4.7	0.0	68.4	798.7	354.4	2589.8	218.5	3162.7	-2364.0
1983	951.3	5.8	12.6	48.1	1017.8	395.1	3632.3	212.2	4239.6	-3221.8
1984	971.1	2.3	0.0	43.0	1016.4	308.1	2235.9	213.7	2757.7	-1741.3
1985	1092.6	0.1	0.0	62.1	1154.8	227.3	2484.1	210.4	2921.8	-1767.0
1986	1166.5	0.1	0.0	69.1	1235.7	155.6	1690.2	134.2	1980.0	-744.3
Average 1980–1986	898.6	5.7	7.1	63.3	974.8	325.4	2377.7	190.0	2893.1	-1918.3

Notes: Nicaragua's figures from 1984 onwards not included.
        *Gross international reserves minus liabilities.
Source: IMF, (1987) International Financial Statistics Yearbook, Washington, D.C., IMF.

TABLE 7.4   Central America: Estimation of Gross Capital Flight*, 1977--1985
(millions of US dollars)

Country	1977	1978	1979	1980	1981	1982	1983	1984	1985	Total
Costa Rica	28	67	66	-162	-128	-2	8	12	55	-56
El Salvador	-24	116	-165	-310	-105	-65	-135	-55	n.a.	-743
Guatemala	14	54	-60	-300	-144	-248	79	-47	-30	-682
Honduras	39	-7	25	-21	15	4	-7	-13	7	42
Nicaragua	-22	-146	-237	-127	-31	-62	-43	n.a.	n.a.	-668
Central America	35	84	-371	-920	-393	-373	-98	n.a.	n.a.	-2036

Note: *Net short term capital movements plus errors and omissions.

Source: IMF, Balance of Payments Statistics, 1985 and 1986.

TABLE 7.5   Central America: Total Outstanding External Debt 1977--1986
(millions of US dollars)

Country	1977	1978	1979	1980	1981	1982	1983	1984	1985	1986
Costa Rica	1499	1870	2233	2209	2687	3188	3532	3752	3742	3739
El Salvador	504	986	939	1176	1608	1808	2023	2095	2162	2093
Guatemala	670	821	939	1053	1385	1841	2149	2505	2624	2641
Honduras	826	980	1280	1388	1588	1986	2162	3992	2803	2931
Nicaragua	1102	1251	1483	1825	2566	3139	3789	4362	4936	5773
Central America	4601	5908	6874	7651	9834	11962	13655	16706	16267	17177

Source: ECLAC Estimates.

TABLE 7.6   Central America: Outstanding Debt by Creditor, 1985
(millions of US dollars)

Country	OECD Countries Govts.	Banks	Multi-lateral	Others*	IMF	Total
Costa Rica	686	2194	738	411	189	4218
El Salvador	629	245	634	232	89	1829
Guatemala	501	2032	711	278	116	3638
Honduras	607	755	1087	193	134	2776
Nicaragua	598	1699	721	2387	0	5405
Central America	3021	6925	3891	3501	528	17866

Note: *Includes mainly CMEA and OPEC countries, and other private debt.

Source: OECD, (1987) External Debt Statistics.

APPENDIX A

Central America: External Indebtedness vis-à-vis Western Europe

The main problem in working out Central America's indebtedness to Western Europe is that the OECD and Bank of International Settlements do not make data on specific creditors available to the public. The World Bank *World Debt Tables* have no breakdown by creditor country so the European share of Central America's debt cannot be calculated. We have calculated two alternative estimates using indirect figures, although both have important limitations and certain inconsistencies. An alternative method of estimation would be to use the data from the five Central Banks of Central America; but this is in some cases confidential and the methodologies would have to be made compatible. Firstly, the BIS quarterly bulletin, *International Banking Developments*, gives total country indebtedness to banks and other financial institutions (see Table 7.A.1). For most countries the coverage does not include liabilities to the United States, so the figures can be treated as an upper limit of total Central American indebtedness with Western Europe. The main limitations of this estimate are that it includes liabilities to other important creditors (i.e. Japan, OPEC members, etc.) and that not all European banks are covered. Secondly, the gross and net flows from developed countries to LDCs since 1977 are shown in the OECD's *Geographical Distribution of Financial Flows to Developing Countries*. By adding up the annual figure for net flows since 1977 (the year in which we supposed a low level of Central America's indebtedness vis-à-vis Western Europe) we can derive a lower limit for the debt figure (see Table 7.A.2). The problem with this approach is that it covers only DAC members (Spain, a relatively important creditor, is not included) and that aggregating annual flows does not ensure an accurate figure for the outstanding balance in a specific year.

For end–1985, the Bank of International Settlements figure is US$ 2.79 billion, while the OECD figure is US$ 1.76 billion. It would reasonable, therefore, to conclude that the current (i.e. end–1987) level of Central American debt with Western Europe is of the order of US$ 2.0 to 2.5 billion.

156

TABLE 7.A.1   Central America: Liabilities to all Non-US Reporting Banks,
               1985-1987 (millions of US dollars)

Countries/Years	Total
Costa Rica	
End of 1985	836
End of 1986	870
June, 1987	862
El Salvador	
End of 1985	218
End of 1986	225
June, 1987	217
Guatemala*	
End of 1985	604
End of 1986	506
June, 1987	477
Honduras	
End of 1985	345
End of 1986	332
June, 1987	288
Nicaragua	
End of 1985	783
End of 1986	564
June, 1987	568
Central America	
End of 1985	2786
End of 1986	2497
June, 1987	2412

Note: *Includes Liabilities to US Banks.

Source: Bank of International Settlements, International Banking
Developments, 2nd Quarter 1987.

TABLE 7.A.2   Central America: Net Financial Receipts from Western European DAC Members, 1977--1985 (millions of US dollars)

Country	1977	1978	1979	1980	1981	1982	1983	1984	1985	Total
Western Europe	75.6	136.1	154.9	213.3	299.5	201.8	120.1	192.7	347.1	1741.1
Austria	0.8	2.9	0.5	0.6	1.3	9.1	9.6	0.9	4.8	30.5
Belgium	1.4	7.5	6.4	11.9	-0.5	2.2	-4.4	9.8	-1.4	32.9
Denmark	1.8	0.6	4	17.4	1.7	0.8	0.9	0.2	0.6	28
Finland	0	0	0.6	1	0.6	2.9	1.9	3.1	3.2	13.3
France	0.4	4.8	36	93.7	117.1	104.8	75.8	31.5	153.6	617.7
Germany	19.3	25.5	67.2	29.5	48	39.9	46.6	26.8	39.5	342.3
Italy	57	42.2	13.1	6.9	58.7	-23.5	-28.4	2.6	39	167.6
The Netherlands	4	4.4	12.1	38.2	21.7	27.5	29.2	37.1	36.9	211.1
Norway	1.6	17.9	10.5	0.4	0.4	4.6	3.1	19	17.2	74.7
Sweden	1.4	0.7	7.2	6.7	14	10	11.9	14.5	16.9	83.3
Switzerland	-0.5	24.7	0.2	22.2	30.2	9.4	-35.4	43	17.4	111.2
United Kingdom	-11.6	4.9	-2.9	-15.2	6.3	14.1	9.3	4.2	19.4	28.5

Source: OECD (1981, 1986, 1987), Geographical Distribution of Financial Flows to Developing Countries.

APPENDIX B

Central America: Net International Reserves

The main problem involved in estimating Central America's net international reserves is the lack of systematic and reliable information on short term liabilities; this information is required to adjust the gross international reserves statistics.

There are two sources but each has important limitations and, unfortunately, there is little consistency between them. The first estimate is taken from the Consejo Monetario Centroamericano in their *Boletín Estadístico 1986* (see Table 7.B.1). The problems are: (a) the estimate only covers the period 1981–1986 and does not report on the international position before the crisis of the 1980s; (b) this series is not directly comparable to figures reported in the past by the same source since the latter doe not include liabilities, only gross international reserves.

The second estimate is based on the IMF *International Financial Statistics* (1987) using some of the indicators for countries' international liquidity (see Table 7.3). Three problems are: (a) some of the liabilities included may be medium-term while the BIS figures on short-term liabilities begin in 1983 and the coverage is not satisfactory; (b) the series is incomplete for Nicaragua, and stops in 1983; and (c) there are some international reserve items have been overlooked, such as contributions to the *Fondo Centroamericano de Estabilización Monetaria*.

However, the very broad picture emerging from the figures indicates a serious decline in liquidity between the 1970s and the 1980s; although gross reserves have been more or less maintained, this has been at the cost of excessive short-term borrowing (often from trade suppliers) leading to a serious negative net reserves position. Finally, it would appear to be necessary that the five Central Banks provide data through the CMCA on their net reserve position if a realistic balance of payments support package is to be negotiated with Europe.

TABLE 7.B.1   Central America: Gross and Net International Reserves, 1981--1986
(millions of US dollars)

Year	Costa Rica Gross	Costa Rica Net	El Salvador Gross	El Salvador Net	Guatemala Gross	Guatemala Net	Honduras Gross	Honduras Net	Nicaragua Gross	Nicaragua Net	The Region Gross	The Region Net
1981	279	-185	161	-194	321	25	133	-10	179	-480	1073	-844
1982	406	-47	169	-189	292	-17	145	-102	211	-613	1223	-968
1983	574	93	257	-1	374	-85	136	-115	224	-582	1565	-690
1984	481	162	277	16	413	-113	151	-118	471	-582	1793	-635
1985	579	312	332	96	475	-154	130	-107	477	-801	1993	-654
1986	630	372	364	210	532	51	139	-109	287	-882	1952	-358

<u>Source</u>:   Consejo Monetario Centroamericano, (1986, 1987) <u>Boletín Estadístico</u>.

Notes

1. Cohen (1982b) provides an excellent account of the establishment of the CACM, placing the monetary integration proposals in the context of the original ECLA proposals of the 1950s, the tradition of cooperation between the five central banks, and the pressure from the USA (supported by the IMF and the IBRD) to strengthen the position of multinational corporations (including banks) in the region.

2. Four of the central banks had been founded as a result of the Great Depression (see Bulmer-Thomas, 1984) and were thus familiar with crisis management; central banking in Nicaragua has its origins much later, for during US occupation in the 1920s an externally controlled national bank had been established.

3. The extremely rapid growth of agrarian production, exports and investment (in contrast to the rest of Latin America, the green revolution did take hold) is undeniable, despite the social consequences; as Weeks (1985b), ECLAC (1985) and Bulmer-Thomas (1987a) all recognize.

4. The disastrous social and political effects of this model are well portrayed in Williams (1986). Much of the current instability in the region arises from the contradictions of this model, exacerbated by the attempts by successive US administrations to prevent any alternative from emerging.

5. This process was the basis of the forecasting model which the SIECA used in the mid–1970s with considerable success (Siri, 1979).

6. Durán and Solís (1979) have an application of the IMF model constructed to for the region and applied to Nicaragua in the mid–1970s, which illustrates this argument well.

7. Irvin (1988) gives this as one of the results of his model of Central American political economy. Even Costa Rica was no exception once the welfare budget commitment had been established.

8. This is a central element of the alternative economic strategy for the region put forward in Irvin and Gorostiaga (eds) (1985).

9. Bulmer-Thomas (1987a) has an excellent analysis of this process, which forms the basis of this section.

10. The problem of capital flight is stressed in ECLAC (1985). For the period 1977–1984 Glower (1986) estimates a minimum of US$ 2.2 billion and a maximum of US$ 3.7 billion. For an independent estimate, see Chapman (1987).

11. The chapter in this volume by Bulmer-Thomas implies that export promotion requires differential exchange rates in general, and a differential between that use for CACM trade and world trade, in particular, such as the DICA scheme implies.

12. See the proposals in ECLAC (1985), and also those in PACCA (1984).

13. The Kissinger Report, for instance (US Senate, 1984), recommended that the Central American region (including Panama) would require some US$ 24 billions in fresh capital inflows over the 1984–1990 period in order to regain its productive capacity.

14. Estimated exports value of 1980 plus terms of trade losses during 1981–1985.

15. FitzGerald (1985) shows that this is even true for small Third-World societies constructing socialism.

8

The Reconstruction of the CACM and European Cooperation

Luis René Cáceres and George Irvin

Introduction

The crisis of the 1980s has set back the development of the Central American region by at least two decades. In this chapter it is argued that the fragility of the CACM arises not so much from its maldistributive character as from its extreme vulnerability to fluctuating world market conditions. In the early 1980s, the sharp fall in world market prices for the region's main commodity exports together with the rising cost of overseas borrowing and capital flight set off a spiral of economic contraction and growing indebtedness. It follows that if late–1970 levels of per capita income are to be reached by the early 1990s, massive overseas assistance will be required.

Such assistance, we argue, will be more effective if it is organized on a multilateral rather than a bilateral basis and promotes the economic integration of the five republics. This means reviving intra-regional trade flows and strengthening the integration organizations of the Central American Common Market. In this respect the European Community, itself a common market, has a special role to play.

Three areas are of critical importance. First, assistance is needed in restructuring the accumulated intra-regional trade debt and establishing new arrangements which will, in future, help ensure that the gains from intra-regional trade are more equitably distributed. Secondly, fresh finance is required for the extra-regional import component of renewed CACM trade as well as to help modernize the region's depleted capital stock. Third, what Central America requires

Luis René Cáceres is Head of the Economic Planning Department of the Central American Bank for Economic Integration (BCIE); George Irvin is Associate Professor at the Institute of Social Studies, The Hague, The Netherlands.

163

even more than new aid is a new set of trading arrangements and, in particular, a scheme to stabilize foreign exchange earnings from its principle export commodities.

The chapter comprises two sections. In the first we examine the empirical dimensions of the crisis, the maldistributive nature of the model and its external vulnerability. In the second, external assistance requirements are estimated and compared to the present multilateral and bilateral components of European Community aid towards the region. Detailed proposals are also made about the costs of extending STABEX-type arrangements to Central America (STABEX is the export revenue stabilization scheme operated by the European Community in favor of signatories of the Lomé Convention; i.e., the ACP (African, Caribbean and Pacific) group of countries). A summary and some final remarks are presented in the concluding section.

SECTION I
Internal Inequity and External Vulnerability

Measured at constant prices, the level of GDP per capita in 1985 had declined in each of the five countries to levels prevailing at least a decade (and in some cases several decades) before. As shown in Table 8.1, in 1985, per capita GDP in Guatemala and Costa Rica had fallen back to its 1974 level; in Honduras it had fallen to its 1964 level while the levels for El Salvador and Nicaragua are those of 1964 and 1955 respectively.

In the eight years between 1979 and 1986, publicly guaranteed external debt quadrupled reaching a figure of over US$ 17 billion. Interest and amortization rose nearly sixfold: from US$ 329 million in 1979 to US$ 1.848 billion in 1986, the latter figure representing about half the region's export earnings. Intra-regional trade, for two decades the motor of regional growth, has fallen back to the level first reached thirteen years ago.

Performance in the 1980s stands in sharp contrast to that achieved in the first two decades of the CACM and even in the 1950s. Whereas in 1960 the share of industrial output in GDP was only 12 percent, by 1978 it reached just over 20 percent. Over the same period, the share of the primary sector in GDP fell from one-third to one-quarter. The growth of CACM industry is reflected in the growth of intra-regional trade, which in 1978 was worth US$ 900 million in contrast to a mere US$ 8 million in 1950. By the same token the share of intra-regional in total trade grew from 4 percent in 1950 to 23 percent in 1978.

More important, for Central America as a whole, the share of investment in GDP climbed from 12 percent to 20 percent over this same period.

The dynamism of these years did produce some very real gains for the region. In two of the five republics per capita income trebled over the period 1950–1978 while in the remaining countries it more than doubled. In 1950 only 16 percent of the population lived in urban areas in contrast to 40 percent at the end of the period. Average life expectancy rose from 42 to 60 as incomes and nutritional status improved. The region's economic infrastructure was greatly extended, particularly in areas such as roads and electric power. One could go on citing examples. The real question is why, given these very real accomplishments, was the region unable to develop a self-sustained model of growth capable of propelling it through the 1980s?

The CACM: A Flawed Model?

The Central American model which gave rise to two decades of growth and integration has been characterized elsewhere as 'additive and exclusive;' i.e. one that built upon existing structures without changing them and concentrated the benefits of growth in the hands of the few.[1] In our view, this argument is correct but oversimplifies the problem.

It is true that, with the exception of Costa Rica, little attention was paid to income distribution. Nearly everywhere, high growth rates were accompanied by increases in both relative and absolute deprivation. Increased deprivation was dysfunctional in that it limited the degree to which economic growth could be driven by domestic demand. Equally, increased deprivation led to increased frustration among the 'have-nots' whose claim to a share in this newly found prosperity was answered nearly everywhere by repression. But the key weakness of the model was its extreme vulnerability to changes in the international economic climate, a matter to which we turn in the next section.

Even with respect to the issue of distribution, an important qualification is required. The 'model' to which we refer is a particular model of capitalist growth associated with a small, open economy dependent on primary exports. The CACM cannot be said to have been maldistributive *per se*. To claim that it was, one would need to argue that in the absence of the CACM the region could have attained an equivalent mean level of per capita income with a smaller dispersion. Although this proposition is by its very nature untestable, it seems highly unlikely that in the absence of the CACM the bulk of the population today would be better off.

What is true is that the CACM did not live up to the expectations of many of its most enthusiastic supporters, namely, that accelerated capitalist development would bring both faster growth and greater equity. However, since this is not true for low-to-middle income LDCs in general, there is no reason to suppose that it should be true for Central America in particular.[2] To say this is in no way to deny the reactionary nature of much of regional politics and its prime importance as a factor contributing to the present crisis.

Table 8.2 illustrates the extent to which growth not only excluded wage earners but, in the 1970s, took place at their expense. Between 1967 and 1977 real wages in El Salvador fell by 17 percent, in Guatemala by 34 percent and in Nicaragua by 40 percent.[3] The data for Costa Rica and Honduras show real wages fluctuating over this period with a slight upward trend. Movements in real wages in industry appear to have been particularly important. According to Schulz (1984), in Guatemala and El Salvador there is a significant relationship between working days lost through industrial disputes and falling real wages, while in Costa Rica, by contrast, decrease in industrial disputes is associated with a rise in real wages. The lesson appears to be that Costa Rican capitalists, by accommodating wage demands, benefited from greater socio-political stability which improved the climate of investment and growth.

The evidence on household income distribution for Central America as a whole is summarized in Rosenthal (1985) who has this to say:

> In the 1960s and 1970s . . . the relative share of the poorest two deciles of the population tends to fall sharply while the of the richest two deciles also falls, though less markedly. From the above one can infer that the gap between the top and bottom 20 percent of the distribution was widening. By contrast the relative share of the intermediate strata, particularly the 30 percent above the mode, tends to rise over time. . . .
>
> The distributive structure is so strongly biased that if yearly per capita variations are measured in absolute terms it is seen that increases accruing to the top twenty percent are always greater than increases accruing to any group lower down the scale. This means that unless there is a change in the trend observed over the last thirty years, it will take generations before the gap between the absolute level of per capita income of the top 20 percent and intermediate 30 percent begins to narrow.[4]

The exception is Honduras where the share of the poorest 20 percent rose by 2.3 percent in 1967–1968 and by 4.8 percent in 1976–1979. This is explained mainly by the growth of rural employment as a result of an expanding agricultural frontier and the impact of land reform measures undertaken in the early 1970s.[5]

Nevertheless, at the end of the 1970s the incidence of absolute poverty in the region remained markedly high despite the significant 'modernization' of the region's infrastructure and productive structure. For the region as a whole, at the end of the 1970s it is estimated that three-quarters of the rural population could be classified as living in poverty and over half in conditions of extreme poverty. Although the region's per capita income more than doubled between 1950 and 1978, the absolute number of Central Americans living in poverty increased from 6 million people in 1950 to 13.5 millions in 1980.[6]

There is, therefore, a curious 'looking-glass' quality about the modernization of Central America over this period. Modernization, although undeniable, relies upon structural forces that erode the living standards of the bulk of the population. Hence, because the model is unable to incorporate growing demands for economic citizenship, the rights of political citizenship cannot be widened. With the clear exception of Costa Rica, Central American politics during this period become more divisive and the state plays an increasingly active role in repression. In sum, this is a period of growth, modernization and urbanization characterized by increased relative deprivation and the conspicuous absence of political institutions capable of dealing with the conflicts created by growth. It is therefore not surprising that the period ends with an upheaval resulting from domestic political forces and a severe downturn in the international economic climate.

External Vulnerability

In the absence of any internal mechanisms to sustain growth, the Central American economy has always been extremely vulnerable to changes in the world economy.[7] In essence, this means at least three things. First, there is a close historical relationship between changes in international terms of trade—in effect the prices of a narrow range of goods and services produced and/or consumed by export-agriculture— and the rate of domestic savings and accumulation. Second, 'modernization' does not appear to have led to any significant weakening of this relationship. Put another way, economic policy-makers still have relatively little scope for adjusting to a downturn in world commodity prices other than by curtailing domestic demand. Finally, any significant reduction in Central America's vulnerability would require there to be new opportunities for domestic investment whose profitability does not depend primarily on the fortunes of export agriculture. If few such opportunities exist it is because any downturn in export agriculture acts as a brake on domestic demand and thus on import substitution. The paradoxical conclusion is that in order to become less dependent on primary exports, Central America requires a prolonged period of primary export-led growth to generate the surplus required to finance diversification.

That a strong positive relationship exists between the domestic savings-investment rate and commodity prices can be illustrated most vividly, if somewhat over-simply, by plotting the share of gross savings in national income for each country against the price of the region's single most important commodity export, coffee. Table 8.3 illustrates this relationship for each country. High coffee prices are associated with a high savings ratio and vice-versa. Note that the 'fit' is best in the case of Guatemala where the share of coffee in total exports is the highest of the five countries, though it is still quite good in the case of Honduras where coffee's share is the lowest. Supporting evidence is given by Reynolds who argues:

> A striking feature of econometric models of income determination in the region is the evidence of the continuing dominating effect of terms of trade and other export-related fluctuations in the level of domestic income and product.[8]

More than three decades of growth does not appear to have significantly increased the autonomy of Central American policy makers, i.e. increased their ability to pursue monetary or other targets actively rather that merely to react to changes in external conditions. For example, it might be supposed that the observed deepening of financial markets in Central American in the past two decades would have dampened the fluctuations in the domestic savings-investment process caused by unstable export earnings. Between 1961 and 1981 the ratio of the domestic money supply (measured as M2) to GDP approximately doubled for the five countries; however there is no evidence that financial deepening has strengthened the domestic savings-investment process and made it less vulnerable to a fall in export earnings.[9]

Indeed, there appears to be an inverse relationship between real international interest rates and the rate of growth of GDP, the opposite of what one would expect to result from an easing of 'financial repression.' Separate studies by Loehr (1986) and by Collier (1984) suggest that whatever beneficial effects may exist from allowing domestic interest rates to follow real LIBOR upwards, these are swamped by the effects of a higher LIBOR on the current account balance (both raising the cost of debt service and depressing foreign demand for commodity exports).[10]

A further structural weakness of the Central American model is its high import propensity. Three factors help to explain this phenomenon. First, although industrial import substitution over the past two decades has been accompanied by a sharp fall in the share of consumer goods imports, locally produced products have had a high import content, something which the ruling tariff structure has tended to encourage.[11] Second, the import content of particular export crops— e.g. pesticides and spraying equipment for cotton—is high and, furthermore, because Central America has no shipping facilities, transport charges are a permanent drain on invisible account. Third, regardless of whether investment has been undertaken by domestic or multinational firms, a significant proportion of profit has been remitted abroad and this proportion has tended to increase as the region's political climate has become more unstable.[12]

A recent study by one of the authors has shown that for Honduras, 58 cents out of every export dollar earned in a given year has leaked overseas by the year's end; the corresponding figure for Costa Rica is 60 cents.[13] Another study shows that in the case of El Salvador, one colón of new investment soon gives rise to demand for a stream of imports whose present value is greater than one colón.[14] These studies suggest that external leakages from the circular flow of income are high and, in consequence, the domestic multiplier effect of investment is low.

A key function of the CACM has been to 'internalize' a part of these leakages; i.e. to confine a high proportion of these to within the region thus allowing a rise in investment in one country to raise both its own income and that of its neighbours. Thus, although over the period 1950–1978 the region's import coefficient more than doubled (from 16 to 33 percent), the share of extra-regional in total imports fell.[15] In this sense, the CACM did save foreign exchange and contribute to growth, albeit less effectively than some of its supporters would have wished.

However, the Achilles heel of the CACM does not reside in the high import content of the ISI model nor even in the structural impediments to reaping the alleged gains from financial and economic modernization. As one of the authors has argued elsewhere,[16] the fact the direct and indirect import content of CACM manufactures came very largely from outside the region is quite consistent with a first-stage import-substitution strategy. Such a strategy does not require industrialization to begin with investment in capital goods, in contrast to the balanced growth strategy originally proposed by ECLAC.

Nor does the vulnerability of the model derive from its 'hybrid' nature; i.e. the fact that the requirements of industrial development (including the modernization of the food-producing sector) took second place to those of export agriculture.[17] To adopt a consumer-goods led industrialization strategy is to postpone industrial deepening thus ensuring that the import coefficient will stay high. It follows that for a given set of techniques, wages and external terms of trade, there is a warranted rate of agricultural export growth that will sustain the import capacity required for industrialization to proceed at a given pace. Should the warranted rate not be realized, the gap will need to be filled by foreign borrowing, the servicing which will increase the warranted export growth rate. Unless there is a secular rise in the barter terms of trade, export receipts can only be made to grow by increasing the rate of exploitation. This is of course precisely what happened during the 1970s and what helped set the stage for political crisis.

In short, the failure of the CACM model cannot be attributed to excessive dependency on export agriculture, on the excessive profits of multinational corporations, on financial irresponsibility, excessive borrowing, failure to implement land reform, failure to modernize the region's polity and so on. Important though these things may be, they are not causes of the crisis but, rather, attributes of a particular model of development whose logic we have sketched. In the section which follows we turn to the question of external assistance required in the short to medium term if self-sustained growth is to be achieved in the longer term.

SECTION II

External Assistance Requirements

If Central America is to return to per capita income levels characteristic of the late 1970s within a reasonable period of time—say five to seven years—a very significant injection of foreign aid will be required. Not only is growth a necessary to reduce vulnerability in the sense outlined above, but it is only through renewed growth that a 'vested interest' in peace can be created.

Any recovery program will need to address the twin questions of financing industry's working capital requirements and renewing the region's aging capital stock. At present, the region is experiencing a major liquidity crisis. Gross domestic savings ratios have fallen; between 1979 and 1986 the annual rate of growth of investment for the five republics taken together has been negative in six out of seven years. Equally, over the same period net international reserves have been negative in six out of seven years.

As can be seen in Table 8.4, between 1979 and 1982, the region's net international gold and dollar reserves fell from CA$ 854 million to a negative value of CA$ -660 million (i.e. liabilities exceeded assets).[18] The only country in the region that still enjoyed positive net reserves in 1982 was Guatemala. Since then, except in Guatemala, net reserves have risen slowly. By 1986 Costa Rica and El Salvador were back in the black by an amount which just offset the combined deficit of the other three republics. In 1986, the region enjoyed positive net reserves of CA$ 54 million (CA$ 1 = US$ 1), though it must be noted that this was a year of high coffee prices.

Looking at percentage changes in gross investment (or gross fixed capital formation since inventory changes are negligible) shown in Table 8.5, for the region as a whole real investment in fixed capital has declined continuously between 1979 and 1986, the only exception being 1984 in which a 1.9 percent increase was registered. The cumulative contraction in real fixed investment over the period has been such that in Guatemala and Nicaragua, the absolute value of net investment was the same as in 1970; for El Salvador, Costa Rica and Honduras the corresponding years are 1973, 1974 and 1977 respectively. Figures for the share of gross domestic savings in GDP by country are given in Table 8.6. In four of the six republics, the 1985 figure is lower than that obtaining two decades earlier.

To offset Central America's loss of reserves, declining fixed capital formation, low domestic savings ratios and falling levels of per capita GDP, a massive injection of foreign resources will be required. This is hardly an original conclusion. In early 1984, the Kissinger Commission reported that in order to reach 1980 levels of per capita output by 1990, the isthmus would require some US$ 25 billion in external finance of which about half would come from multilateral agencies, commercial banks and private investment and the remainder from the United States.[19] A later study published by the BCIE suggests that the region needs to attract resource inflows on the order of US$ 4 billion per annum.[20]

In practice, total annual regional inflows have only amounted to about half this figure while, given recent trends in commercial lending, it seems unlikely that the international private banking community will increase its lending to the region. Aid disbursements by the region's main official multilateral donors, the World Bank and the Inter-American Development Bank, have averaged just over US$ 400 million per annum over the period 1980–1985, or one-tenth of the

BCIE's target figure. Hence not only is the inflow insufficient, but there is little prospect of the situation improving. This situation has persisted despite various calls to the international community including that issued at the Brussels meeting in 1983 promoted by the IDB,[21] the efforts of the Contadora Group which led to the setting up of CADESCA,[22] the cooperative program with the European Community initiated at San José in September 1984,[23] and BCIE's repeated efforts to recruit new members from the ranks of the industrialized countries.

Recently, though, as the Esquipulas peace process has gained momentum (particularly after Esquipulas II in August 1987, and Esquipulas III in January 1988), there have been signs that the international community might be willing to provide financial assistance in support of the peace process. This was the message of the Latin American heads of state (known as the Group of Eight) which met at Acapulco in November 1987 and which speaks explicitly of the need for an emergency aid package, for new trade and aid relationships between Central and Latin America, and for efforts to strengthen Central American economic integration and revive intra-regional trade.[24] This was also the message of UN Resolution 42/1 which called for a Special Plan of Action to be presented to the General Assembly at the end of April 1988.[25] Finally, it is in this spirit which the Hamburg meeting between European Community Foreign Ministers and those of the Central American isthmus held 28 February–1 March 1988, has discussed the possibility of a significant increase in multilateral aid.[26]

The Special Role of the European Community

Total European aid for the five Central American republics and Panama (together known as the countries of the Central American isthmus) is made up of multilateral and bilateral programs. The multilateral program is in the hands of the European Community whose executive agency, the European Commission in Brussels, administers a budget the bulk of which is divided among the six recipients but part of which is earmarked for the region as a whole. In addition, each European member state has its own bilateral aid program towards the individual countries of the region (though the size and composition of these programs varies considerably between EC member states).

From Tables 8.7 and 8.8 two things will be apparent. First, the bilateral programs of the member states have traditionally been larger than multilateral program administered by Brussels. Second, the bulk of multilateral aid has been divided up between the recipients. In recent years, more emphasis has been placed on the multilateral program and, within this, on designing regional projects and programs rather than merely dividing up the aid between the recipients. Economic cooperation between the EC and the five republics has come to focus increasingly on four areas: financial and technical cooperation, support for regional integration, improved trade relations and social and humanitarian aid. Because the fourth of these areas is relatively uncontentious, our discussion will be confined to financial cooperation, regional integration and new trade arrangements with Europe.

Financial Cooperation and the BCIE

If future European economic assistance to the region is to assume a more clearly defined multilateral and regional character, it will make sense to channel extra resources through existing integration organizations such as the BCIE. This is in part because multilateral aid tends to be more efficient than bilateral aid.[27] It is also because BCIE is the region's only multilateral recipient body. Moreover, since the onset of the crisis, the BCIE has found itself in the difficult position of having to tend to greater needs on a tighter budget.

In order to draw in new resources, in August 1983, BCIE's Board of Governors agreed to widen membership of the BCIE to include countries outside the region. Because, formally speaking, the incorporation of such members as normal shareholders involves the lengthy process of renegotiating the terms of the Treaty under which the Bank established, in February 1985 the Board of Governors decided to create the *Fondo para el Desarrollo Económico y Social* (FONDESCA), a special fund jointly administered by the Bank and its extra-regional members. In September 1986, Mexico joined FONDESCA subscribing US$ 57.6 million of which US$ 14.4 million was in cash. Argentina followed suit in November 1987, with a contribution similar in size to that of Mexico. In December 1987, Venezuela set up a trust (*fideicomismo*) within BCIE as a first step in becoming a full member.

The BCIE is by far the largest public financial institution in Central America, with assets totalling CA$ 1.45 billion as per December 1987. Its lending has been targeted principally at projects and programs of a regional character. But, as the regional economic crisis developed, the Bank has played an increasingly active role in other areas. For example, in 1981, the BCIE established the *Fondo del Mercado Común* in order to refinance some of its member-states' unsettled accounts with the Central American Clearing House (CCC). (Unfortunately, as regional trade continued to decline and imbalances were exacerbated, this line of finance was soon exhausted). It is envisaged that in future the Bank will play an increasingly important role not only in financing projects but in advising member states on the coordination of financial and trade policy, export promotion and technology transfer.

Hence, the incorporation of members from outside the region is more than an operation for tapping extra-regional finance. New members have an important say in policy formulation. In this sense, the eventual incorporation of European members is desirable not only because it would provide new equity capital and enable the Bank to increase its borrowing in the commercial market but also because it would enable Europe to put into practice the principles of development partnership affirmed at numerous junctures in the San José process. It is worth noting that the communiqué that emerged from the Guatemala Meeting of Foreign Ministers (San José III) in February 1987, welcomed the interest shown by certain EC member-states in joining the BCIE and supporting its work.

Over the next quinquennium, 1988–1992, the BCIE's lending target for the region is of the order of CA$ 1 billion, a quite considerable sum although it falls far short of the region's target resource requirement. The principle sources of finance envisaged include CA$ 100 million in new capital subscribed by member-states within the region, CA$ 133 million in repayments on outstanding loans, CA$ 160 million in capital subscribed by new members outside the region and CA$ 607 million from bilateral and multilateral sources.[28] As will be seen in Table 8.9, the envisaged pattern of lending calls for about one-quarter of this total to be invested in housing and other forms of social infrastructure, just over one-third in economic infrastructure and the remainder to be divided between agriculture and industry.

Europe can also play an important role in providing technical assistance. The need to find short-term remedies for pressing economic problems has left the region short of well-designed projects. There is, for example, an urgent need to establish a regional resource inventory and carry out basic studies in such areas as land use, water-resource development, geothermal energy, offshore and inland fisheries, reforestation and so forth. One proposal is to establish a Technical Cooperation Fund as a means of strengthening the region's project and program design capacity. However, it should be stressed that the region's economic problems cannot be cured merely by designing and financing more projects. On the contrary, to implement more projects at this stage may prove counterproductive if this diverts attention from the real need for improved macroeconomic decision-making at a regional level.

European Aid for Integration

It has been argued that Central America cannot and should not return to a 1960s-style CACM. This is not to say that economic integration should be struck from the agenda. That the CACM helped stimulate growth is undeniable. In a seminal article, Cline (1978) demonstrated that the static and dynamic benefits of CACM integration were worth about US$ 200 million in the early 1970s or about 4 percent of Gross Regional Product.[29] A more recent piece by one of the present authors estimates that for the period 1965–1968, the CACM added 1.2 percent on average to the annual growth rate of the region's countries.[30]

The reactivation of intra-regional trade is particularly important since for the region taken as a whole such growth would save foreign-exchange. Cline (1988) has estimated that an extra US$ 250 million in intra-regional trade growth would substitute almost entirely for extra-regional imports and add about half a percentage point to the regional GDP growth rate. Given the very low rates of regional GDP growth experienced in recent years, an increment of this magnitude would constitute a substantial improvement. Such growth would be relatively costless since it would make use of underemployed men and machines.

The collapse of regional trade is closely tied to the deterioration in international market conditions, which has left the region critically short of foreign exchange. Not only have deficit countries in the region lacked the foreign exchange to buy imports from their neighbors but, even surplus countries have been unwilling to export to their neighbors for fear of not being paid. The result has been the growth of unsettled intra-regional accounts (at present worth some CA$ 750 million), the collapse of multilateral trading arrangements—most conspicuously the Central American Clearing House (CCC)—and the proliferation of bilateral 'compensated' trade agreements, usually of a short-lived nature. Moreover, even assuming an exporter still has regional clients, foreign exchange in the form of working capital to finance imported raw materials and maintain machinery will still be required.

The irony is that the most of CA$ 750 million shortfall in savings which appears on the books as payments arrears to the CCC was incurred over the period 1979–1982 when the region lost CA$ 1.9 billion in net reserves, a sum easily covered by terms of trade loss and/or capital flight.[31] Arguably, then, this shortfall in savings—which caused the CACM to seize up—accrued to the rest of the world in the form of lower commodity prices and higher bank deposits. It is therefore not entirely unreasonable for the region to ask the Europe, one of the region's main trading partners, to help towards refinancing the *Fondo Centroamericano del Mercado Común* (FCMC).

It might be objected that, because about half of the CA$ 750 million in intra-regional debt is between two countries (Nicaragua and Costa Rica) and the export capacity of the debtor country is severely limited, to refinance the debt would be to throw good money after bad. However, such an objection misses the point that any scheme designed to reflate regional trade will need to incorporate mechanisms which reduce (and eventually eliminate) structural imbalances.

Various detailed schemes for settling this problem have been advanced by the regional integration organizations; for present purposes, it will suffice to sketch the principles involved. In part, trade imbalances reflects the very severe discrepancies that have arisen between countries in setting realistic exchange rates. Table 8.10 shows how real exchange rates moved over the period 1978–1984, the period in which structural deficits accumulated. It will be seen that in four out of five cases, the real exchange rate rose. That country in which it rose the most experienced the most serious trade deficit. By contrast, Costa Rica has managed a substantial real devaluation and has moved into intra-regional trade surplus. Adequate exchange rate management thus needs to be an integral part of any package designed to reactivate trade.

The difficulty is that exchange rate policy is designed very largely to restore equilibrium on the extra-regional account and that the exchange rate structure which will do this is not necessarily the same as the exchange rate structure which will eliminate structural disequilibria in intra-regional trade. This is why, in separate chapters in this volume, Bulmer-Thomas has examined the logic of untying intra-regional and extra-regional exchange rates while Fuentes has described the DICA scheme which, in practice, should have this effect.

In any case, it is likely that exchange rate adjustment will need to be accompanied by institutional measures to deal with structural imbalances in intra-regional trade. One suggestion is that any country running a regional surplus for more than two or three successive years be required to increase its purchases of deficit country exports, or else use its surplus (in the form of joint investment ventures) to help the deficit countries build up the necessary export capacity.

In fact, these notions are based on the experience of the European Payments Union established in 1950 to deal with structural disequilibria in trade. The key principle of the European scheme was that responsibility for adjustment did not rest exclusively with deficit countries but required surplus countries to liberalize their trade policies. Moreover, the Executive Council of the European Payments Union enjoyed wide powers and played an important role in coordinating the economic policies of member states. These arrangements were remarkably successful in promoting intra-European trade, ensuring currency convertibility and saving on foreign-exchange use.[32]

Settling outstanding intra-regional debt is only one dimension of reviving CACM trade. Even if the debt problem was to be settled tomorrow, there would remain the further problem of financing the extra-regional import component of expanded intra-regional trade. This comprises two elements: the purchase of raw materials and other inputs and the modernization of Central America's aging industrial plant. At present, the BCIE is administering an EC funded scheme for support to small and medium-scale industry worth some ECU 15 million (US$ 17 million). However, in a joint document prepared by the region's main integration bodies, an additional program involves ECU 76 million for upgrading existing plant and ECU 40 million for financing extra-regional raw material imports.[33]

This is not the place to set out more detailed proposals on the terms under which the European Community and its member states might contribute towards reactivating regional trade through refinancing intra-regional trade debts via the *Fondo Centroamericano del Mercado Común* and providing fresh funds for extra-regional imports. Suffice it to say that the scheme advanced in the chapter by FitzGerald and Croes for recycling Central American debt service payments to EC member-states as the basis for financing a Central American Reconstruction Fund is a particularly interesting proposal which merits careful study. Below, we turn to the final and perhaps the most important area in which Europe could make a decisive contribution, trade.

Trading Arrangements with Europe: Stabilizing Export Receipts

Trade between the five republics and the European Community at present is worth about US$ 2 billion annually. Four commodities— coffee, bananas, cotton and sugar—account for about 90 percent of Central American exports to the EC. Hence, while it may be important for Central America to develop new export lines in order to diversify trade, export earnings will be determined for some time to come by the price of traditional commodities. Although the evidence for a long-term secular decline in the region's terms of trade is mixed, there is no doubt that terms of trade have declined very sharply in the past decade which, coupled with the volatility of export prices, goes far to explain the present crisis. To take but one example, the value of Central American coffee exports to the EC fell from US\$ 585 million in 1980 to US\$ 391 million in 1983 before rising to US\$ 420 million in 1985. In short, the most important determinants of Central American economic performance remain international terms of trade movements and, more generally, the business cycle in the industrialized countries.[34]

At the San José III meeting (Guatemala, February 1987), the Foreign Ministers' Meeting recognized the need to pay particular attention to problems arising from fluctuating export earnings within the context of the cooperative program with the countries of the isthmus. Logically, this should imply the willingness of the EC countries to extend facilities to compensate for fluctuations in export prices received by its Central American trading partners similar to the STABEX facility which the Community at present extends to the ACP countries (signatories of the Lomé Agreements).

The estimated cost of STABEX for 1985–1990 is about ECU 925 million and, in the past, about two-thirds of this aid has gone to 10 countries.[35] Broadly speaking, STABEX is designed to compensate ACP (Africa Caribbean and Pacific) countries for any loss in earning incurred if the price of that commodity falls 6.5 percent below its average price in the past four years. For a commodity to qualify, it must be agricultural—though tobacco, sugar, citrus fruit and meat are excluded—and earnings from that commodity must account for an agreed minimum percentage of the country's total export earnings subject to various criteria (e.g. its per capita income level, whether it is landlocked, and so on). Although the facility was originally intended to be a revolving buffer fund (countries paying in excess earning in years of higher than average prices), in practice the EC pays out compensation in the form of grants the use of which is left to the discretion of the recipient.

If a STABEX-type scheme were extended to Central America, in practice the only commodity to qualify for significant compensation would be coffee which accounts for about half of the region's exports to the European Community. Table 8.11 shows our own estimate of the costs of such a scheme which over the period 1977–1985 would have been US\$ 465 million or approximately US\$ 50 million (ECU 40 million) per annum. The years have been chosen to produce a deliberately high estimate since the period includes 1977 (in which price was high thus raising the four year average) and excludes 1986 (in which price rose so that no compensation would have been paid). Hence it is probably reasonable to use this as a valid current cost.

On the assumption that total EC bilateral and multilateral aid to the region were to rise from about ECU 150 million in 1987 to ECU 200 million in 1988—now possible more likely after the San José IV (Hamburg) meeting—the extension of a STABEX-type facility to the region could be accommodated comfortably within this rise.

The standard arguments against such a measure are that it is inequitable, it is too expensive and it would be opposed by the ACP states. The inequity argument states that because El Salvador is the region's main coffee exporter, Europe would be subsidizing the Salvadorean oligarchy. This is misleading on two counts. First, although coffee accounts for over 60 percent of El Salvador's export receipts, the average figure for Central America is 40 percent. The country which would benefit least is Honduras which earns only about one-quarter of its export revenue from coffee. Second, compensation is not paid to growers but to governments. Indeed, there would be a strong case for paying compensation into a common Central American fund such as the *Fondo Centroamericano del Mercado Común*.

The argument that the scheme is too expensive depends on whether the aid is considered additional. Since EC aid to the region for 1988 is programmed to rise but the precise nature of the programs to be funded remains to be negotiated, it is difficult to argue on an *a priori* basis that extending a STABEX-type scheme would increase the total cost of the aid package. Indeed, given that at present the region's absorptive capacity for project aid is limited, the opportunity cost (i.e. project benefits foregone) of extending a STABEX-type facility to the region are probably close to zero. Moreover, the effective future cost of the scheme depends on such factors as whether it is operated using current intervention price levels and whether compensation is paid out entirely in the form of grants. The term 'STABEX-type scheme' is chosen with care. There is much to be said for negotiating a scheme which differs significantly from that now applied to the ACP countries.

Finally, we would argue that such a scheme need not be opposed by the ACP countries for at least three reasons. First, a price stabilization scheme for Central American coffee would only threaten ACP coffee producers if it were to undercut their market. This need not be so since African robustas and Central American aromatics constitute different market segments. Moreover, to the extent that the intervention level was raised or grant element reduced in the Central American case, ACP countries would retain their preferential treatment. Finally, it might be recalled that the ACP states were nearly unanimous in their support of the UN General Assembly Resolution 42/204 calling for "extraordinary, additional and complementary" aid to Central America.

Conclusions

In the first section of this chapter we argued that the high growth rates achieved by the CACM countries in the 1960s and early 1970s were largely the result of favorable world market conditions of the time. By contrast, when external conditions worsened after the first oil shock, the region for a time was able to cushion the impact of the downturn in world trade by cutting real wages at home and borrowing more abroad. But growing poverty in the midst of plenty heightened social tensions and, well before the second oil shock, political unrest was causing local capital to flee the region. After 1979, the combination of political turmoil, capital flight, deteriorating terms of trade and dearer credit combined to produce the most serious economic decline experienced since the 1930s.

Although it would be misleading to suggest that a clear chain of causality can be discerned in these events, different theories do lead to different recommendations for policy. For example, we have argued that it is not helpful to attribute the model's collapse to an excessive emphasis on export agriculture and therefore to recommend that, in future, resources should be directed exclusively toward alleviating the poverty of the peasantry. Everybody would agree that the latter is a *worthy* objective. But we would argue the logic of any small, open economy model dictates that if poverty is to be alleviated, resources must first go to generating the necessary foreign exchange surplus. Such a surplus can then be applied to diversifying exports on the one hand (thus reducing vulnerability to export earnings fluctuations) and to modernizing peasant agriculture and redistributing land assets on the other.

There are two key points to be retained from the second section of this chapter. The first is that world market conditions may be so unstable that the surplus required to diversify export production cannot be generated. This is where the role of the international community is crucial. Vulnerability can only be reduced where primary product consuming countries agree to cooperate with producer countries in order to stabilize prices. Nor should STABEX-type arrangements be seen as aid (even though in practice both producer and consumer countries tend to consider them as such). Commodity price stabilization merely means that consumers agree to give up windfall income gains in the short term for more a more stable stream of future income. The general logic is that applicable to any form of insurance and, just as there are economies of scale in universal insurance coverage, so too are there economies of scale for Europeans in widening STABEX-type coverage.

The second key point follows from the first. Momentum towards region economic integration can only be sustained under conditions of extra-regional balance. Once the extra-regional account is under strain, there will be a natural tendency for each country to adopt policies which restore its own foreign exchange position at the expense of its neighbors. As evidence, one need merely cite the collapse of multilateral trade arrangements within the CACM.

However, we believe that the decline of the CACM is reversible, particularly if new extra-regional trade arrangements are combined with assistance to renew intra-regional trade in a manner which resolves the intra-regional debt problem. An important contribution to settling this problem might be for European creditor states to agree to a recycling of Central American sovereign debt (as suggested in the Chapter by FitzGerald and Croes) as a *quid pro quo* for Central American creditors agreeing to the recycling of intra-regional debt.

Central America possesses the requisite administrative capacity to renew the integration process including the *Fondo Centroamericano del Mercado Común*. It possesses a regionally-defined investment program for renewing its manufacturing plant. It has rationalized its common external tariff. Intra-regional debt negotiations are now taking place. The first steps have been taken in putting into effect a new mechanism for settling intra-regional obligations which would save foreign exchange. The set of declarations which have emerged from the Esquipulas process suggest that the political climate is more favorable now than it has been for some years.

By supporting the recent resolution of the General Assembly on an emergency program for Central America, the international community has agreed in principle to make resources available. It would be most unfortunate if full advantage were not taken of this conjuncture of favorable circumstances in order to help the region back to its feet.

TABLE 8.1   1985 Real GDP Per Capita and Previous Year in which Same
Level was Reached (in 1975 US dollars)

	1985 GDP Per Capita	Year in which 1985 Figure Last Reached
Costa Rica	998	1974
Guatemala	598	1974
Nicaragua	434	1955
Honduras	372	1968
El Salvador	348	1964

Source: CEPAL (1986d), 'América Latina y El Caribe: Escenarios del Crecimiento Económico, 1986--1995,' LC/r 558, México: 11 de diciembre.

TABLE 8.2   Central America: Index of Real Wages, 1963--1978

(1975 = 100)

Year	Costa Rica	El Salvador	Guatemala	Honduras	Nicaragua
1963	80	90	-	-	92
1967	-	105	112	-	137
1970	96	96	113	-	121
1971	107	94	115	-	119
1972	103	98	115	96	114
1973	100	100	100	100	100
1974	108	92	91	71	100
1975	91	90	84	82	106
1976	103	95	81	94	106
1977	113	88	78	88	97
1978	-	87	-	103	-

Source: See Booth (1984), pp. 351--365.

TABLE 8.3   Central America: Gross Domestic Savings Rate and
             International Coffee Prices, 1960--1982

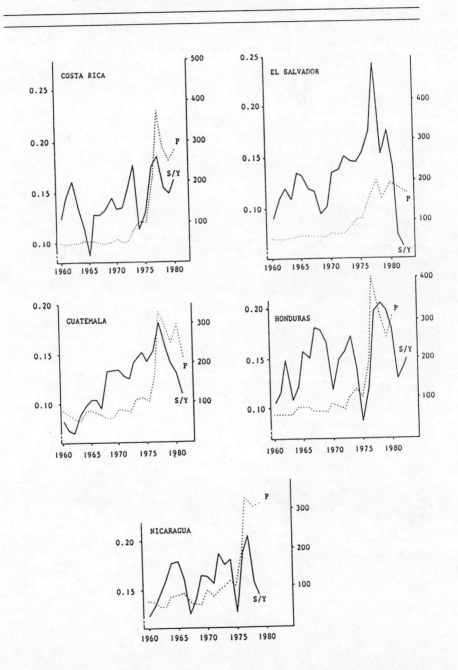

TABLE 8.4   Central America: Net Gold and Dollar Reserves 1979--1986
             (millions of CA$)

Year	Costa Rica	El Salvador	Guatemala	Honduras	Nicaragua	Central America
1979	59	171	723	129	-227	855
1980	-139	-25	400	75	-423	-112
1981	-185	-149	63	3	-366	-634
1982	-47	-79	21	-90	-466	-661
1983	93	121	-48	-121	-395	-350
1984	162	129	-25	-128	-385	-247
1985	312	176	-66	-117	-504	-199
1986	371	251	-26	-119	-423	54

Source: Central Banks and BCIE.

TABLE 8.5   Real Rates of Growth of Gross Investment, 1979--1986
             (percent over previous year)

Year	Costa Rica	El Salvador	Guatemala	Honduras	Nicaragua	Central America
1979	15.3	-15.6	-5.1	2.6	-65.0	-4.8
1980	-9.4	-28.0	-9.9	14.5	139.8	-3.2
1981	-24.9	-10.8	7.8	-18.8	62.9	-2.3
1982	-38.2	-7.6	-8.7	-16.2	18.4	-17.3
1983	-7.2	5.5	-28.8	-1.6	10.8	-10.7
1984	-25.0	2.3	-11.2	7.1	-2.2	1.9
1985	-5.0	7.8	-3.2	-6.6	-9.4	-2.8
1986	-8.2	1.4	-2.2	-7.6	-8.7	-0.6

Source: Central Banks, Planning Ministries and BCIE.

TABLE 8.6   Gross Domestic Savings Ratio: 1965, 1985 (percent of GDP)

Year	Costa Rica	El Salvador	Guatemala	Honduras	Nicaragua
1965	9	12	10	15	18
1985	22	6	9	13	-2

Source: World Bank (1987), World Development Report, p. 237.

TABLE 8.7   European Community Multilateral Aid to the Countries of the Central American Isthmus, 1979--1986 (thousands of ECU)

	1979	1980	1981	1982	1983	1984	1985	1986	TOTAL
Costa Rica	160	240	280	18560	740	270	13986	699	34935
El Salvador	630	2410	3900	5260	2420	4820	8912	14790	43142
Guatemala	170	260	170	1060	1720	2100	1385	15974	22839
Honduras	6780	11920	4070	25460	14476	3350	4758	13370	84184
Nicaragua	7110	9750	18940	19100	15230	10780	20878	23090	124878
Panama	90	210	150	170	240	0	0	310	1170
Total Country	14940	24790	27510	69610	34826	21320	49919	68233	311148
Regional	1600	700	1980	13510	3351	20300	26983	5058	73482
% Regional	9.7	2.7	6.7	16.3	8.8	48.8	35.1	6.9	19.1
Total	16540	25490	29490	83120	38177	41620	76902	73291	384630

Source: Cáceres (1987), p. 32.

TABLE 8.8   Bilateral Aid from EC Member States to the Countries of the Central American Isthmus, 1979--1984 (thousands of ECU)

	1979	1980	1981	1982	1983	1984	Total
Costa Rica	10.5	15.7	19.2	13.8	11.0	12.1	82.3
El Salvador	11.6	4.0	3.2	3.4	5.5	4.6	32.3
Guatemala	8.4	10.3	8.3	7.4	7.2	6.3	47.9
Honduras	5.8	13.1	8.1	13.4	13.6	16.8	70.8
Nicaragua	27.7	25.1	36.4	44.3	37.3	37.8	208.6
Panama	1.5	1.6	1.8	1.6	2.1	5.3	13.9
Total	65.5	69.8	77.0	83.9	76.7	82.9	455.8

Source: Cáceres (1987), p. 33.

TABLE 8.9   Projected Composition of BCIE Lending, 1987--1992
(thousands of CA$)

	1987--88	1988--89	1989--90	1990--91	1991--92	Total
Agriculture and Livestock	0.5	15.0	43.0	54.0	73.0	185.5
Manufacture	10.0	23.0	43.0	52.0	65.5	193.5
Infrastructure	83.2	65.8	69.5	68.3	73.0	359.8
Social Dev.	9.2	22.0	31.5	37.0	45.0	144.7
Housing	25.8	21.5	19.0	21.7	28.5	116.5
Total	128.7	147.3	206.0	233.0	285.0	1000.0

Source: Cáceres (1987), p. 37.

TABLE 8.10   Central America: Real Exchange Rate Movements, 1978--1984

	1978	1979	1980	1981	1982	1983	1984	1978--84*
Guatemala	1.00	1.60	1.15	1.14	0.98	0.91	0.89	-0.11
El Salvador	2.50	2.50	2.44	2.25	1.91	1.20	1.55	-0.38
Honduras	2.00	2.11	2.28	2.32	2.03	1.70	1.58	-0.21
Nicaragua	7.03	6.94	6.26	4.83	3.74	2.83	1.64	-0.77
Costa Rica	8.57	7.85	7.80	16.65	17.20	13.49	13.35	0.56

Note: *Positive number signifies a real devaluation.

Source: Saidi, N. and W. Loehr (1985), 'Research on a Trade Financing
Facility for Central America,' BCIE: mimeo.

TABLE 8.11   Central America: Hypothetical Compensation for Loss
of Coffee Export Revenue, 1977--1985 (millions of US dollars)

Year	Value of Exports	Reference Level	Compensated Revenue Loss
1977	729	–	–
1978	563	–	–
1979	670	–	–
1980	585	637	–
1981	486	576	151
1982	447	547	129
1983	391	477	156
1984	477	450	–
1985	421	434	29
Total			465

Source: GAC (1988), p. 19.

Notes

1. Some of the more perceptive analyses of the present crisis include: CEPAL (1985); CEPAL (1981b); Vega Carballo (1985); Bulmer-Thomas (1985b); Schulz (1984); and López (1986).

2. The view that the size distribution of income will improve only once a country reaches a relatively high level of per capita income is originally attributed to Kuznets (1963); it is of course implicit in much classical writing and underlies the Lewis model.

3. Indirect evidence of falling real wages is provided by data on per capita consumption of basic grains for the five republics taken together. Taking 1965 as the base year, the 1975 indices for maize and beans are 87 and 81 respectively.

4. See Rosenthal (1985), pp. 19–38.

5. On the distribution of income in Honduras and the relative absence of social confrontation see Schulz (1984).

6. See Rosenthal (1985), pp. 19–38.

7. See Bulmer-Thomas (1987b).

8. Reynolds quoted in Bulmer-Thomas (1985a), p. 195. Also, for a detailed analysis of the relationship between fluctuations in savings rates and real income and fluctuations in coffee export earnings see Ramírez (1987), pp. 161–188.

9. For figures on the increase in the ratio of the money supply to GDP over the period 1961–1981 see Cáceres (1987).

10. Loehr (1986) is an econometric study which finds a significant relationship between a rise in real LIBOR (the six month rate adjusted by the US inflation rate), a slowdown in economic activity in developed countries and an increase in the current account deficit of the Central American countries. In much the same vein, Collier (1984) shows a rise in international interest rates to have a negative impact on growth which is greater in the developing than in the developed countries.

11. It is not until relatively recently that reforms to the Common External Tariff have removed extreme discrepancies in the structure of effective protection.

12. Indeed it is possible that net capital remitted by local firms may actually be greater than that of foreign firms although, to our knowledge, no study has been carried out which addresses this question directly.

13. See Cáceres and Seninger (1982).

14. See Cáceres (1980), chapter 5.

15. See CEPAL (1985).

16. See Irvin (1988).

17. The 'hybrid growth' thesis is central to the argument put by Victor Bulmer-Thomas in his excellent book on the political economy of the region. See Bulmer-Thomas (1987b).

18. The *peso centroamericano* (CA$) is a nominal unit of account equal to the US dollar.

19. See United States Senate (1984), pp. 53-54.

20. See *Revista de Integración y Desarrollo de Centroamérica*, Nos. 29 and 35.

21. See IDB (1983).

22. See SELA (1983).

23. A copy of the Communiqué is published in Pierre (1985).

24. See CCIC (1987), a document prepared by an inter-institutional committee supported by CEPAL for the Group of Eight Meeting in Acapulco in October 1987.

25. See note 4 in Chapter 1 of this book (Irvin and Holland).

26. See Hamburg (1988), the Communiqué issued at the Hamburg Meeting, 23 February–1 March 1988.

27. For evidence that bilateral aid tends to substitute for domestic savings while multilateral aid tends to complement such savings, see Bowles (1987).

28. See BCIE (1987).

29. See Cline (1978).

30. The figures for the average annual contribution of the CACM to each country's growth for 1965–1968 are as follows: Guatemala, 1.67 percent; El Salvador, 2.21 percent; Honduras, 0.53 percent; Nicaragua, 1.13 percent; Costa Rica, 0.44 percent; see Cáceres (1980), p. 63.

31. See Bulmer-Thomas (1987b), pp. 237–240.

32. For a good account of the functioning of the European Payments Union see Bloomfield (1984).

33. See SIECA/BCIE/ICAITI (1987).

34. In a recent study carried out by the Economic Commission for Latin America and the Caribbean on the five Central American countries, Haiti and the Dominican Republic using data for the period 1970–1985, regressing their GDP growth on that in seven industrialized countries (their main trading partners) and on movements in net barter terms of trade yields an R^2 of 0.98. See CEPAL (1986d).

35. See Hewitt (1987).

References

AISA (Asesoría Económica Internacional, S.A.) (1985) 'Modernización y Reestructuración del Sector Industrial en Costa Rica' San José diciembre.

Balassa, B. (1979) *Inter-Industry Trade and the Integration of Developing Countries in the World Economy* World Bank Working Paper no. 316, Washington, D.C.: International Bank for Reconstruction and Development.

Baloyra, E. A. (1983) 'Reactionary Despotism in Central America' *Journal of Latin American Studies* vol. 5, no. 2.

Behrman J. and J. A. Hanson (eds) (1979) *Short Term Macroeconomic Policy in Latin America* Cambridge, Mass.: Ballinger.

BCIE (Banco Centroamericano de Integración Económica) (1987) 'Propuesta de un Nuevo Llamamiento de Capital del Banco Centroamericano de Integración Económica' doc. no. BCIE-PLAN-PROFI-031/87, 7 de noviembre.

BID (Banco Interamericano de Desarrollo) (1986) *Progreso Económico y Social en América Latina, Informe 1986* Washington, D.C.: Banco Interamericano de Desarrollo.

Bloomfield, A. I. (1984) 'La Experiencia de la Unión Europea de Pagos y su Posible Aplicabilidad a América Latina' *Integración Latinoamericana* no. 95, octubre.

Bodenheimer, S. (1974) 'El Mercomún y la Ayuda Centroamericana' in R. Menjivar (ed) *La inversión extranjera en Centroamérica* San José: EDUCA.

Booth, J. A. (1984) 'Trickle-up Income Distribution and Development in Central America During the 1960s and 1970s' in M. A. Seligson (ed) *The Gap Between the Rich and the Poor* Boulder: Westview.

Bowles, P. (1987) 'Foreign Aid and Domestic Savings in Less Developed Countries; Some Tests for Causality' *World Development* vol. 15, no. 6, June.

Brundenius, C. (1985) 'Estrategia del Desarrollo Industrial en Nicaragua' *Cuadernos de Pensamiento Propio* no. 8, INIES/CRIES, Managua, enero.

Bulmer-Thomas, V. (1976) 'The Structure of Protection in Costa Rica—a New Approach to Calculating the Effective Rate of Protection' *Journal of Economic Studies* no. 3, pp. 13–28.

Bulmer-Thomas, V. (1979) 'Export Promotion versus Import Substitution in the Central American Common Market' *Journal of Economic Studies* no. 6.

Bulmer-Thomas, V. (1982a) 'The Central American Common Market' in A. El-Agraa (ed) *International Economic Integration* London: Macmillan.

Bulmer-Thomas, V. (1982b) *Input-Output Analysis in Developing Countries* London: John Wiley.

Bulmer-Thomas, V. (1984) 'Central America in the Inter-War Years' in R. Thorp (ed) *Latin America in the 1930s: the Periphery in World Crisis* London: Macmillan.

Bulmer-Thomas, V. (1985a) 'Central American Integration, Trade Diversification and the World Market' in G. Irvin and X. Gorostiaga (eds).

Bulmer-Thomas, V. (1985b) 'Centroamérica desde 1920: Desarrollo Económico en el Largo Plazo' *Anuario de Estudios Centroamericanos* San José, vol. 11, fascículo 1.

Bulmer-Thomas, V. (1986) 'Economic Relations between Central America and Western Europe' paper delivered to the CRIES/ASERCCA Conference on Central American Integration, Managua, November.

Bulmer-Thomas, V. (1987a) 'The Balance of Payments Crisis and Adjustment Programmes in Central America' in R. Thorp and L. Whitehead (eds) *Latin American Debt and the Adjustment Crisis* London: Macmillan.

Bulmer-Thomas, V. (1987b) *The Political Economy of Central America since 1920* Cambridge: Cambridge University Press.

Caballeros, R. (1987) 'External debt in Central America' *CEPAL Review* no. 32, August.

Cáceres, L. R. (1980) *Integración Económica y Subdesarrollo en Centroamérica* México: Fondo de Cultura Económica.

Cáceres, L. R. (1987) 'Consideraciones sobre la Cooperación de la Comunidad Europea a Centroamérica' mimeo, Tegucigalpa: BCIE, 25 de enero.

Cáceres, L. R. and C. Imendia (1987) 'Vinculación Comercial e Integración Económica en Centroamérica: una Aplicación del Análisis de Flujo de Transacciones' *Cuadernos de Economía y Finanzas* Tegucigalpa: División de Planificación, Banco Centroamericano de Integración Económica, Cuaderno no. 2, marzo.

Cáceres, L. R. y S. Seninger (1982) 'Redes Interregionales, Estructuras Jerárquicas y Fuga de la Riqueza en Centroamérica: un Análisis de Cadena de Markov' *El Trimestre Económico* vol. 49, no. 3, julio-septiembre.

Castillo, C. M. (1985) 'La Integración Económica de Centroamérica en la Siguiente Etapa: Problemas y Oportunidades' paper prepared for the Inter-American Development Bank, San José.

Castillo, C. M. (1986) 'Central America: Perspectives for Economic and Social Development' paper prepared for 'Beyond the Debt Crisis—Latin America: The Next Ten Years' Conference sponsored by the IDB and the International Herald Tribune, Paris, 27–28 January.

CCIC (Comité de Cooperación del Istmo Centroamericano) (1987) 'La Integración Centroamericana y las Relaciones Económicas con el Resto de América Latina' México: CEPAL, 16 de octubre.

CEFSA (Consultores Económicos y Financieros S.A.) (1983) 'La Industrialización en el Período de Reajuste Estructural, 1980–1990' in IDB (1983) *Industrialización y Desarrollo* Washington: Inter-American Development Bank.

Central American Report (weekly newsletter) Guatemala: INFORPRESS Centroamericana.

CEPAL (Comisión Económica para América Latina y El Caribe) (1956) *La Integración Económica de Centroamérica* México.

CEPAL (1981a) 'Reflexiones sobre la Situación Actual y las Perspectivas del Proceso de Integración Centroamericana' (Memorándum dirigido a los Ministros Responsables de la Integración Económica Centroamericana) E/CEPAL/CCE/403, México, junio.

CEPAL (1981b) 'Istmo Centroamericano: el Carácter de la Crisis Económica Actual, de los Desafíos que Plantea y la Cooperación International que Demanda' E/CEPAL/G. 1184, 26 de agosto.

CEPAL (1983a) *Industrialización en Centroamérica 1960– 1980* Serie Estudios e Informes de la CEPAL no. 30, Santiago de Chile.

CEPAL (1983b) *Centroamérica: la Exportación de Productos Industriales y las Políticas de Promoción en el Contexto del Proceso de Integración Económica* México.

CEPAL (1984) 'La crisis en Centroamérica: Orígenes, Alcances y Consecuencias' *Revista de la CEPAL* no. 22, Santiago de Chile, abril.

CEPAL (1985) 'Centroamérica: Bases de una Política de Reactivación y Desarrolllo' (LC/MEX/G.1/Rev.1) México, 20 de mayo. CEPAL (1986a) *Estudio Económico de América Latina y El Caribe 1985* Santiago de Chile.

CEPAL (1986b) 'Central America: Bases for a Reactivation and Development Policy' *CEPAL Review* no. 28, Santiago de Chile, April.

CEPAL (1986c) 'Preliminary Overview of the Latin American Economy 1986' *Notas Sobre la Economía y el Desarrollo* no. 438/439, Santiago de Chile, diciembre.

CEPAL (1986d) 'América Latina y El Caribe; Escenarios del Crecimiento Económico; 1986–1995' doc. no. LC/R-558, México, 11 de diciembre.

CEPAL (1987a) 'Central America: Notes on Economic Developments in 1986' *Notas Sobre la Economía y el Desarrollo* no. 444, Santiago de Chile, marzo.

CEPAL (1987b) 'Balance Preliminar de la Economía de América Latina, 1986' Santiago de Chile, marzo.

CEPAL (1987c) 'Integración e Industrialización en América Latina: Más Allá del Ajuste' *Cuadernos de Ciencias Sociales* no. 6, San José: FLACSO.

CEPAL/CEMLA (Comisión Económica para América Latina y El Caribe/Centro de Estudios Monetarios Latino Americano) (1983) 'Integración Monetaria y Comercio Intrarregional en Centroamérica' México, febrero.

CEPAL/SIECA (Comisión Económica para América Latina y El Caribe/Secretaría permanente de la Integración Económica Centroamericana) (1964) 'Los Problemas de la Política Industrial Centroamericana' *Economic Bulletin for Latin America* vol. 9, no. 1, Santiago de Chile.

Chapman, R. (1987) 'Central America: a Review of the Economic Situation' in R. Rausch (ed) *Europe and the Crisis in Central America and the Caribbean* Marburg: Philipps-Universitat.

Checchi and Co. (1985) 'Research on a Trade Financing Facility in Central America' Report presented to ROCAP (USAID) Washington, D.C., March.

Cline, W. R. (1978) 'Benefits and Costs of Economic Integration in Central

America' in W. R. Cline and E. Delgado (eds) *Economic Integration in Central America* Washington, D.C.: Brookings Institution.

Cline, W. R. (1988) 'El Papel de la Integración Económica en el Desarrollo Centroamericano' *Revista de la Integración y el Desarrollo de Centroamérica* no. 39, Tegucigalpa: BCIE.

Cline, W. R. and E. Delgado (eds) (1978) *Economic Integration in Central America* Washington, D.C.: Brookings Institution.

Consejo Monetario Centroamericano (1985) *Boletín Estadístico 1984* San José.

Cohen, I. and G. Rosenthal (1977) 'Reflexiones Sobre el Marco Conceptual de la Integración Económica Centroamericana' *Revista de la CEPAL* no. 3, primer semestre.

Cohen, I. (1981) 'Apuntes Sobre la Definición de la Integración' *Revista de la CEPAL* no. 15, diciembre.

Cohen, I. (1982a) 'Comentarios a Eduardo Lizano . . .' mimeo, México.

Cohen, I. (1982b) *Regional Integration in Central America* Lexington, Mass.: Lexington Books.

Collier, P. (1984) 'Growth of Developing Countries and World Interest Rates' *Journal of Macroeconomics* vol. 6, no. 4, autumn.

Delgado, E. (1981) Evolución del Mercado Común Centroamericano y Desarrollo Equilibrado, San José: EDUCA.

Demas, W. (1984) 'Adjustment and Recovery in the CARICOM Economies' Caribbean Development Bank, May.

DiPalma, G. and L. Whitehead (eds) (1986) *The Central American Impasse* London: Croom Helm.

Durán L. and J. F. Solís (1979) 'An Econometric Model for Nicaragua' in J. Behrman and J. A. Hanson (eds) *Short-term Macroeconomic Policy in Latin America* Cambridge, Mass.: Ballinger.

ECLA (U.N. Economic Commission for Latin America) (1983) *The Crisis in Central America: its Origins, Scope and Consequences* Mexico.

ECLAC (U.N. Economic Commission for Latin America and the Caribbean) (1985) *Central America: Bases for Reactivation and Development* 85-3-404, Santiago de Chile.

FAO (U.N. Food and Agricultural Organization) (1987) *Agriculture: Toward 2000* Rome: FAO.

FitzGerald, E. V. K. (1985) 'The Problem of Balance in the Peripheral Socialist Economy: a Conceptual Note' *World Development* vol. 13, no. 1.

Fuentes, J. A. (1986) 'La Desviación del Comercio Intracentroamericano' Proyecto SIECA/Fundación Ford, San José, 7 de noviembre.

GAC (Grupo de Asesoría a la Comunidad Europea) (1988) *Informe de Resultados del Seminario 'El Mecanismo del Derecho de Importación Centroamericana (DICA) y la Reactivación Comercial en el Mercado Común Centroamericano* I.S.S, La Haya, 10 de febrero.

Glower, C. (1986) 'La Fuga de Capital en Centroamérica 1977– 1984' *Cuadernos de Economía y Finanzas* no. 1, Tegucigalpa: BCIE.

Grabendorff, W., H. W. Krumwiede and J. Todt (eds) (1984) *Political Change in Central America: Internal and External Dimensions* Boulder: Westview.

Griffith-Jones, S. (1981) *The Role of Finance in the Transition to Socialism* London: Frances Pinter.

Guerra Borges, A. (1968) 'Industria y Política Industrial' *Economía* no. 17, Guatemala: Instituto de Investigaciones Económicas.

Guerra Borges, A. (1975) 'Materiales para el Estudio de la Especialización e Interdependencia Industrial en Centroamérica' (in) *Ensayos Sobre la Integración Económica* Guatemala: Editorial Universitaria.

Guerra Borges, A. (1986) 'Exenciones arancelarias en Guatemala' *Integración Latinoamericana* no. 111, Buenos Aires: Instituto para la Integración de América Latina.

Guerra Borges, A. (forthcoming) 'Centroamérica: Controversia Sobre Políticas de Desarrollo' Occasional Paper Series, Florida International University: Center for Latin American and Caribbean Studies.

Hamburg (1988) 'Joint Economic Communiqué from the European Community and the Countries Party to the General Treaty on Central American Integration and Panama Resulting from the Conference on Political Dialogue and Economic Cooperation between the European Community and its Member States, the Central American States and the States of the Contadora Group, Held in Hamburg on 29 February and 1 March 1988' Brussels: European Commission DG-1.

Hewitt, A. (1987) 'STABEX and Commodity Export Compensation Schemes: Prospects for Globalization' *World Development* vol. 15, no. 12, May.

Hintermeister, A. (1987) 'Rural Poverty and Export Farming in Guatemala' in P. Peek (ed) *Rural Poverty in Central America: Causes and Policy Alternatives* Geneva: ILO.

Hirschman, A. O. (1977) 'Comentarios de Albert O. Hirschman' *Revista de la CEPAL* no. 3.

Holland, S. (ed) (1983) *Out of Crisis; a Project for European Recovery* London: Spokesman Books.

IDB (Inter-American Development Bank) (1983) *Special Programme Meeting for the Development of Central America, Summary* Brussels, 13-15 September 1983, mimeo ICA-5, Washington, D.C.: 11 October.

IDB (1983) *Industrialización y Desarrollo* Washington: IDB.

IDB (1987) *Economic and Social Progress Annual Report 1987* Washington: IDB, forthcoming.

Instituto para la Integración de América Latina (1986) *Exenciones Arancelarias e Integración* Buenos Aires: Instituto para la Integración de América Latina.

IRELA (Instituto de Relaciones Europeo Latinoamericanas) (1985) 'Bibliography of Western European-Latin American Relations' Working Paper DT1, Madrid: IRELA.

IRELA (1987) 'San José III: Possibilities for Cooperation between the EC and the Central American Isthmus' dossier no. 9, February.

Irvin, G. (1988) 'ECLAC and the Political Economy of the Central American Common Market' *Latin American Research Review* vol. 23, no. 3, autumn.

Irvin, G. and X. Gorostiaga (eds) (1985) *Towards an Alternative for Central America and the Caribbean* London: Allen & Unwin.

Kristol, I. (1985) 'Should Europe be Concerned about Central America?' in A. J. Pierre (ed) (1985).

Kuznets, S. (1963) 'Quantitative Aspects of the Growth of Nations; Distribution of Income Size' *Economic Development and Cultural Change* vol. 11, no. 2, January.

Lara, C. (1977) 'Comentarios de Cristóbal Lara' *Revista de la CEPAL* no. 3.

Linder, S. B. (1961) *An Essay on Trade and Transformation* New York: Almquist and Wicksell.

Lizano, E. (1982) 'El Mercado Común Centroamericano en una época de Turbulencia' mimeo, San José, marzo.

Loehr, W. (1986) 'Balance de la Cuenta Corriente en Centroamérica 1969–1984: Influencias Domésticas y Externas' *Revista de Integración y el Desarrollo de Centroamérica* no. 36, Tegucigalpa: BCIE.

López, J. R. (1986) 'Los Orígenes Económicos de la Crisis en Centroamérica' Documento de Trabajo, San José: ICADIS.

Manley, M. and W. Brandt (1985) *Global Challenge; from Crisis to Cooperation: Breaking through the North-South Stalemate* London: Pan Books.

Medal, J. L. (1985) *La Revolución Nicaraguense: Balance Económico y Alternativas Futuras* Managua: Instituto Nacional de Investigaciones Económicas y Sociales.

Nassau Declaration (1984) 'The Nassau Understanding: Structural Adjustment and Closer Integration for Accelerated Development in the Caribbean Community' Nassau, 7 July.

PACCA (1984) *Changing Course: a Blueprint for Peace in Central America and the Caribbean* Washington: Institute for Policy Studies.

Peek, P. (ed) (1987) *Rural Poverty in Central America: Causes and Policy Alternatives* Geneva: ILO.

Pierre, A. J. (ed) (1985) *Third World Instability; Central America as a European-American Issue* New York: New York University Press.

Ramirez, D. G. (1987) 'Consideraciones Sobre el Endeudamiento Externo de Centroamérica' en R. Rodríguez Céspedes y M. A. Carrillo (eds) *Deuda Externa: el Caso de los Países Peque;atnos Latinoamericanos* Tegucigalpa: BCIE.

Ramsett, D. (1969) *Regional Industrial Development in Central America: a Case Study of the Integration Industries Scheme* London: Praeger.

República de Costa Rica (1983) *Convenio de Crédito Revolutivo Suscrito entre el Banco Central de Costa Rica, la República de Costa Rica y los Bancos Acreedores* mimeo, San José: 24 de noviembre.

Rosenthal, G. (1983) 'Comentarios de Gert Rosenthal' in IDB, *Industrialización y Desarrollo* Washington, D.C.: Inter-American Development Bank.

Rosenthal, G. (1985) 'Principales Rasgos de la Evolución de las Economías Centroamericanas desde la Postguerra' en CECADE/CIDE, *Centroamérica: Crisis y Política Internacional* México: Siglo Veintiuno.

Seers, D. (1983) *The Political Economy of Nationalism* New York: Oxford University Press.

Schulz, D. E. (1984) 'Ten Theories in Search of Central American Reality' in D.

E. Schulz and D. M. Graham (eds) *Revolution and Counterrevolution in Central America and the Caribbean* Boulder: Westview.

SELA (Sistema Económico Latino Americano) (1983) *Reunión de Consulta y Constitución del Comité de Apoyo al Desarrollo Económico y Social de Centroamérica (CADESCA)* Panamá, 13 a 15 de diciembre.

SIECA (Secretaría de Integración Económica Centroamericana) (1974) *El Desarrollo Integrado de Centroamérica en la Presente Década* Buenos Aires: Instituto para la Integración de América Latina/SIECA.

SIECA (1984) 'Series Estadísticas Seleccionadas de Centroamérica' no. 19, Guatemala: SIECA.

SIECA (1985a) *La Complementación Industrial en Centroamérica* Cuadernos de la SIECA no. 16, Guatemala: SIECA.

SIECA (1985b) 'Estadísticas Analíticas del Comercio Intracentroamericano' Guatemala: marzo.

SIECA (1985c) 'Estadísticas Macroeconómicas de Centroamérica 1980–1984' Guatemala: junio.

SIECA/BCIE/ICAITA (Secretaría Permanente de Integración Económica Centroamericana/Banco Centroamericano de Integración Económico/Instituto Centroamericano de Investigación y Tecnología Industrial) (1987) 'Propuesta para Reactivar la Producción Industrial y el Intercambio de Bienes Complementarios en la Región Centroamericana; Documento Base' Guatemala: SIECA, 28 de octubre.

Singh, S. (1983) 'Sub-Saharan Agriculture: Synthesis and Trade Prospects' *World Bank Staff Working Papers* no. 608.

Siri, G. (1975) 'Minimodelos de Dependencia Externa de las Economías Centroamericanas' Guatemala: SIECA.

Siri, G. (1979) 'A Minimodel of External Dependence of the Central American Economies' in J. Behrman and J. A. Hanson (eds) *Short-term Macroeconomic Policy in Latin America* Cambridge, Mass.: Ballinger.

This Week: Central America and Panama (weekly report) Guatemala.

Torres Rivas, E. (1984) 'The Beginning of Industrialization in Central America' *Working Paper no. 141* Washington, D.C.: The Wilson Center.

U.S. Senate (1984) *Report of the National Bipartisan Commission on Central America* (the Kissinger report) Washington, D.C.: U.S. Senate.

Vega Carballo, J. L. (1985) 'Algunas Anti-tesis Sobre la Crisis Centroamericana' *Anuario de Estudios Centroamericanos* San José, vol. 11.

Valdés, A. (1987) 'Agriculture in the Uruguay Round; Interests of Developing Countries' *The World Bank Economic Review* vol. 1, no. 4.

Weeks, J. (1985a) 'The Central American Economies in 1983 and 1984' in J. W. Hopkins (ed) (1985) *Latin America and Caribbean Contemporary Record* New York: Holmes and Meier.

Weeks, J. (1985b) *The Economies of Central America* New York: Holmes and Meier.

Weeks, J. (1986a) 'An Interpretation of the Central American Crisis' *Latin American Research Review* vol. 21, no. 3.

Weeks, J. (1986b) 'The Central American Economies in 1984 and 1985' in J. W.

Hopkins (ed) (1986) *Latin America and Caribbean Contemporary Record* New York: Holmes and Meier.

Weeks, J. (1987) 'Rural Poverty, Growth, and Equity' paper prepared for the FAO document *Agriculture: Toward 2000* Washington, D.C., February.

Weinert, R. (1983) 'Nicaragua's Debt Renegotiation' *Cambridge Journal of Economics* vol. V, no. 1.

Williams, R. G. (1986) *Export Agriculture and the Crisis in Central America* Chapel Hill: University of North Carolina Press.

World Bank (1967) *Economic Development and Prospects for Central America* vol. IV, Industry, Washington, D.C.: IBRD.

World Bank (1972) *Report of the Industrial Finance Mission to Central America; The Common Market and its Future* Washington, D.C.: IBRD.

World Bank (1983) 'The Outlook for Primary Commodities' *World Bank Staff Commodity Working Paper* no. 9.

World Bank (1987) *World Development Report* Washington, D.C.: IBRD.

*Series in Political Economy
and Economic Development in Latin America*

Series Editor
Andrew Zimbalist
Smith College

Through country case studies and regional analyses this series will contribute to a deeper understanding of development issues in Latin America. Shifting political environments, increasing economic interdependence, and the difficulties with regard to debt, foreign investment, and trade policy demand novel conceptualizations of development strategies and potentials for the region. Individual volumes in this series will explore the deficiencies in conventional formulations of the Latin American development experience by examining new evidence and material. Topics will include, among others, women and development in Latin America; the impact of IMF interventions; the effects of redemocratization on development; Cubanology and Cuban political economy; Nicaraguan political economy; and individual case studies on development and debt policy in various countries in the region.

Index